D0953596

CARL VAN VECHTEN
AND THE
HARLEM RENAISSANCE

CARL VAN VECHTEN AND THE HARLEM RENAISSANCE

A PORTRAIT IN BLACK AND WHITE

EMILY BERNARD

Yale UNIVERSITY PRESS

NEW HAVEN AND LONDON

Published with assistance from the foundation established in memory of Philip Hamilton McMillan of the Class of 1894, Yale College.

Yale University Press books may be purchased in quantity for educational, business, or promotional use. For information, please e-mail sales.press@yale.edu (U.S. office) or sales@yaleup.co.uk (U.K. office).

Set in Meridien type by Westchester Book Group.
Printed in the United States of America.

Library of Congress Cataloging-in-Publication Data

Bernard, Emily, 1967–
    Carl Van Vechten and the Harlem Renaissance : a portrait in black and white / Emily Bernard.
    p. cm.
  Includes bibliographical references and index.
  ISBN 978-0-300-12199-5 (cloth : alk. paper)   1. Van Vechten, Carl, 1880–1964—Criticism and interpretation.   2. African Americans—New York (State)—New York—Intellectual life.   3. Harlem (New York, N.Y.)—Intellectual life—20th century.   4 African Americans in literature.   5. Harlem Renaissance.   I. Title.
  PS3543.A653Z59 2012
  813'.52—dc23

                                                              2011034190

A catalogue record for this book is available from the British Library.

This paper meets the requirements of ANSI/NISO Z39.481–992 (Permanence of Paper).

10 9 8 7 6 5 4 3 2 1

For Giulia and Isabella, who promised me that, if I couldn't, they would finish this book for me when they got bigger

If Carl was a people instead of a person,
I could then say, these are my people.
—*Zora Neale Hurston*

I am large, I contain multitudes.
—*Walt Whitman*

CONTENTS

ACKNOWLEDGMENTS

I am pleased to acknowledge the individuals who helped me to see this book to completion. I am indebted to my editor, Ileene Smith, who always had faith in me and this book, and surely must be the most patient and supportive editor in the world. I thank Rachel Cohen for introducing me to Ileene and setting this ball in motion. Ileene's assistant, John Palmer, went above and beyond his duties with unflagging kindness and boundless good nature. Senior editor Margaret Otzel offered beneficence when I needed it. Robin DuBlanc is a rigorous copy editor whose skills are almost as great as her kindness. All of the accuracies in this book are hers; all of the mistakes are mine. The same is true of the research assistants I have worked with over the years, most prominently Grace Grundhauser and Emma Hansen. Bess Malson-Huddle prepared the index with facility and finesse. Many thanks to publicist Ivan Lett for his passion and enthusiasm.

Without a fellowship from the Ford Foundation, and a year at Yale University as the James Weldon Johnson Senior Research Fellow in African American Studies at the Beinecke Library, I would not have been able to finish this book. I have been fortunate also to have had extensive aid and advocacy from the administration at the University of Vermont—from Wanda Heading-Grant, in particular. I could not have had more fantastic colleagues in the English department, in particular Hilary Neroni and Todd McGowan, who carefully and enthusiastically read multiple versions of this work over the years of its evolution and enriched this book—and the life of its author— with their insights and advice. Major Jackson endured countless conversations about Carl Van Vechten and, like Hilary and Todd, is a prime example of commitment, fortitude, and passion as a writer and a friend. Greg Bottoms also braved multiple monologues on the virtues of Carl Van Vechten, and I thank him for his interest and tolerance. Loka Losambe is a surpassing mentor, a wonderful neighbor, and a paradigm of intellectual rigor. I have been fortunate to have outstanding students at the University of Vermont. They remind me why I got into this line of work in the first place.

I am lucky, too, for the friendship of so many people who have contributed in large and small ways as I made my way to the finish line. First, I must thank the Zeifs, in particular Loree, Molly, and Maddie; Caitlin Shelburne; Yem Berhame; Anh Ducharme; Zu Xhou; and my in-laws, Clara Gennari and Joan Tyer, for supportively caring for my daughters at crucial periods when I needed solitude to work. In this regard, I will never be able to repay John Gennari, who is as loving a father as he is a husband. Elizabeth Alexander has always been as remarkable as a friend as she is a scholar and writer. Edi Giunta was astoundingly generous, offering her home as a writing sanctuary and her friendship as a marvelous place to land. Hazel Georgia Ryerson inspired me with her brilliance and imagination. Margaux Fragoso talked me through some desperate moments. Davida Pines has always been a beacon of intellectual grace and perseverance. Ellie DesPrez has provided constant encouragement for many years. Sandhya Shukla read and critiqued early versions of this manuscript, and I am grateful to her. Other invaluable readers include: Maurice Berger, Sarah Elizabeth Lewis, Margo Thompson, and Carla Kaplan. Nancy Carnevale put aside her own work to help me with mine. Ken Schneider lent assistance as well as benevolence. My gratitude to those listed above is bottomless, and so is my regret that I do not have the space to list the many others whose friendship I hold dear, and whose forgiveness I beg for having disappeared for so long while I struggled to complete this book.

Without Kathy Pfeiffer's ingenuity, the most enjoyable parts of this book would not exist. George Hutchinson is a valued friend and an exemplar of excellence in scholarship and intellectual curiosity. His work on the Harlem Renaissance has served as an inspiration. The same is true for the eminent scholars and writers Elizabeth Alexander, Hazel V. Carby, Rachel Cohen, Thadious Davis, Henry Louis Gates Jr., the late Nathan Huggins, Carla Kaplan, Bruce Kellner, David Levering Lewis, Arnold Rampersad, Robert B. Stepto, Amrijit Singh, Cary D. Wintz, and so many others, like Thomas Wirth, who kindly endured my tedious questions, and Susan Curtis, whose work on African Americans in theater was enlightening, as was her correspondence on the same subject. Richard Brodhead found the time to respond to my inquiries with characteristic charity and good cheer.

Good cheer appears to be a job requirement for staff members at the Beinecke Rare Book and Manuscript Library at Yale University. I am indebted to the resourceful and diligent archivists who tend the James Weldon Johnson Collection. Louise Bernard and Nancy Kuhl gave of their time when they had none to give. The staff of the Manuscripts and Archives Division at the New York Public Library was inordinately helpful. The same is true of the archivists affiliated with the Oral History Office at Columbia University. Finally, staff members at the Bailey/Howe Library at the University of Vermont made it their missions, it seemed, to solve various mysteries that had me stumped. Beth M. Howse, Special Collections Librarian, John Hope and Aurelia E. Franklin Library, Fisk University; Diana Lachatanere, Assistant Director for Collections and Services, the Schomburg Center for Research in Black Culture; Richard Workman, Associate Librarian at the Harry Ransom Center at the University of Texas at Austin; Jennifer Chang Rowley at Random House, Inc.; and Craig Tenney at Harold Ober Associates were all wonderfully attentive to my eleventh-hour requests. I thank Faith Childs for her expertise and unwavering good counsel. I thank Bruce Kellner for ten years of friendship. My debt to him is colossal.

I cannot express enough gratitude for my families, both Gennaris and Bernards. My brothers, James and Warren, are solid and true both as siblings and as friends. My late mother was here at the start, and I know she is here at the end as well. My father sets an example in his commitment to and faith in the value of meaningful work. My daughters Giulia and Isabella greeted me after preschool with "Mommy, how is your work?" and then right-sized me with "Mommy, when is your career going to be *over?*"

Most of all, I thank John Gennari, without whose forbearance and discerning eye this book would not exist. He is a true "friend of my mind," as Sixo describes the Thirty-Mile woman in *Beloved,* and for many years his scholarship, talent, and magnanimity have enriched my life and served as models for me.

Finally, I would like to acknowledge the institutions and individuals that granted me permission to quote from the correspondence that appears in this book: the Amistad Research Center; the Carl Van Vechten Trust; Harold Ober Associates; the Harry Ransom Humanities Research Center; Jeh Vincent Johnson; the Moorland-Spingarn Research Center; the National Association for the Advancement of Colored People (NAACP); Carla L. Peterson; Random House; the Schomburg Center for Research in Black Culture; the Stewart and Walrond families; Manuscripts and Archives, Yale University Library; and the Zora Neale Hurston Trust.

Excerpts from the correspondence of Claude McKay are reprinted courtesy of the Literary Representative for the Works of Claude McKay, Schomburg Center for Research in Black Culture, The New York Public Library, Astor, Lenox and Tilden Foundations.

Excerpts from "Advertisement for the Waldorf-Astoria," "Prelude to Our Age," and "The Weary Blues" from *The Collected Poems of Langston Hughes* by Langston Hughes, edited by Arnold Rampersad with David Roessel, Associate Editor, copyright © 1994 by the Estate of Langston Hughes, are used by permission of Alfred A. Knopf, a division of Random House, Inc., and Harold Ober Associates.

Excerpts from *Remember Me to Harlem,* edited by Emily Bernard, copyright © 2001 by Emily Bernard and the Estate of Langston Hughes, used by permission of Alfred A. Knopf, a division of Random House, Inc., and Harold Ober Associates.

EX LIBRIS
CARL VAN VECHTEN

Bookplate by Prentiss Taylor (Yale Collection of American Literature, Beinecke Rare Book Manuscript Library. Courtesy of the Carl Vechten Trust.)

INTRODUCTION

This book is a portrait of a once-controversial figure, Carl Van Vechten, a white man with a passion for blackness. Van Vechten played a crucial role in helping the Harlem Renaissance, a black movement, come to understand itself. This book is not a comprehensive history of an entire life, but rather a chronicle of one of his lives, his black life, that began in his childhood and thrived until his death.

Van Vechten has been viewed with suspicion, particularly because of his audaciously titled and deliberately provocative 1926 novel *Nigger Heaven*. As I was writing this book, people all across the racial spectrum asked me whether I consider Van Vechten a racial voyeur and sexual predator, an acolyte of primitivism who misused his black artist friends and pushed them to make art that fulfilled his beliefs in racial stereotypes. Yes, friends and acquaintances conceded, Van Vechten's enthusiasm for blacks may have catapulted many careers, but at what cost to the racial integrity of those artists, and to the Harlem Renaissance as a whole?

These suspicions have merit. Particularly in his early writing about blackness, Van Vechten insisted that black people were born entertainers and sexually free. He thought that black singers should stick to their "natural" talents, like spirituals, jazz, and blues. He saw Harlem as a mecca of exotica, as did many other white pleasure seekers who made pilgrimages uptown. As a gay man, Van Vechten was attracted to the tolerant atmosphere toward homosexuality that colored Harlem nightlife. But while Van Vechten's early interest in blackness was certainly inspired by sexual desire and his fascination with what he perceived as black primitivism, these features were not what sustained his interest in African American people and culture. Most important, these aspects were matched by his conviction that blackness was a central feature of Americanness, hardly a popular perspective during his lifetime. My story is not an attempt to answer the simplistic question of whether Carl Van Vechten was a good or bad force in the lives of black people during the Harlem Renaissance and beyond. Instead, my ambition in this book is to enlarge that question into something much richer and more nuanced: a tale about the messy realities of race, and the complicated tangle of black and white.

Van Vechten's ideas about black art matured as he became familiar with black artists. His expanding personal world created a dramatic change in the way he experienced race and racial difference. He described a remarkable moment of transformation to William Ingersoll, who interviewed him in 1960: "I remember once coming home almost jubilantly after a night in Harlem, and telling my wife in great glee that I hated a Negro, I'd found one I hated. And I felt that was my complete emancipation, because now I could select my friends and not have to know them all. . . . Up to that time I had considered them all as one. Now, I feel about them exactly the way I feel about white people—I like some, am uninterested in others, and some of them I find very distasteful. But at that time I hadn't got around to that."[1]

Van Vechten's experience was quite a shift, one that not everyone can make even in the twenty-first century. Perhaps this is because when we talk about race at all, we necessarily invoke a set of assumptions about group identity. Whether we consider these assumptions positive or negative, they serve as an attempt to organize a diverse group of people under a single umbrella. Any discussion that involves terms like "the black community" or "black people" is an exercise, however harmless, in defining African Americans as a homogeneous cluster with an unchanging set of characteristics—characteristics that are necessarily distinguishable from other racial groups. In some respects, it is impossible to talk about racial sameness—to assert that black and white people are fundamentally alike—without talking about racial difference—to imply that, in their very state of being black or white, the two groups are fundamentally different. This is the riddle of race, a trap in which Carl Van Vechten was ensnared. He may have exulted the first time he discovered that blacks were just like whites, but if he had really felt that, he would not have become attached to them. Carl Van Vechten believed that black and white people were different. He also believed they were alike. This essential contradiction describes him, as it still may describe many of us, and it is implicit in the enduring debates about the nature of black art.

This book has assumed many different forms over the years. At first, I tried to fit this story into the structure of academic discourse. But after many drafts, I realized that a narrative had emerged, not an argument, and it was perfectly capable of telling itself. After that revelation, whenever I felt myself trying to argue a point, I did my best to pull back and allow a subtler and more fascinating story to unfold.

The story I tell is grounded, for the most part, in the dramas occasioned by the Harlem Renaissance, as it is called today, or the Negro Renaissance, as it was called by many people in the 1920s, when it first came into being. In these pages, I have focused on writing, the black and white of things: the articles, fiction, essays, and letters that Carl Van Vechten wrote to black people and about black culture, and the writing of the black people who wrote to and about him. I have turned to the written word out of personal preference, and also because I believe that the material on which I have drawn offers the most compelling portal onto the story I have chosen to tell.

Van Vechten's correspondence with his black friends of the Harlem Renaissance plays a central role in this book. In general, Carl Van Vechten was an impassioned correspondent. Some of his letters are full of vituperation, and others shine with exuberance. The range in tone of his letters mirrors the array of colors he used to decorate his stationery: emerald blue, tomato red, and lime green, among others. His idiosyncrasies extended to his punctuation. He rarely used apostrophes, so that "don't" is often "dont," and he often did not underline the titles of books or plays. He was inconsistent with commas and periods, sometimes using dashes in their places. I have not corrected these lapses so as to preserve the integrity of the personality of his correspondence.

Van Vechten's letters are a record of his personal style, and they reveal the flesh and blood relationships between Van Vechten and his black friends that make the story of his involvement in the world of black art in the 1920s much bigger than a question of "good" or "bad." Friendship was Van Vechten's forte; in his personal relationships, Van Vechten (known as "Carlo" to his friends) was doggedly faithful and bracingly honest. Such was the case in the relationships between Van Vechten and many Harlem Renaissance figures, and it is in these private relationships I have been most interested. For instance, many histories of the Harlem Renaissance note that Van Vechten introduced the readers of *Vanity Fair* to the elegant and very traditional poetry of Countee Cullen in 1925. More interesting to me are the letters between them, such as one that Cullen wrote to Van Vechten within weeks of the *Vanity Fair* piece, asking him for current Harlem gossip. "You with your excellent entrée to all social functions of color, must know more about Lenox and Seventh Avenue gossip than Eric Walrond," Cullen wrote.[2] Cullen was ambivalent about Van Vechten. He considered him a friend but he also ardently disagreed with him over one of the issues about which they both cared most: the relationship between race and art.

Guyanese-born writer Eric Walrond, on the other hand, shared Van Vechten's views on the subject. He published a strong collection of stories, *Tropic Death*, in 1926, after having first shown it to Van Vechten for his appraisal. Walrond was known as a confident and worldly man, but to Van Vechten he revealed his insecurities; once he asked for reassurance after he mistook a woman at one of Van Vechten's parties for Blanche Knopf, wife of Alfred A. Knopf, Van Vechten's friend and publisher, and herself an advocate for black literature at the Knopf firm. Alarmed by the degree of Walrond's embarrassment, Van Vechten abandoned his friends one night to go to Walrond to console him. Walrond thanked him in a letter: "I am sure no man could wish for a diviner manifestation of interest and concern."[3] Van Vechten gave him sympathy, but also told him to toughen up.

Just as much as his correspondence, this story has also been greatly enriched by the private anecdotes Van Vechten entrusted to his diaries, which he called daybooks. For instance, the influential painter Aaron Douglas, whose career Van Vechten promoted, not only did the illustrations for *Nigger Heaven*, he also painted a mural in Van Vechten's bathroom, as Van Vechten noted in an August 8, 1927, entry. Scholars of the Harlem Renaissance have recorded the fact that Van Vechten took *The Walls of Jericho*, the first novel of black writer and physician Rudolph Fisher, to Alfred A. Knopf, who accepted it immediately. But just as interesting to me is the fact that Fisher inherited a set of evening clothes from Van Vechten.

Fisher called Van Vechten "the only pro-Negro Nordic on earth with whom I am constantly comfortable," a sentiment shared by many of Van Vechten's close friends.[4] Race was a theme that floated in and out of the friendships between Van Vechten and his black friends, many of whom saw no racial divide between themselves and Van Vechten. This was true of Zora Neale Hurston, who was certain that she knew him better than anyone else.[5] A persistent thread in the following pages has to do with the intimate relationships Van Vechten enjoyed with several black women in his life. Besides Hurston, Van Vechten was close to internationally acclaimed performer Ethel Waters, illustrious hostess A'Lelia Walker, retiring novelist Nella Larsen, glamorous actress and teacher Dorothy Peterson, and popular musician and Harlem provocateur Nora Holt, who described her feelings about him in a 1954 letter: "I will never change for my heart has always possessed you even though I know I share you with many people who love you almost as much as I. This love has fluctuated from the erotic to the spirituelle and reached an adulation akin to a saint conditioned by the culture of our own day."[6]

A few major players in this story appear in part 1, "A Niche Somewhere," which begins with a biographical sketch of Van Vechten's life as well as the genesis of the Harlem Renaissance, and where they came to meet. Van Vechten had a close professional and personal relationship with James Weldon Johnson, a statesman and artist whose talents were expansive. Johnson published the novel *The Autobiography of an Ex-Coloured Man* anonymously in 1912; it was reissued with his name attached in 1927, at the behest of Carl Van Vechten. W. E. B. Du Bois, editor of the *Crisis* and visionary of the Negro Renaissance, believed that black artists should focus on art that would uplift the race. Van Vechten was as turned off by Du Bois's elitism as Du Bois was disgusted by what he saw as Van Vechten's penchant for depravity. Langston Hughes was a friend and co-conspirator for forty years and, like many other black friends, stood by Van Vechten's side during the controversy over *Nigger Heaven*.

Hughes, Du Bois, and Johnson were important to Van Vechten as people, but most important to the first section of this book are their ideas about the relationship between race and art, an issue that consumed Van Vechten. As well as Van Vechten, Du Bois, and Johnson, Langston Hughes, George Schuyler, Alain Locke, and others also wrestled with the meaning of black art during the 1920s. The arguments they had—in person and on the page—constituted the true force of the Harlem Renaissance, which is often remembered as a period of celebration, but was just as much, if not more, an occasion for intriguing conflicts. The conflicts were in place before Carl Van Vechten arrived on the scene, but his 1926 novel *Nigger Heaven* brought these disagreements to a boiling point.

I have devoted part 2, "*Nigger Heaven*," to the novel, but not just in terms of its plot. Even more, I have been interested in the way that *Nigger Heaven* became something of a rallying cry for African American writers who admired it, like Langston Hughes, George Schuyler, and Wallace Thurman, as well as for critics who despised it, like W. E. B. Du Bois and others. For Carl Van Vechten, *Nigger Heaven* was a declaration of his right to write about black Harlem life just as he pleased. For black writers, the novel was their way of declaring the same, and they gloried in the scandal that Van Vechten had created—although Van Vechten himself was distressed by it—because the book afforded them an opportunity to distance themselves from conservatives who thought that black stories should be written only by black people.

No one was more inspired by *Nigger Heaven* than Wallace Thurman, a witty and depressive novelist and journalist, who used the novel and Van Vechten to poke his finger in the eye of Harlem Renaissance conservatives. He and Nella Larsen play important roles in "Letters from Blacks," part 3, which culminates in a discussion of the evolution of the James Weldon Johnson Memorial Collection of Negro Arts and Letters, as it was called then, or the James Weldon Johnson Memorial Collection, as it is called now, which is a preeminent collection of African American cultural materials. Van Vechten conceived of the collection and worked tirelessly to build it—and to secure a place at the Yale University library for a black person to curate it. In this second ambition he failed. But no studies of the Harlem Renaissance—or much other scholarship on African American lives and literature in general— would exist today if not for this collection, the most formidable assemblage of black materials housed at a largely white institution. Van Vechten named the collection in honor of James Weldon Johnson partly to pay homage to his late friend, who had died in 1938, but also because he understood that if the collection bore his name, a substantial number of black people might be reluctant to contribute to it: in many quarters, his reputation had never recovered from the debacle of *Nigger Heaven.*

Subsequent generations have viewed Van Vechten, his novel, and what they symbolized as indications of what was wrong with the Harlem Renaissance, an assessment based on sexuality as much as race: black sociologist Harold Cruse diagnosed the Negro Renaissance as "emasculated," and all Harlem-based creative innovations as "whitened."[7] Cruse's words, published in his pioneering 1967 study, *The Crisis of the Negro Intellectual,* set a tone. Van Vechten plays a role in *Mumbo Jumbo,* a cornerstone novel in African American literature, published in 1972 by Ishmael Reed. In the novel, Carl Van Vechten is Hinckle Von Vampton, the greatest threat to Jes Grew, which is black esprit de corps. Explicitly and implicitly, Carl Van Vechten has come to symbolize an anxiety about the insidious and undermining nature of white influence on black cultural integrity, which has been a central theme throughout the evolution of black life in the United States.

Carl Van Vechten symbolizes a problem, yet he was also a person, as singular as anyone, and like any person, he was saddled with a complex personality and a host of contradictions. And if *Nigger Heaven* tells a true story about its author and his intentions, then his private history tells another story, a chronicle of a man who was defined by an intimate life lived in color, as much as a public life lived in black and white.

1 A NICHE SOMEWHERE

BEGINNINGS

By the time of his death in 1964, Carl Van Vechten had been a far-sighted journalist, a best-selling novelist, a consummate host, an exhaustive archivist, a prescient photographer, and a Negrophile bar none. But long before he was any of these things, he was an unusual boy growing up in Cedar Rapids, Iowa, in the late nineteenth century.

"I was born in a town in Iowa where at least half the population is of Slavic origin and I was brought up on Bohemian lullabies. When our cook was in good humor she sang lusty Czech airs."[1] In the mid-1870s, great numbers of immigrants from eastern Europe, former citizens of the Austro-Hungarian Empire called Bohemians, transformed the demographics of Iowa. The Van Vechtens, however, were among the earliest American pioneers. Carl was a descendant of Teunis Dircksen, the first of the clan to emigrate from Holland, who took up residence in New York in 1638. Charles Duane Van Vechten, Carl's father, moved his family to Iowa in 1877, in the middle of that wave of immigration.

As young men, Charles and his brother Giles had worked in a lumber mill operated by their father in Mattawan, Michigan.

When the senior Van Vechten died, Giles left Michigan to pursue larger ambitions, eventually becoming a successful banker in Cedar Rapids, Iowa. By the time Charles Van Vechten arrived, a year after his brother, Cedar Rapids had evolved from a small village of several hundred residents to a city with a population of between ten and eleven thousand, all within thirty years. The Van Vechtens' first residence was a simple clapboard house, close to a slaughterhouse and the railroad tracks. It was not long before Charles moved his family into an elegant Victorian home far away from the factory smoke and the train soot. The house was a gift from Carl's uncle Giles. Charles Van Vechten became an insurance agent and, like his brother, one of the most successful businessmen in Iowa.

The Van Vechten family that arrived in Cedar Rapids in 1877 consisted of Charles, his wife, Ada, and their two children: Ralph, born in 1862, and Emma, born in 1864. Carl was not born until 1880, when his mother was thirty-nine years old. "Late children are popularly supposed to be the best," he would say eighty years later, "they seem to resist more."[2]

Resistance was in his blood. Charles and Ada Van Vechten were freethinkers who rejected the status quo when it came to accepted ideas about blacks and women. His parents set examples that Carl would follow for the rest of his life. Carl always remembered how his father instructed him to refer to the black yardman as "Mr. Oliphant" and the laundress as "Mrs. Sercey" at a time when it was uncommon for whites to refer to blacks with honorifics. Charles Van Vechten donated money to the Piney Woods School in Mississippi, an elementary school for black children, which was founded in 1909 by Laurence Clifton Jones and remains in operation to this day. In 1960, Carl described his father as sober and kindhearted, a man with "no prejudice whatever."[3] Years later, Charles would implore his son not to call his fifth novel, the only novel devoted to African American life, *Nigger Heaven*. He diagnosed the title as a symptom of his son's stubbornness, and warned him that it would be seen as a sign of disrespect toward black people. Carl ignored his father's advice.

Ada Amanda Fitch Van Vechten was a suffragist who kept company with abolitionists. She had attended Kalamazoo College, where she had known Lucy Stone, who was not only a well-known abolitionist and advocate for women's rights but also the first American woman on record to keep her own name after marriage. Carl's mother was as much a student of culture as of politics. She circulated through women's clubs in Iowa, giving talks on such subjects as oriental rugs, single-handedly elevating aesthetics in the state, Carl recalled. She marshaled community interest for a public library in Cedar Rapids, solicited the necessary funds from Andrew Carnegie, and obtained the requisite governmental support to maintain it. She remains one of the great heroes of Cedar Rapids history. "Nevertheless, she was in no sense of the word a public character," Carl remembered in old age. "Her home was her one real interest. All my early life centered around her."[4]

"He seems very bright in imitating: he will bleat like a lamb, bark like a dog, or mew like a kitten," wrote Ada Van Vechten in her diary about her year-old son.[5] In adulthood, Carl would sometimes bark when he was enthusiastic and sign his letters with "Woof! Woof!"

As an author of letters, Carl would grow up to resemble his father, a prolific and faithful correspondent who kept every missive. "He wrote boxes and boxes of letters to my mother at one period—which were always preserved in the attic," Carl recalled. When he was a child, Ada brought the boxes down for her son to see. "Observing me, my father, sentimental but shy of showing it, demanded that the letters be burned and burned they were while my mother wept softly, for she could not bear the idea of their being destroyed."[6]

From his mother, Carl learned the art of collecting. Ada had a remarkable tin trunk, the details of which he lovingly recalled in "The Tin Trunk," an essay included in *Sacred and Profane Memories,* a 1932 collection that consists mainly of revisions of previously published pieces (not essays, he said), whose unifying theme is "things remembered." In "The Tin Trunk," Carl remembered how Ada would take the trunk down from the top shelf of the closet on rainy days. The trunk was less a trunk than a box, but its role in Carl's childhood was mighty. It was a repository of the past: daguerreotypes, which occupied most of the space; letters; hair clippings from family heads; old jewelry; pieces of dresses; pictures; and a silver dollar from 1880, the year of his birth: "Each object had its own history and my mother used to relate these histories to me while I pored over the contents of the box, handling each object as gently and reverently as if it had been a religious relic and I a devout Catholic."[7]

Carl often lingered over a ferrotype of his father, taken when Charles was around twenty. He saw in it a spiritual, even mystical quality. But the image he cherished the most was a daguerre-otype of his mother set in a small, oval, plum-colored velvet case. The image captured his mother at eighteen, "an exquisite, roguish portrait which might have been that of a Parisian beauty of the Second Empire. The honest eyes, full of character, were black and round and full, with a suggestion of witchery playing over their surface. The black hair, parted in the middle over the forehead, was smooth and glossy. The nose was strong, but not too strong, and the lips seemed to quiver with interest and emotion."[8]

Carl experimented with simple box cameras as a child, and in high school moved on to the Kodak, which was first available for sale in 1888. In the early 1930s, he would turn his full attention to photography and amass a collection of twenty thousand pictures, many of which are portraits of prominent American writers and entertainers, among them Sammy Davis Jr., Eugene O'Neill, Aaron Copland, Bessie Smith, Leonard Bernstein, Billie Holiday, Gertrude Stein, Joe Louis, and Marlon Brando. He called his passion for photography an addiction (the same word he used to describe the "violent" interest in Negroes that arrested him in the early 1920s). In his passions, Carl Van Vechten was meticulous and thorough. Early in his career as a photographer, Van Vechten determined to photograph every prominent African American he could persuade to sit for him. When necessary, he badgered. Most people surrendered.

So much younger than his siblings, Carl grew up essentially as an only child. Impressions of his brother, Ralph, as "a thin, serious-looking boy in his youth," and his sister, Emma, as "a roly-poly, curly-headed blonde," were gleaned from tintypes and anecdotes. Both of his siblings married when he was a toddler. With no other children to influence him, Carl flourished in the company of the adults around him. His Grandmother Fitch took up residence with her daughter's family once she became a widow. She was an unusual woman, a pipe smoker with a penchant for urinating on the front lawn. She predicted that her grandson would wind up in the gallows. Carl adored her.[9]

Carl himself was unusual, given to attracting and enjoying attention. At thirteen, he was a looming six feet tall. He had the "blank stare of an animal, as steady as a cat's, as cold as a snake's," writes biographer Bruce Kellner. His unnerving expression was coupled with two big, protruding front teeth, which would become his trademark as an adult. Twelve years of attempts to straighten them proved unsuccessful. Carl did not try to hide his strange looks; instead he cultivated them. He grew one long fingernail, on the pinky of his right hand. He wore his pants tight, his collars high, and pointed patent-leather boots.[10] Others considered him odd; he enjoyed the attention. He was spectacular, and it satisfied him. He had good friends; his best friend was Anna Snyder, who would become his first wife. They married in 1907 and divorced in 1912, and Van Vechten was ordered to pay twenty-five dollars a week in alimony, which he, then working as an arts critic for the *New York Times*, could not afford.

Snyder and Van Vechten had been compatible, just not completely, he said later. Anna Snyder was six feet tall, "serenely handsome and friendly," according to Bruce Kellner.[11] Their shared desire to escape Cedar Rapids simply did not prove to be

Carl Van Vechten in 1899 (Manuscripts and Archives Division, The New York Public Library, Astor, Lenox and Tilden Foundations. Courtesy of the Carl Van Vechten Trust.)

sufficient foundation for the marriage. Two months after they divorced, Van Vechten met Russian actress Fania Marinoff, whom he married in 1914. Van Vechten and Snyder had separated without acrimony, but when Van Vechten and Marinoff married, Snyder demanded the back alimony Carl owed her. She sued him, and Van Vechten spent four months in jail.

Van Vechten and Marinoff had a passionate marriage, though it was not always sexual. Over successive generations, homosexual, bisexual, gay, and queer are all terms that have been used by many contemporary scholars and writers to describe the sexual identity of Carl Van Vechten. He had sexual affairs with men, including Jimmie Cole, a black prostitute with whom he spent many evenings just after the heyday of the Negro Renaissance had passed. He began a long-term relationship in 1919 with Donald Angus, a nineteen-year-old lover of opera and music, who regularly accompanied Van Vechten to nightclubs and parties in Harlem. The intensity of their affair diminished after a year, but Angus remained close friends with Van Vechten for the rest of his life, maintaining a friendship with Marinoff, too, until she died in 1971. Van Vechten had a more sustained relationship with Mark Lutz, a journalist based in Virginia. The two men exchanged daily letters for thirty-three years, long after the end of their sexual relationship. Van Vechten had one more lasting relationship with a man, Saul Mauriber, a decorator and designer who would eventually become his lighting assistant. At the end of her life, Marinoff told Bruce Kellner that she had never fully understood her marriage. "It was a sexual marriage, yes," she said, "for a long time, but more important it was a spiritual marriage."[12]

When Van Vechten had an opportunity to describe his life with Marinoff (as he usually referred to her), he began his narration from the year of their marriage, which was when, he said, his life really began:

> Since then we have quarreled almost incessantly about important and unimportant matters. Seemingly, we agree about few subjects, but Fania is a maid of many moods, and a few minutes after a violent discussion she is all smiles and charm. She is enchanting in this aspect and the other aspect is soon forgotten. . . . Fania's native intelligence is great; her

opinions frequently worthless, but her volatile temperament and her really considerable charm provide her in the end with a mellow background. She has great beauty and loves to surround herself with beautiful objects. She holds elegant dress in great esteem, but never dresses in fashion, being more concerned with personal taste and a very good idea of what suits her. We are a mutual admiration society: I am passionate in praise of her acting and she is consistent in her regard for my books. She is more frequently governed by her heart, I by my head. We have been married for forty-six years and no two people could stay married for forty-six years without feelings generally affectionate towards one another.[13]

In 1932 Marinoff spoke to a reporter at the *New York World-Telegram* about her marriage. " 'It is nice to have been married for so long to a man as difficult as my husband,' Fania Marinoff said, tapping her wooden dressing table with her knuckles, 'and I hope it will stay as it is. We have found that a sense of humor is better than separate apartments.' "[14] Carl Van Vechten and Fania Marinoff had just celebrated fifty years of marriage when he died in 1964.

"Where was he going? What was he going to do? He did not know. He did not care," muses Gareth Johns, the main character in *The Tattooed Countess*, a 1924 bildungsroman by Carl Van Vechten that contains similarities to his own life story. Gareth has no direction, but he "harbored no doubts, no fears. His vivid imagination assured him that he would find his niche some-where, once he was free from the bondage which this town and his family life entailed."[15] Like Gareth, Carl would first choose Chicago. But while he longed for escape from Iowa as a boy, Carl would remember its charms as an adult. In a travel essay called "The Folksongs of Iowa," he wrote, "Indeed, to me the Iowa scene boasts a peculiar picturesqueness which I do not find elsewhere in the United States." He contrasted the state with Pennsylvania and Connecticut which, to him, bore the overwhelming mark of England, while Iowa "remains essentially American."[16]

Carl enrolled in the University of Chicago at the age of nine-teen, but formal education was not on his mind. He went to Chicago for the art. He had become fascinated with the opera as a teenager—even aspired to become a singer—and Chicago pro-vided opportunities to attend the theater, art galleries, and con-certs, activities not available in Cedar Rapids.

Carl began to prepare himself for a career in journalism while he was a student at the University of Chicago. Writing had always been a passion. "I cannot remember the time when I was not trying to write," he would recall, "often with no reasonable amount of skill." Although he would entertain other ambitions—to be an actor, a composer, and a concert musician ("careers which I was not encouraged to follow")—writing was a calling.[17] Not long after graduation, he was hired at the *Chicago American* (which was bought by the *Chicago Tribune* in 1956), from which he would be discharged three years later for "lowering the tone of the Hearst newspapers," according to a note from the manag-ing editor, after Carl wrote an article in which he mocked the wardrobes of women at an annual horse fair that was attended by the wife of the business manager. Bruce Kellner writes that this story was "apocryphal," but Carl enjoyed telling it all the same.[18]

Undeterred, and feeling he had exhausted every opportunity available to him in the Midwest, he took a train to New York, where he eventually found a job at the *New York Times*. Carl would continue to write for various newspapers for ten years, establishing a reputation as a critic of theater, music, and drama. In 1914 he published a review of *Granny Maumee*, a "Negro drama" written by Ridgely Torrence, describing it as "the most important contribution which has yet been made to the American stage."[19] At the time, the stage of his own life had been lit up with color.

Carl had first been exposed to black entertainment as a child in Cedar Rapids, when he had seen the soprano Sissieretta Jones, the first black performer to sing at Carnegie Hall. At the University of Chicago, he discovered the comedy of Bert Williams and George Walker, who comprised the popular comedy-dance team known as the Williams & Walker Company. "The two comedians headed a large troupe of blacks and offered musical entertainment in a sense sophisticated but which did not dilute the essential charm, the primitive appeal of the Negro," he wrote in a 1920 essay, "The Negro Theatre."[20]

In a college writing course, Carl composed two stories about his personal experiences with the black people he knew at the time. "Biondina" is a portrait of the eponymous central character, a "very pretty child of six with big brown eyes and decidedly coquettish ways." Biondina is the daughter of the real-life cook and housekeeper at his fraternity, Aurelia Veta Clement. The girl is "spoiled"; she gets what she wants and bewitches every man with whom she comes into contact. She charms with her talent for conversation and precocious discretion. She is as serious as she is innocent. The short piece ends when Biondina runs to her mother and asks incredulously, "Mama, do mens kiss girls?"[21]

A far more substantial piece is "The Inky Ones," a fictionalized account of his experiences with Biondina's mother, whom the narrator describes as "the first black person who had come within my ken." In the story, Clement is Mrs. Manchester, or Sidonia to her friends. She captivates Wallace, the main character, based on Carl himself, and it is through his careful study of her body and manner that he begins to consider himself an expert on all black people. At times Wallace indulges in sociology: "They are a good-hearted set—these negroes—with an overestimated idea of a white man's importance which is bred into them I suppose—it is amusing." He waxes romantic: "I always wished that I had a mammy like the children in the south—Two or three dusky matrons with ample bosoms." Perhaps most strikingly, this story contains the first stirrings of the pleasure in a status that he would cultivate for the rest of his life—that of an exceptional white person among black people. When he escorted Mrs. Manchester to "colohed affahs," he said, "I was invariably mistaken for a coon."[22] Van Vechten's language in his early writing, of course, is born of ignorance and not of malice. Many years later, he would evaluate his body of college writing: "My themes were pretty dreadful—I have retained some of them, probably the best: so I am not criticizing from memory—but my energy in creating them was enormous, and once or twice I almost hit on something in the way of an idea."[23]

Mrs. Clement/Manchester introduced Carl to the black social world of Chicago. "I used to go downtown sometimes to night clubs and I met a woman whom I got to be very fond of and liked very much," Van Vechten said of black singer Carita Day. "She was a fascinating person and sang like an angel."[24] Day and her husband were once hired to perform at a party at his fraternity, where she sang and her husband, Ernest Hogan, played the piano.

By 1920, Carl had become an advocate for black artists. Although it was an unusual road for a white person of his era to take, it was not, in fact, surprising for Carl Van Vechten, considering his background. His childhood had prepared him to go against the current. Early on, he had learned from his parents to respect black people and to challenge the social conventions that considered blacks and whites to be naturally and forever separate. It may also be true that early attraction to blackness, as well as his eagerness to introduce black people and their art forms to white people, was inspired by his adolescent desire to attract attention, when he learned to take pleasure in creating a spectacle. Whatever its inspiration, thus began the era of Van Vechten's passionate attachment to blackness. In the 1920s, he described the virtues of spirituals, ragtime, blues, and jazz in the pages of *Vanity Fair*, calling black music the only authentic American.

Van Vechten had been making bold statements about art since the 1910s. He was the first serious American ballet critic, and the first in this country to recognize the particular genius of Gertrude Stein, with whom he developed a very close relationship. He appreciated the unique gifts of Isadora Duncan, Anna Pavlova, Igor Stravinsky, Vaslav Nijinsky and the Ballets Russes, and the ragtime and jazz of George Gershwin well before it became fashionable to do so. But Carl Van Vechten was not only a critic; he also wrote fiction. His first novel, *Peter Whiffle,* would make him a best-selling author. His fifth novel, *Nigger Heaven,* his only novel devoted to black life, would make him notorious.

Carl Van Vechten gave up writing in the early 1930s. Many years before, he had predicted the same outcome for his interest in black art. "Jazz, the blues, Negro spirituals, all stimulate me enormously for the moment. Doubtless, I shall discard them too in time," he wrote to the journalist H. L. Mencken in 1925.[25] He was wrong. Ten years after he published his review of *Granny Maumee,* the biography of Carl Van Vechten and the biography of the Harlem Renaissance would merge, and it would become impossible to tell the story of this singular black movement without telling the story of one singular white man.

SPECTACLES IN BLACK

"Harlem is the city of constant surprises, a city of ecstatic moments and diverting phenomena. It is a city in which anything might happen and everything does," marveled Harlem Renaissance writer Wallace Thurman, who would become a fan of Van Vechten and his *Nigger Heaven,* which was essentially its author's attempt to celebrate Harlem and its thriving, fascinating culture.[26]

The Harlem Renaissance was occasioned by the historical phenomenon known as the Great Migration, which saw almost 2 million black people fleeing southern poverty and racial violence between World War I and 1940. Chicago, Detroit, Philadelphia, and Washington, D.C., were among the destinations for black migrants seeking something better than what was possible for them in the South. World War I had left factories and packinghouses empty of white men, so agents from the North and Midwest came south to recruit black workers, who then found themselves, upon arriving in their new cities, being used as scabs to break labor unions. Racial tensions led to race riots that erupted all over the country, among the most memorable being the 1917 and 1919 riots in East St. Louis and Chicago, respectively. But in general the northern cities offered a way out of the degradation that characterized black life in the South, as well as the concrete benefits of better wages, the freedom to vote, and improved quality of elementary and secondary schools.

The Great Migration changed the character of black life in cities all over the country. But there was no other place like the two-mile neighborhood at the northern tip of Manhattan called Harlem. Between 1920 and 1930, the black population in Harlem increased by 40 percent. With the infusion of new black residents, Harlem neighborhoods became home to the most diverse black population in the country. Laborers fresh from the South rubbed elbows with African Americans who had known wealth, independence, and social prestige for generations. Immigrants from the West Indies and Africa encountered black people with entirely different sensibilities and customs. Some of these subcultures blended harmoniously while others did so grudgingly, but all of this mixing provided excellent fodder for African American artists determined to translate the cultural upheaval they saw around them into art. During the 1920s, Harlem claimed over two hundred thousand black residents.

New black communities all over the country were producing art, music, and theater that reflected the energy of the changing demographics produced by the Great Migration. Black people were making culture that was, in turn, creating a change in the collective racial self, claimed Harlem Renaissance writers. "In the very process of being transplanted, the Negro is being transformed," observed Alain Locke, a Harvard-trained philosopher and editor of the 1925 anthology *The New Negro,* the first substantial collection of Harlem Renaissance art and literature.[27] In a review of *The New Negro* for the *New York Herald Tribune,* Carl Van Vechten called it "a remarkable book." He applauded Locke's work: "He has put not merely the best foot of the new Negro forward; he has put all his feet forward."[28]

Alain Locke adopted the term *New Negro* from writers like A. Philip Randolph, a socialist who had founded the radical magazine the *Messenger* and who would found the Brotherhood of Sleeping Car Porters, an independent union of sleeping-car porters and maids. A few years before *The New Negro* was published, Randolph had used the term to describe a postwar generation that believed in militant action to further black political and personal self-actualization. In "A New Crowd—A New Negro," a 1919 article published in the *Messenger,* Randolph details the differences between Old and New Negroes. He criticizes the "Old Negro" for his political conservatism, politics of accommodation, opposition to organized labor, and dependence upon white benefactors who had nothing but disdain for the working class.[29]

The Old Negro as conceptualized by Alain Locke was more cultural than political. As he explains in his introduction to *The New Negro:* "The Old Negro, we must remember, was a creature of moral debate and historical controversy. He had been a stock figure perpetuated as an historical fiction partly in innocent sentimentalism, partly in deliberate reactionism."[30] Sambos, pickaninnies, bucks, mammies, Uncle Toms: these were racial archetypes that dominated the cultural landscape of the American South, in broadsides, advertisements, and minstrel shows (which featured white performers in blackface)—and, with the debut of D. W. Griffith's groundbreaking 1915 film *Birth of a Nation,* they permeated the film industry as well. It was these stereotypes that the "New Negro" was meant to correct. It was the collective "best foot forward" effort that Van Vechten saw at work in *The New Negro,* and that W. E. B. Du Bois espoused in his own writings on the state of black America.

Does the act of naming affect lived experience, or change the material conditions of black people in this country? Whether yes or no, in the history of black American experience naming has always been a central way to talk back to and deflect an internalized sense of inferiority. In both its political and cultural incarnations, the New Negro was largely an invention, but it was also real because black people felt it was real, and it represented a transformation in black identity that was an essential principle of the Harlem Renaissance.

Harlem itself had gone through a variety of ethnic incarnations before it became Thurman's city of constant surprises. Like the Van Vechten clan, Harlem was Dutch in origin, once called Nieuv Haarlem, after the city of Haarlem in the Netherlands. Then it was German, then Irish, then Jewish. Harlem became known as "the black mecca" only after a considerable real estate war and subsequent white flight out of its neighborhoods. Like the rest of New York, Harlem was a study in extremes. Fifth Avenue was poor and overcrowded. St. Nicholas Avenue, however, was a showplace, sleek and lined with attractive well-kept brownstones.

For many black people, Harlem was as much a fantasy as a reality. "I was in love with Harlem long before I got there," Langston Hughes wrote in a retrospective essay, "My Early Days in Harlem," in 1963.[31] Hughes arrived in Harlem in 1921, fresh from an unhappy visit with his father in Mexico. In his 1940 autobiography, *The Big Sea,* he described the thrill of his first subway ride and what greeted him once he arrived at 135th Street. "I went up the steps and out into the bright September sunlight. Harlem! I stood there, dropped my bags, took a deep breath and felt happy again." Ostensibly, Hughes had come to New York to begin college at Columbia University, but he found its size alienating and its atmosphere chilly with racism. He left college and plunged into Harlem, where, as he said, "I began life on my own."[32]

In *The Big Sea,* Hughes revealed that his inspiration for attending college in New York was *Shuffle Along,* a 1921 Broadway musical revue that "gave just the proper push—a pre-Charleston kick—to that Negro vogue of the 20s." It was "a honey of a show," Hughes remembered. "Swift, bright, funny, rollicking, and gay, with a dozen danceable, singable tunes."[33] *Shuffle Along* was not the first Broadway production written and performed by black people. It was preceded by two 1898 musicals: *Clorindy: The Origin of the Cakewalk,* with music by Will Marion Cook and lyrics by Paul Laurence Dunbar; and *A Trip to Coontown,* which was a product of the collaboration of songwriters Bob Cole and Billy Johnson. But *Shuffle Along* was new, "epoch-making," according to writer and statesman James Weldon Johnson.[34] Its unmemorable plot revolved around two grocery store owners running for mayor of the fictional Jimtown, Mississippi. The show was distinguished from its predecessors by its outstanding roster of talent, record-breaking sales, and extraordinary score, which was written by Noble Sissle and Eubie Blake (Aubrey Lyles and Flournoy Miller wrote the book) and yielded hits like "I'm Just Wild about Harry," "Love Will Find a Way," and the eponymous "Shuffle Along." The well-known choir director Hall Johnson and composer William Grant Still performed in the orchestra. Singer and dancer Florence Mills became an international sensation as a result of the show, whose chorus featured a then-unknown talent called Josephine Baker. *Shuffle Along,* which ran for over five hundred performances, proved that white people would pay to see an all-black show. It was succeeded by several similar shows whose producers hoped to take advantage of the interest *Shuffle Along* had created, but none of them met with comparable success.

Carl Van Vechten reviewed *Shuffle Along* in "Prescription for the Negro Theatre," a 1925 article he wrote for *Vanity Fair*. He agreed with Johnson and Hughes that the revue was exceptional for its performers and score in general, but he described "Love Will Find a Way" as "moth-eaten," and he faulted the show, whose comedians "blacked their faces and carmined and enlarged their lips," for its perpetuation of minstrel stereotypes.[35]

"Harlem is not to be seen. Or heard. It must be felt," insisted Wallace Thurman, who arrived in Harlem in 1925 via Salt Lake City, Boise, Chicago, Omaha, Pasadena, and Los Angeles. He called Harlem the greatest Negro center in the world, "a cosmos within itself," the promised land.[36] The black cosmos of Harlem flourished alongside earthly social and political institutions devoted to race uplift, such as: the National Association for the Advancement of Colored People (NAACP), the National Urban League, and the Universal Negro Improvement Association (UNIA). Each organization was committed to its own brand of race uplift work, and each had its own personality, which was embodied both by the individuals most closely associated with it, and the magazines and newspapers it produced.

The NAACP had its most visible spokesperson in W. E. B. Du Bois, editor of the *Crisis,* the house organ of the NAACP, with whom Van Vechten would have a critical falling-out over *Nigger Heaven*. The National Urban League had educator and writer Charles S. Johnson, who edited its magazine, *Opportunity*. Johnson admired *Nigger Heaven* and supported its author's right to use the title, as did Wallace Thurman. Van Vechten, who had little interest in politics, had no relationship with A. Philip Randolph or Marcus Garvey, who founded and led the UNIA and who edited the organization's weekly newspaper, *Negro World.*

All of these organizations and magazines were unmatched in their dedication to social and political progress for black people. In addition, the *Crisis, Opportunity,* and the *Messenger* were deeply committed to the identification and development of African American literature and art. For most African American writers, getting a book published was the ultimate goal, but newspapers and magazines reached the broadest audiences and therefore constituted primary outlets for black authors seeking a hearing. The flourishing of Harlem Renaissance literature could have taken place only in New York. By the 1920s the city had supplanted Boston as the center of American publishing, and Van Vechten played an important role as an informal scout for black literature at the preeminent publishing firm run by Alfred A. Knopf, who was a good friend of Van Vechten's and the publisher of most of his books.

Daytime Harlem reverberated with sober conversations about the state of the race. At night, however, Harlem roared. It was in constant motion; inside cabarets, buffet flats, speakeasies, and ballrooms, each dancer, singer, and musician seemed more ingenious than the last. "This was the era in which was achieved the Harlem of story and song," declared James Weldon Johnson in his 1933 autobiography, *Along This Way.* He described the Harlem Renaissance as an epoch when "Harlem's fame for exotic flavor and colorful sensuousness was spread to all parts of the world."[37] In "Spectacles in Color," a chapter in his autobiography *The Big Sea,* Langston Hughes captured the particular social alchemy of Harlem during the 1920s in his descriptions of a Harlem drag ball, lodge parties, funerals, weddings, and the enterprising ways of George Wilson Becton, a popular Harlem evangelist. "Harlem likes spectacles of one kind or another—but then so does all the world"[38] In no small part, the world that came to enjoy the spectacle of Harlem was white. Over the years, Harlem changed color completely, wrote Claude McKay, who was famously blunt and temperamental. "Harlem is an all-white picnic ground and with no apparent gain to the blacks," he wrote in 1937.[39]

White interest in Harlem created the central paradox of the Harlem Renaissance. Though white financial support was essential to its success, the cost was extreme. All of Harlem's nightclubs benefited financially from white curiosity. But some nightclubs catered primarily to whites and forced black patrons to sit in segregated "Jim Crow" sections. The Cotton Club, for instance, was famous for its array of black talent, such as Duke Ellington, Cab Calloway, and Count Basie, but it catered to white clientele by keeping black patrons, when they were admitted at all, out of sight.

Most white tourists who came to Harlem to look at black people did not see them as equals, sometimes not even as fellow human beings. Langston Hughes described the phenomenon in *The Big Sea:* "So Harlem Negroes did not like the Cotton Club and never appreciated its Jim Crow policy in the very heart of their dark community. Nor did ordinary Negroes like the growing influx of whites toward Harlem after sundown, flooding the little cabarets and bars where formerly only colored people laughed and sang, and where now the strangers were given the best ringside tables to sit and stare at the Negro customers—like amusing animals in a zoo."[40] Blacks in Harlem found white presumption obnoxious. "It is actually amazing what number of white people will assure you that they have seen and are authorities on Harlem and things Harlemese," wrote Wallace Thurman.[41] Black writer Rudolph Fisher was similarly frustrated. "I am actually stared at, I frequently feel uncomfortable and out of place, and when I go out on the floor to dance I am lost in a sea of white faces."[42] White tourists assumed their welcome in Harlem after dark. Black patrons endured white presence with quiet resentment. "But they didn't say it out loud," explained Langston Hughes, "for Negroes are practically never rude to white people."[43]

There were blacks who stoked white eagerness to enjoy black spectacles uptown, however. Black characters jeer at Caleb Johnson, a "colored social worker" in "Who's Passing for Who?" a 1952 short story by Hughes set during the Harlem Renaissance. Caleb "was always dragging around with him some nondescript white person or two, inviting them to dinner, showing them Harlem, ending up at the Savoy—much to the displeasure of whatever friends of his might be out that evening for fun, not sociology." The narrator and his cohort roll their eyes at Caleb, but they themselves enjoy the white spectators' fascination with their company and conversation. Later the whites get the best of them when they pretend to be black—"We've just been *passing* for white for the last fifteen years"—and seduce their black companions into relaxing their "professionally self-conscious 'Negro' manners." Finally, they confess their whiteness and speed downtown, disappearing into the white world below 125th Street, and leaving the narrator and his friends mystified and undone.[44]

Carl Van Vechten ushered numerous whites to Harlem—he called it his fate. His unofficial tours were famous and captured the attention of black songwriter Andy Razaf, whose popular "Go Harlem!" encouraged listeners to "Go inspectin' like Van Vechten." At the request of publisher Bennet Cerf, Van Vechten once escorted William Faulkner uptown. Faulkner embarrassed him. "In the first place, he was quite drunk," Van Vechten explained. "Anyway, I did take him, and every place I took him into, the first thing he did was ask the entertainer to sing 'The St. Louis Blues.'" Van Vechten tried and failed to restrain him. "But at least nobody got sore," he remembered, "because he wasn't unpleasant."[45]

"Rent parties," thrown ostensibly to raise rent money for the host, became important avenues for African Americans to congregate privately, away from the curious gazes of white people. And some black nightclubs managed to hold on to a sense of racial integrity. In his autobiography, *A Long Way from Home,* Claude McKay described an evening out with white mentor and friend Max Eastman, who was then editor of the socialist magazine *New Masses.* He tried to take Eastman with him to Ned's, "one place of amusement in Harlem in which white people were not allowed." They were turned away. Ironically, Eastman was heartened by the experience. "He said he was happy that there was one place in Harlem that had the guts to keep white people out," remembered McKay.[46]

Rent parties and clubs like Ned's successfully gave blacks in Harlem reprieve from inquiring white eyes. But every black person who lived in Harlem during the Negro Renaissance had to wrestle, on some level, with a paradox that defined the period: the black spectacle that we now call the Harlem Renaissance would not have been as dazzling without white spectators. There was no white witness more important than Carl Van Vechten.

SOMETHING NEW, SOMETHING TRUE

April 5, 1917. James Weldon Johnson called it "the date of the most important single event in the entire history of the Negro in American theatre." It was the opening night of *Granny Maumee* at New York's Garden Theatre in Madison Square Garden. "It was the first time anywhere in the United States for Negro actors in the dramatic theatre to command the serious attention of the critics and of the general press and public," remembered Johnson in *Black Manhattan,* his 1930 study of New York. In one night, with one play, "the stereotyped traditions regarding the Negro's histrionic limitations were smashed," wrote Johnson, a sober man not given to hyperbole, unlike Carl Van Vechten, who had seen the play when it was first staged in 1914 at the Stage Society in New York.[47] Written by white playwright Ridgely Torrence, *Granny Maumee* was the centerpiece of the trilogy *Three Plays for a Negro Theater.* W. E. B. Du Bois who, like Johnson, attended the play on opening night in 1917, pronounced the trilogy a breakthrough and "epoch making," just as

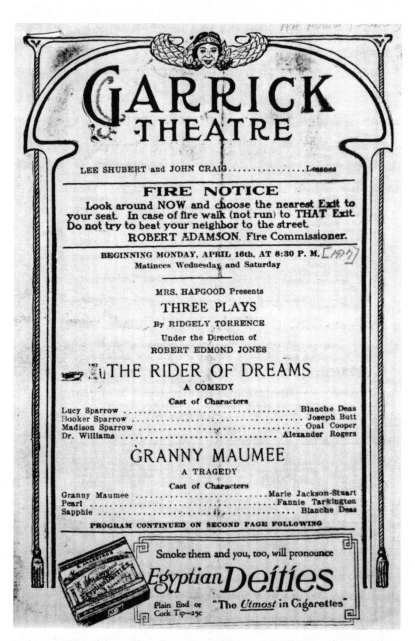

1917 playbill for *Granny Maumee* (Yale Collection of American Literature, Beinecke Rare Book and Manuscript Library. Courtesy of the Carl Van Vechten Trust.)

Johnson had described *Shuffle Along*.[48] Carl Van Vechten, W. E. B. Du Bois, and James Weldon Johnson all admired the play for the same reason. To them, it represented the birth of black pride and the death of black shame. That one play could accomplish so much testifies to how urgently black intellectuals hungered for change in public presentations of black people; it was a hunger intense enough to make the Harlem Renaissance seem inevitable.

The 1917 cast of *Granny Maumee* was not the first black cast to appear before a white Broadway audience, but it was the first to represent black people and their lives with texture and seriousness, according to its fans. The play represented such an enormous challenge to the traditional representation of black people that the actors feared retribution. Backstage, Torrence would remember, the cast was gripped with stage fright, certain that "Negroes trying to be serious before an audience of white people who had never known them on the stage except as clowns, would be jeered and hooted off the boards."[49] Most of the cast members asked their families not to attend opening night, so as not to be forced to witness the actors' humiliation.

But no one in the audience wanted to shame the actors that night. Instead of jeers and boos, the cast was showered with applause; the leads were called out for standing ovations. Torrence received numerous notes of congratulation, and the early reviews in the mainstream press were overwhelmingly enthusiastic. A reporter for the *New York Evening Post* called the trilogy "singular" and "remarkable in many ways." The response from the black press, in particular, was glowing. Like Johnson, Du Bois, and Van Vechten, black critics believed that the plays represented something true and unvarnished about black life. Lester Walton, drama critic for the black newspaper *New York Age*, for instance, called *Three Plays for a Negro Theater* "an unqualified success."[50]

Granny Maumee opens with the eponymous protagonist readying her log cabin in anticipation of the return of her great-granddaughter Sapphie, and Sapphie's baby boy. Granny is blind, "with white hair and a face so seared by burns that it masks her great age."[51] The backstory unfolds through a conversation between Granny and Pearl, her other great-granddaughter. Granny lost her sight when she tried to protect her son Sam from a lynch mob that burned him alive for a crime he did not commit. When Sapphie arrives, Granny implores God to restore her sight so that she can see the boy. God complies.

The baby that Granny is suddenly able to behold, however, is more white than black. And even though the child's white father is kind, his grandfather was the leader of the mob that murdered Sam. The baby's light skin alone is enough to inspire fury in Granny. Once she learns of the boy's lineage, her fury ascends to murderous rage. She turns to voodoo. "Debbils calls out debbils," she tells a terrified Sapphie.[52]

The spirit of her dead son delivers Granny from her hunger for revenge. "Go back, w'ite man, an' sin no mo'," she commands the baby's father as he knocks at the door.[53] The intensity of the moment is more than Granny can bear. Reduced to a shell, she dies when she has surrendered her anger. As her spent form lies on the floor, the curtain descends.

"The sweep of this drama is great; it is a satisfactory presentation of a big theme," wrote Carl Van Vechten in "The Negro Theatre," an essay that appeared in his 1920 collection, *In the Garret,* and into which he incorporated his 1914 review of the show for the *New York Press.* Van Vechten was impressed by the voodoo and magic in *Granny Maumee.* He liked the fact that the "proud Negro grandmother" does not believe in white superiority, that she is, in fact, disgusted by her great-great-grandson's pale skin. He appreciated the references to the story of Moses and the burning bush. It was a tour de force, he announced to his readers. "So far as I know this was the first serious attempt to depict the Negro, from his own point of view."[54]

Van Vechten's admiration for the play proved a springboard to a broader issue. "I was seized with the idea of founding a real Negro theatre, in which Negroes should act in real Negro plays, as the Irish of the Abbey Theatre had produced characteristic Irish plays," he wrote.[55] Van Vechten saw no contradiction in the idea that this real black institution would need him as its architect. And in fact, he was a member of the steering committee that in 1925 founded the Krigwa Little Theater Group, whose purpose was to produce plays by, for, and about blacks. Torrence, Johnson, and Du Bois were also members of the committee.

In the original 1914 production of *Granny Maumee* that Carl Van Vechten saw at the Stage Society of New York, all of the actors were whites in blackface. The minstrel tradition had been one of the most popular forms of American entertainment since the nineteenth century, so Torrence's decision to use white actors was a practical one, a guarantee that his work would be staged.[56] When producer Emilie Hapgood (whose brother-in-law Hutchins Hapgood was a good friend of Van Vechten's) and director Robert Edmond Jones—two powerful figures in the world of New York theater—got involved, Torrence was in a strong position to push for an all-black cast. In the trilogy's 1917 incarnation, all of the actors, and even the stagehands, were black. *Three Plays* may have had a long life if not for the fact that the day after its debut the United States declared war on Germany. After a few successful days at the Garden, Hapgood moved the plays closer to the theater district at the Garrick Theatre, which was managed by Lee Shubert. *Three Plays for a Negro Theater* could not compete with the theater of war, however, and the production closed after one week.

Carl Van Vechten and Ridgely Torrence were both white men who believed in the Americanness of African Americans at a time in national history when such a belief was not a given. They found inspiration in the arts. "To the Negroes, indeed, we are indebted for the rhythm of our best music, the only American music," wrote Carl Van Vechten in 1921, though the music of the American Indian, too, he said, "has a folk quality."[57] Torrence conceived of *Three Plays* during a research trip in Ohio, his home state, when he began gathering black folk materials and became convinced that African Americans could be considered American "folk"—natives with an indigenous culture and an authentic worldview grounded in the land itself. Like his producer and director, Torrence was an advocate of the New Movement in the Theater, whose intent was to establish a genuine American theater in the way that other national theaters existed—on the basis of a folk tradition made into art. Like the Negro Renaissance, the New Movement in the Theater was an attempt to make something new out of what already existed.

For Van Vechten, Du Bois, and Johnson, *Granny Maumee* was fresh because it revised what was old. The story—with white villains and proud black heroes—turned racial stereotypes on their heads and put black self-respect on display. By the time he published "The Negro Theatre," Van Vechten believed, like his Harlem Renaissance contemporaries, that it was crucial to the integrity of black theater that racial stereotypes should die. But he also believed they should survive.

THE NEGRO AS HE IS

"The Negro Theatre" was Van Vechten's first extensive published essay on black art and culture. It included Van Vechten's review of *Granny Maumee* for the *New York Press* as well as a review of *My Friend from Kentucky* (commonly known as *The Darktown Follies*), a 1913 show produced by black songwriter J. Leubrie Hill. "How the darkies danced, sang, and cavorted. Real nigger stuff, this, done with spontaneity and joy in the doing," Van Vechten remembered of the show. *My Friend from Kentucky* was mesmerizing, he said—"distinctly" coon, but there were elements he called derivative, "an imitation of the white man's theatre": the "sprinkling of girls in long satin gowns to [Hill's] otherwise entirely fresh Negro salad." But overall, *My Friend from Kentucky* was remarkable because it was the first black-produced theatrical attempt "to present the Negro as he really is and not as he wants to be on stage." According to Van Vechten, the Negro *wanted* to command the stage by singing conventional hymns in long satin gowns. The authentic Negro, on the other hand, pranced and strutted, threw "his chest and buttocks out in opposite directions," as did George Walker of the Williams & Walker Company, which had so enchanted Van Vechten as a college student.[58]

Van Vechten called *My Friend from Kentucky* a revival of the authentic black entertainment perfected by Williams & Walker. The genius of Williams and Walker lay in their mastery of minstrelsy and in how precisely they performed acts that were "reminiscences of the plantation" and evocations of the "coon." But Van Vechten also saw that the "coon" performed by Bert Williams and George Walker was artificial. If Williams and Walker recalled the minstrel tradition and plantation stereotypes, they did so with great deliberation and awareness. Van Vechten praised Williams for his "pantomimic powers" and his careful development of scene. He quoted Eleanora Duse, the great Italian actress, who pronounced Williams America's finest actor. Walker may have cut a "barbaric" figure, Van Vechten wrote, but he did so with much calculation, and his act "created a bond between Africa and Broadway."[59] The essential Negro charm of the Williams & Walker Company, as Van Vechten understood it, was counterfeit. Van Vechten appreciated the artistry of the artifice, the genius in the clown. But at the same time as he believed the stereotypes were artificial, he also felt strongly that they represented something elemental about blackness itself.

Five years after he published "The Negro Theatre," Van Vechten sent the essay to his then new friend James Weldon Johnson and, in an inscription, asked Johnson to evaluate his ideas within the context of his earlier ignorance. At the time, the two men were both deeply involved in the debates surrounding black art, culture, and identity that lay at the heart of the Negro Renaissance. "You state in your very nice inscription that many of the views that you have expressed on the Negro have been considerably altered by your recent experiences," responded Johnson to Van Vechten's request. "I am quite sure they have, and I am quite curious and anxious to have you write on the subject now out of your larger knowledge and more intimate experiences. Besides, as I once said to you, no acknowledged American novelist has yet made use of this material."[60] If Johnson had any reservations about "The Negro Theatre," he did not admit them to Van Vechten. In fact, the two men developed a close friendship that would thrive for thirteen years, until Johnson's death in 1938. In large part, their friendship evolved out of their similar beliefs about black art and about the importance—and insignificance—of racial difference.

AN OPPORTUNITY

Ten years after Carl Van Vechten published his review of *Granny Maumee,* a pivotal chapter in the story of the Harlem Renaissance unfolded. Charles S. Johnson, editor of *Opportunity* magazine, remembered the evening of March 21, 1924, as "one of the most significant and dramatic of the announcements of the renaissance."[61] He was the principal architect of the evening's event, a dinner that would serve as the "coming out" ceremony for the Negro Renaissance, the first formal event held to present the new generation of black writers. Carl Van Vechten was across town that night, at Madison Square Garden, watching Abe Goldstein take the world bantamweight title away from Joe Lynch. He was five months shy of meeting Walter White (the writer and NAACP official who would initiate him into the world of Harlem), and probably unaware that fifteen blocks south, an event was taking place that would shape much of the course of the rest of his life.

Charles S. Johnson and Alain Locke had collaborated on the event, deciding that the date of the dinner should coincide with the publication of *There Is Confusion*, the first novel written by Jessie Fauset. Straitlaced and prolific—she would go on to write three more novels, poetry, and essays—Fauset edited the *Brownie's Book*, a magazine for black children, from 1920 to 1921, and also served as the literary editor of the *Crisis* between 1919 and 1926, when Du Bois became deeply involved in the Pan-African Congress movement. Claude McKay, whose work she championed, considered her "prim and dainty as a primrose" and precious, like her novels, which she began to publish at the age of forty-two.[62] Like Du Bois, she straddled two generations, the Victorian and the modern, characterized by two competing worldviews. She would always feel cheated by the fact that the celebration of the publication of her first novel faded into little more than an afterthought as the event evolved to take on a larger significance.

One hundred and ten members of the New York literati, black and white, attended the dinner, which was held at the

Civic Club, the only elite club in Manhattan that welcomed both blacks and women. Black and white editors, writers, and publishers inspired the crowd with their common faith that a new era for black art had begun. Along with Jessie Fauset, Countee Cullen, Langston Hughes, and short-story writer Eric Walrond were among the black writers present to embody the new spirit, while mentors like Locke, Charles S. Johnson, James Weldon Johnson, and Du Bois explained to the crowd the meaning of that new spirit. Locke said, "They sense within their group— spiritual wealth which if they can properly expound, will be ample for a new judgment and re-appraisal of the race."[63] All four men believed that the beginning of creative freedom for black artists was near.

Alain Locke served as master of ceremonies for the evening at Charles S. Johnson's urging. Johnson described Locke as a man of "mellow maturity and esthetic sophistication."[64] Van Vechten appreciated Locke for his gossip. He recorded a visit from Locke in an October 31, 1925, daybook entry, shortly after he had begun work on *Nigger Heaven*. Locke stopped by and discussed "the character of Langston Hughes at some length, telling me extraordinary things about Countee Cullen . . . about Claude McKay, etc. I liked him much better than I ever have before."[65] Zora Neale Hurston, who was not present at the event, described Locke as a "malicious little snot" in a letter to James Weldon Johnson. "So far as the young writers are concerned," she wrote, "he runs a mental pawnshop. He lends out his patronage and takes in ideas which he soon passes off as his own."[66] But on that evening of March 21, 1924, Locke, who was the first African American Phi Beta Kappa, was all charm, moving easily among the interracial crowd of literary stars, which included literary critic Van Wyck Brooks, playwright Eugene O'Neill, journalist and social activist Paul Kellogg, novelist Fannie Hurst, philosopher John Dewey, James Weldon Johnson, W. E. B. Du Bois, and critic and writer Carl Van Doren.

Over the course of the evening, young poet Gwendolyn Bennett recited her poem "To Usward": "We claim no part with racial dearth / We want to sing the songs of birth!" After dinner, Van Doren, who would win the Pulitzer Prize in 1938 for his biography of Benjamin Franklin, rose to speak. "The Negroes, it must be remembered," he told the crowd, "are our oldest American minority."[67] He was a compelling speaker; Claude McKay praised him for being "practical-minded in the pleasant canny Yankee way."[68] Like Ridgely Torrence and Carl Van Vechten, Van Doren believed that it was because most black people lived their lives on the margins and not in the mainstream that they had unique perspectives and gifts to offer white Americans. "What American literature decidedly needs at the moment is color, music, gusto, the free expression of gay or desperate moods," he declared. "If the Negroes are not in a position to contribute these items, I do not know which Americans are."[69] The bell for new black art was sounded.

After the dinner, Paul Kellogg, editor of the sociological periodical *Survey Graphic*, proposed devoting an entire issue of his magazine to African American culture, suggesting that Charles S. Johnson serve as editor. Johnson enlisted Alain Locke to help him assemble the issue. In March 1925, a special edition of *Survey*

Graphic, entitled "Harlem: Mecca of the New Negro," was released. It would become the most widely read issue in the magazine's history. Months later, Locke expanded this special edition into an arts anthology, *The New Negro,* which features portrait drawings as well as essays, poetry, and fiction, and includes the work of many key writers and artists of the Harlem Renaissance, such as Countee Cullen, W. E. B. Du Bois, Aaron Douglas, Langston Hughes, Zora Neale Hurston, James Weldon Johnson, Claude McKay, Winold Reiss, and Jean Toomer. Van Vechten told Alain Locke that he would contribute an article about the influence of the Negro on American art for the anthology, but he was preoccupied with his other writing, including his article "Prescription for a Negro Theatre," which would be published in *Vanity Fair* in October.

The impact of *The New Negro* on the Harlem Renaissance is irrefutable—as is, evidently, the malice of its editor, as described by Hurston. In a few years, Locke would do everything he could to undermine Langston Hughes in his then-unraveling relationship with their mutual patron Charlotte Osgood Mason as an attempt to remain in her favor. Still, Langston Hughes would remember Locke as one of the "midwives" of the movement, a list that also included Jessie Fauset and Charles S. Johnson, but not Carl Van Vechten.[70]

Inspired by the success of his 1924 dinner, Charles S. Johnson decided that *Opportunity* would host a literary contest. The first announcement for the contest appeared in the August 1924 issue. Ultimately, twenty-four respected white and black editors, publishers, and artists served as contest judges in five categories: essays, short stories, poetry, drama, and personal experiences. The wife of Henry Goddard Leach, editor of *Forum* magazine, contributed the prize money, which came to a very attractive 470 dollars, roughly 6,000 dollars today.

The awards ceremony, held in May 1925, was a resounding success. Three hundred and sixteen people turned up to witness the future of black writing. Talented young writers, among them Sterling Brown (who, many years later, would proudly and bitterly denounce the Harlem Renaissance, largely because of what he perceived as Carl Van Vechten's powerful influence over the period), E. Franklin Frazier, Zora Neale Hurston, Eric Walrond, Countee Cullen, and Langston Hughes, all accepted awards that evening. Cullen and Hughes, the most well-known poets of the era, dominated the poetry category. Both Cullen and Hughes had created a stir with poems written in 1921 when they were just teenagers, but besides their gift for poetry they had little else in common, as is reflected in their poetic styles. Cullen, an admirer of John Keats, preferred traditional structures, while Hughes was less concerned with meter than he was with translating the blues idiom onto the page. Hughes took first prize for what would become one of his signature poems, "The Weary Blues." The poem is a portrait of a Harlem piano player whose haunting lyrics include the lines:

> Droning a drowsy syncopated tune,
> Rocking back and forth to a mellow croon,
> I heard a Negro play. [71]

Like Hughes and Cullen—like the Negro Renaissance as a whole—the highbrow event was a study in contrasts: at the end of the evening, Charles S. Johnson announced that Casper Holstein, king of the Harlem numbers racket, would fund the second annual *Opportunity* contest. Holstein was eager to participate in the exciting new world of black art, and his contributions made the *Opportunity* awards possible, but his generosity never earned him an invitation into the upper-crust circles of Harlem.

At the 1925 *Opportunity* awards dinner, Carl Van Vechten took the first chance he had to reintroduce himself to Langston Hughes, who had read some of his poetry that evening. Van Vechten, moved by Hughes's words, recommended to Alfred A. Knopf, his friend and publisher, that he consider them for publication. Van Vechten invited Hughes to visit him at his apartment the next morning. Over the next two days, Hughes would visit twice; he and Van Vechten discussed the manuscript that would become Hughes's first book, *The Weary Blues*. It took Knopf only two weeks to decide to accept the manuscript. The 1925 *Opportunity* awards dinner led to a professional and personal relationship between Van Vechten and Hughes that would last for the rest of their lives.

The two had actually met several months earlier. Van Vechten's friend Walter White had introduced them at a benefit party for the NAACP at Arthur "Happy" Rhone's nightclub on 143rd Street and Lenox Avenue in Harlem. "In about a week after that I knew practically every famous Negro in New York because Walter was a hustler," Van Vechten recalled in 1960.[72] After he mastered the Walter White hustle, Carl Van Vechten's diary entries began to take on a change in color. As a natural collector he was meticulous, and Van Vechten kept a record of every

Negro he encountered, as well as new white acquaintances. That November night at Happy Rhone's was particularly fruitful. He checked off his accomplishments: "W. E. B. Du Bois (met), Countee Cullen (met), Kingston Hughes (met), Florence Mills (met), Rosamond Johnson (met), Bill Robinson (met)."[73] "Kingston" Hughes was, of course, Langston Hughes.

The friendship between Carl Van Vechten and Walter White was mutually beneficial. Van Vechten was a veritable celebrity in 1924, the author of the best-selling 1922 novel *Peter Whiffle* as well as a substantial body of well-regarded dance, theater, and music criticism, and a general man about town. Van Vechten was not just a celebrity—he was a white celebrity, and interracialism was considered fashionable in the sophisticated social circles in which New Negro artists traveled. For his part, Van Vechten was somewhat awestruck with White, as he revealed in a letter to his friend writer Edna Kenton a few days after meeting White. "He speaks French and talks about Debussy and Marcel Proust in an offhand way," he marveled. "An entirely new kind of Negro to me."[74] At first, the two men got on like "a house afire," Van Vechten said. White was charming, if forward. "The first thing he did was always to call you by your first name and that made you feel rather as if you were intimate. He's the only person living that calls Mrs. Roosevelt 'Eleanor,'" Van Vechten said.[75] It was White's way of breaking down racial barriers. Carl became disillusioned with White over the years, and in 1960 remembered him as a show-off and a blowhard. But the 1924 party at Happy Rhone's was a time for celebration. It was a time to laud not only the exceptional black artists present, but even more what they represented, which was nothing less than the incarnation of a common dream of the New Negro, a dream that had actually been brewing for nearly a century. In order to come true, this black dream needed white dreamers—during the New Negro movement, the most important white visionary was Carl Van Vechten.

THESE ARE MY PEOPLE

There were other white visionaries, men and women who were excited by the flowering world of black art and music in New York. Some of these visionaries were enthusiastic enough to lend financial support to individual artists. Mrs. Charlotte Osgood Mason, for instance, was a wealthy Park Avenue widow who had an avid interest in Negroes, which grew out of her equally avid interest in Native Americans. In both cultures, she saw a spirit of primitivism, which she insisted her black protégés reproduce in their art. She depended upon Alain Locke, whose career she supported and whose informal role in her life was to introduce her to black artists whose work he thought would please her. For a time, Mason provided financial support to the artists Aaron Douglas and Richmond Barthé, noted choral director and composer Hall Johnson, and even the cantankerous novelist Claude McKay. Mason was exacting and controlling; she was a patronizing patron. She insisted that her black protégés call her "Godmother." In turn, she referred to them as her "Godchildren" and required them, at least metaphorically, to sit at the feet of her throne, from which she expounded on the primitive essence of black art. Langston Hughes and Zora Neale

Hurston were two of Mason's Godchildren, and they tried and failed to please her. Hughes earned her scorn and lost her support and friendship when he abandoned primitivism and began to incorporate politics into his poetry.

Charlotte Mason is a uniquely disquieting example of what it meant to be a white patron of black art during the Harlem Renaissance. On the other side of the spectrum lay the Spingarn brothers, Joel and Arthur, and Joel's wife, Amy, each one a philanthropist and committed believer in the importance of black cultural and political progress. Joel served the NAACP as chairman of the board, treasurer, secretary, and president, successively. Arthur provided the NAACP free legal counsel and served as both its vice president and president, taking over after his brother died in 1939. Joel and Amy established literary awards for black writers, and it was Amy who rescued Hughes when Mason cut him off. Joel created the Spingarn Medal, which is still awarded annually by the NAACP to honor black achievement. Recipients have included W. E. B. Du Bois, James Weldon Johnson, and Walter White.

Some black artists were supported by whites in ways that were perhaps more valuable than money. Claude McKay's career was boosted by his friendship with Max Eastman, who, as editor of the *Liberator*, published McKay's famous poem "If We Must Die" in 1919. H. L. Mencken promoted the work of several Harlem Renaissance writers, most prominently George Schuyler, whose articles appeared often in the magazine Mencken edited, *American Mercury*. Harlem Renaissance writers were indebted to publishers like Horace Liveright and Alfred Knopf, who took a particular interest in black writing. If it hadn't been for Carl Van Vechten's close relationship with Alfred and Blanche Knopf, the careers of several important writers of the Negro Renaissance, such as Langston Hughes, Nella Larsen, and Rudolph Fisher, may not have been the same.

Carl Van Vechten did not establish formal financial relationships with the black artists he admired. Instead, when a new black artist excited him, he often sought to establish a personal relationship with him or her. His friendships with blacks were also mentorships in most cases, but he was always primarily a fan, and he promoted the work of the black artists he admired just as any powerful friend and fan would, as he also did for white artists, such as Gertrude Stein. But his relationships with black artists were naturally always complicated by the racial imbalances that structured the world in which they lived. By the time Van Vechten fell in love with blackness, he was aware of his power to help black artists, and sometimes he expected something in return.

Van Vechten single-handedly jump-started what would become the magnificent career of the actor and singer Paul Robeson. Van Vechten and Fania Marinoff met Paul Robeson through Walter White in early 1925, when White and his wife, Gladys, hosted a party at which Robeson and his wife, Essie, were also present. Van Vechten and Marinoff were both enchanted with Robeson's stunning voice and commanding presence and, by April of that year, Van Vechten had arranged for Robeson's first public concert, which took place in downtown New York at the Greenwich Village Theatre. At the time, Robeson was well known as an actor but not as a singer. Six months after they met, Van Vechten called Robeson one of his best friends.

Van Vechten and Essie conspired together to build Robeson's career, and she became particularly close to Van Vechten. She confided in him about her marital troubles, many of which were brought on by Paul's infidelities. Two years after the historic concert at the Greenwich Village Theatre, Robeson remembered his debt to Van Vechten, and thanked him for his "unselfish interest" in his career. "It was you who made me sing," he wrote in a letter to Carl.[76] But as Robeson became more and more famous, he seemed to lose interest in both Carl and Fania. Van Vechten became bitter and complained to Marinoff about what he perceived as Paul's growing self-centeredness. "The point about Paul is that he only wants to talk about himself and how he's improving and how he is working on new songs and he can't talk to his old friends that way because they've heard this story so long," he wrote in a 1929 letter to his wife.[77] If Van Vechten was bitter, Marinoff was enraged—she called Robeson "weak, selfish, indulgent, lazy—really if it were not for his meagre talent and his great charm he would be just the traditional 'lowdown worthless nigger.'"[78] Van Vechten exulted when Robeson lost favor with the white American public after his political views shifted to the far left. As Van Vechten saw it, he had helped to make Paul a star—but more than gratitude, he wanted Paul's attention and affection. He did not like to be ignored.

Blues singer and actor Ethel Waters lavished Van Vechten with the attention he craved and the loyalty he expected in her

1951 biography *His Eye Is on the Sparrow*, in which she described the evolution of their friendship. It began on a night when she, backstage at the Lafayette Theatre, was informed by a stagehand that "a white man named Carl Van Vechten wanted to see me." It was 1925, and she was coming off a midnight performance of the musical *Plantation Revue;* she was not interested in meeting another tedious white fan. White people, in general, annoyed her. They were "full of mental pains and psychic aches" and had "all but forgotten what it was like to breathe freely and with pleasure." She pitied them. "They seemed to get little fun out of life and were desperately lonely," she said. "Often when I worked in night clubs I'd look around at those pale faces and weary eyes and I'd think, 'They are only here to kill time.'"[79]

Waters knew who Carl Van Vechten was. She had heard of *Nigger Heaven,* which she despised, even though she hadn't read it, but curiosity overcame her, and she agreed to meet the author despite her antipathy toward his book. Waters was happy to discover that Van Vechten was nothing like she expected him to be. "When Carl Van Vechten talked to me that evening in my dressing room I sensed that he was more like my Greenwich Village friends than the night-clubbing crowd I'd watched. He was rich, but that hadn't got him down. Carl had great life in him and enthusiasm."[80] On that evening, she had no idea that he was so enthusiastic about her that he had purchased a bust of her by Italian sculptor Antonio Salamme, who also created a life-size statue of Paul Robeson.

She saw the bust when she attended the first of many dinner parties at Van Vechten's home, where she met white cultural luminaries such as playwright Eugene O'Neill, composer Cole Porter, novelists Somerset Maugham and Sinclair Lewis, the Knopfs, and journalist Heywood Broun. Van Vechten's apartment was "filled with beautiful things," she remembered in *His Eye Is on the Sparrow:* "paintings, rare old books, sculptures, antiques. But none of those meant a damn thing to me." She wasn't impressed with the food, either. "It was rich white folks' food" like caviar which, she told Carl, "looked like buckshot." The meal started with borsch. *"Cold Borsch!* That is nothing but beet soup and clabber. Served cold, it is enough to kill your gizzard for a week." "But what *do* you like to eat, Ethel?" Carl asked her after that evening. She invited him to her house and served him baked ham, string beans, iced tea, and lemon meringue pie. He loved it, she said, and her "informal way of living."[81]

Van Vechten did everything he could to promote Waters's career. He advertised her talents to the readers of *Vanity Fair* in a March 1926 essay, "Negro 'Blues' Singers," the fourth in his series on black art, in which he described Waters as "superior to any other woman stage singer of her race."[82] He even took out an ad in the *New York Times* praising her performance in the 1939 Broadway show *Mamba's Daughters.* Waters became close to both Carl and Fania, and in her autobiography, she called them her dearest friends. But it was Carl to whom she was truly devoted. "Sometimes it seems to me that Carl is the only person in the world who ever has understood the shyness deep down in me," she wrote. Van Vechten commemorated each of her opening nights on Broadway by sending her a pair of antique earrings. When she got around to reading *Nigger Heaven,* she called it "a

Endorsement of Ethel Waters in *Mamba's Daughters, New York Times,* January 6, 1939 (Yale Collection of American Literature, Beinecke Rare Book and Manuscript Library. Courtesy of the Carl Van Vechten Trust.)

sympathetic study of the way Negroes were forced to live in Harlem."[83]

Zora Neale Hurston admired Ethel Waters as much as Van Vechten did, but unlike Van Vechten, Hurston was "too timid to go backstage and haunt her, so I wrote her letters and she just plain ignored me." Eventually, Van Vechten gave a dinner party to introduce Waters and Hurston. Hurston discovered that Waters, the consummate performer, was also an essentially shy person: "She is one of the strangest bundles of people that I have ever met."[84]

As did Ethel Waters, Hurston paid tribute to Van Vechten in her autobiography, *Dust Tracks on a Road*, in a chapter called "The Inside Light—Being a Salute to Friendship," which appears in the appendix of the book. "With the exception of Godmother," Hurston wrote, "Carl Van Vechten has bawled me out more times than anyone else I know. He has not been one of those white 'friends of the Negro' who seeks to earn it cheaply by being eternally complimentary." As a friend, he was forthright, she said, and without ambivalence when it came to his affections. "If he is not interested in you one way or another, he will tell you that, too, in the most off-hand manner, but he is as true as the equator if he is for you. I offer him and his wife Fania Marinoff my humble and sincere thanks."[85] "If Carl was a people instead of a person, I could then say, these are my people," Hurston once said.[86]

Van Vechten was as enthusiastic about Hurston as he was about Waters. "Zora is picturesque, witty, electric, indiscreet, and unreliable. The latter quality offers material for discussion; the former qualities induce her friends to forgive and love her." Like Van Vechten's wife, Hurston had a dramatic taste in clothing that he appreciated. "She once appeared at a party we were giving attired in a wide Seminole Indian skirt, contrived of a thousand patches; still another time in a Norwegian skiing outfit, with a cap over her ears."[87] Van Vechten also admired Hurston as a writer—and as a fellow iconoclast with a similarly wicked sense of humor. She once dubbed the New Negro writers of the 1920s "the Niggerati," and christened Van Vechten their king.[88]

Hurston sought Van Vechten's help during hard times. In 1930, she had a falling-out with Langston Hughes when they were composing *Mule Bone,* a play that would never be staged in the authors' lifetimes. In large part, their disagreement concerned Louise Thompson, who served as secretary to Hughes and Hurston during their collaboration. At the time, all three of them were being subsidized by Charlotte Mason. Hurston came to believe that Hughes had given Thompson too great a role in the composition of the play. Hughes said that Hurston began to act suspiciously, and then tried to pass *Mule Bone* off as her own creation. Hurston threw a veritable tantrum when she went to Van Vechten's apartment to solicit his support. But Van Vechten's loyalties were divided between the two writers, and he did his best to remain neutral. Years later, he considered the whole incident as simply more evidence of Hurston's charming flair for drama.

Like Waters and most of his other black friends, Hurston would always remain loyal to Van Vechten, and would prove an ardent supporter during the controversy that followed the publication of *Nigger Heaven*. But there were other black artists of the period who experienced a different Carl Van Vechten than the one Hurston and Waters described in their autobiographies, the Van Vechten who was disappointed in Paul Robeson's failure to satisfy his considerable need for adulation. Black artist Bruce Nugent, roguish, becoming, and openly gay, described a 1936 encounter with Van Vechten to biographer Thomas Wirth. At the time, Van Vechten was fifty-six and Nugent thirty. "If you had just patted me on the head and said, 'Carl, you're a nice boy,' you could have had anything you wanted. You could have gone to Paris," Van Vechten told Nugent as he put his hand on the younger man's shoulder. Nugent didn't interpret Van Vechten's statement as a sexual overture, but he told Wirth that it was well known that Van Vechten expected a certain kind of "knee-bending," and Nugent simply refused to comply.[89]

Carl Van Vechten did not sit on a throne and require the black artists whom he helped to kiss his figurative ring, like Charlotte Mason. But from Nugent's perspective, it is possible to construe the effusive homage some black Harlem Renaissance artists paid to Van Vechten as a "kind of knee-bending," an earnest effort on the part of black artists like Waters, Hurston, and others to please a powerful man who had the resources at his disposal to promote their careers. But perhaps it is also true that many friendships, regardless of race, are complicated by imbalances in power at one point or another, and that these imbalances may generate excessive gratitude or bitter resentment. What is certainly true is that Van Vechten's relationships with individual black artists of the Harlem Renaissance were inconsistent, changeable, and complicated, just like the relationship between black art and white influence itself.

I MET YOU AT CARL VAN VECHTEN'S

When Van Vechten became enchanted with a black artist, he wanted his other friends, black and white, to meet him or her. In the mid-1920s, he and Fania Marinoff created an interracial world at their home on West 55th Street, which Walter White dubbed the midtown office of the NAACP. Blacks and whites gathered at the Van Vechtens' and from there often took the party up to Harlem.

"I don't think I've given any parties since 1923, until the present, without asking several Negroes," Van Vechten remembered in 1960.[90] He was famous for his parties, which were numerous and eventful, particularly during the Prohibition years. Van Vechten had a bootlegger who ran a speakeasy in the West Forties.[91] He and Fania had prodigious and eclectic guest lists, which included painter Salvador Dalí, singer Bessie Smith, and publisher Horace Liveright. Before their estrangement, Paul Robeson was a frequent guest, and could often be persuaded to sing. Van Vechten saw James Weldon Johnson regularly, and the two men often talked into the early hours of the morning. The liquor flowed freely, and for Carl, there were plenty of mornings like this one in 1925: "Up at 10, with a hangover & remorse."[92] He woke up after many parties too drunk to remember what had happened the night before.

Entryway of Carl Van Vechten and Fania Marinoff's West 55th Street apartment; portrait of Van Vechten by Martha Baker (Yale Collection of American Literature, Beinecke Rare Book and Manuscript Library. Courtesy of the Carl Van Vechten Trust.)

Drawing room of West 55th Street apartment (Yale Collection of American Literature, Beinecke Rare Book and Manuscript Library. Courtesy of the Carl Van Vechten Trust.)

Van Vechten played host often to Langston Hughes and Zora Neale Hurston. On July 4, 1925, he received one of many visits from George Gershwin, during which the composer rehearsed songs he was working on. At one going-away party, the scintillating Nora Holt shook the house with a rendition of the popular blues song "My Daddy Rocks Me with One Steady Roll," to the confusion of Alice Foote MacDougall, an enterprising restaurateur and successful coffee wholesaler, who thought the song was a spiritual.[93] In August 1925, Holt wrote to thank Marinoff for a party during which the blues singer Clara Smith sang the wildly popular song "Downhearted Blues": "I faintly remember the place disappearing while Clara Smith moaned, I never loved but three mens in my life. I am sure I detested all men at that moment—all but Carl and I forgive him almost everything, even taking my salad away and biting my neck."[94]

The parties at the Van Vechten–Marinoff home on West 55th Street changed Langston Hughes's life. "Your party was like a dream," he wrote to Van Vechten in December 1925, several months into their friendship. He thanked Van Vechten for giving him the chance to meet the actress Marie Doro, one of his childhood idols.[95] Van Vechten's parties were events at which unusual, uncomfortable, and amusing things would happen, planned and spontaneous. There was a gossip party, at which guests repeated or invented rumors about other guests, "who were sure to go right over and tell them all about it," Hughes remembered in The Big Sea. Hughes described another party during which a woman with a pistol in her purse waited in the hall all night for her cheating husband, who never showed up.[96]

A "fat friend" party Carl once gave for the singers Mamie Smith and Marguerite d'Alvarez did not make it into *The Big Sea;* Van Vechten asked Hughes to excise the anecdote in a 1939 letter. "Marguerite has fallen on evil days," he wrote, "is most melancholy, and this would hurt her very much."[97]

At another party, Van Vechten refused a latecomer—Rudolph Valentino. Van Vechten could not abide tardiness or any kind of carelessness with social engagements. In "The Reminiscences of Carl Van Vechten," Oral Carl quoted the silent-film actor Ward McAllister, who once said, "A dinner invitation is a sacred obligation; if you die, send your executor."[98]

"The Twenties were famous for parties; everybody both gave and went to them; there was always plenty to eat and drink, lots of talk and certainly a good deal of lewd behavior," Van Vechten remembered years later.[99] In his daybook, he recounted one "very gay" party in 1927 in which everybody took off their clothes.[100] Carl himself misbehaved often at parties. A few months after *Nigger Heaven* was published, he showed up drunk at an otherwise sober private party in Harlem and so disgusted one guest that she wrote a letter to the editor of the black Harlem newspaper, the *New York Age.* "I am a white woman," she wrote, "and this was my first introduction to a Harlem social gathering. It is not a matter for congratulation that a delightful, high-toned function should have been tarnished—even in this slight degree—by one of my own race."[101]

When he got drunk, Carl could be nasty, as he was during one evening with Hughes, Hurston, and others. "I get very drunk & abusive & finally pass out," he admitted in a 1926 daybook entry.[102] He sometimes became abusive with Marinoff, who would retreat to the house of a close friend for the night. Two months before *Nigger Heaven* was published, they got into a fight and Marinoff left, saying she was leaving him for good. After she left, he couldn't sleep and paced the floor well into the night. "She says she is through forever," he wrote in his daybook the next morning. "If she is what is there in life for me?"[103] They soon reconciled and he was never violent with his wife again, although they continued to quarrel, often in public.

Fania had wearied of the New York social scene by the early 1930s. "I have memories of hundreds of parties in apartments, night clubs, honky tonks, speakeasies—in Harlem, in the Village," she told a reporter for the *New York World-Telegram* in 1932. "It was a phase in the life of this generation. It was very hollow. I never liked it." She said that she and her husband had stopped drinking by that point, but it was a struggle for Carl, and his daybooks in the late 1920s contain a record of his on-again, off-again success with sobriety. Still, the public pronouncement of the end of high living for Fania and Carl was impressive enough for a Cleveland newspaper to carry the headline: "They'll Gin No More: Van Vechtens, Sick of Speakeasies, Quit Drinking."[104]

Both Carl and Fania took pride in the sober side of their parties. As a host, Van Vechten was a genius, using his parties as occasions for a brand of "social work" that not only helped secure support for black artists but also helped break down racial barriers in essential, interpersonal ways, an achievement that legal changes alone simply cannot accomplish. At West 55th

Street, black artists were able to meet powerful whites on the most intimate terms, and cocktails were garnished with a twist of race uplift, whether the guests knew it or not. Black newspapers and magazines kept a careful watch of Van Vechten's interracial social life throughout his life. In 1938, the *New York Amsterdam News* reported: "Zora Neale Hurston . . . paused long enough to attend a dinner which Carl Van Vechten of 'Nigger Heaven' fame gave in her honor." In 1942, the *New York Age* announced: "Socialites Attend Carl Van Vechten Dinner." And in 1960, *Jet* magazine contained a notice of Van Vechten's eightieth birthday celebration.[105]

New York legends were born at 150 West 55th Street. A piece in a 1927 issue of the *New Yorker* entitled "Reunion" reported: "One of the embarrassing moments which the tabloids have not recounted concerns a matron, who, having been away from the city, returned, to be greeted at the Grand Central by one of the darker red-caps. 'How do you do, Mrs. S——,' he murmured, cheerily, and, noting her amazement, added: 'I met you at Carl Van Vechten's!' Of course she remembered. On the way to the cabstand she debated whether it would be proper to tip a social acquaintance. She decided that, in this instance, she should, and a quarter was accepted with due gratitude."[106] Langston Hughes applauded the social politics he saw at the heart of the West 55th Street parties, describing these events as evidence of real democracy at work. Blues singer Ethel Waters remembered how Van Vechten was "credited with knowing at the time more about Harlem than any other white man except the captain of the Harlem police station."[107]

In 1960, Van Vechten responded to a question posed by William Ingersoll about whether the purpose of his mixed parties was to improve race relations: "Well, I always had something like that in mind, but I had my own pleasure too."[108] Pleasure was his motivation, and the urgent and seemingly boundless nature of his desire to know black people would always arouse suspicion among both blacks and whites.

Against the backdrop of Jim Crow segregation, interracial socializing was an act of rebellion. Black and Tans were social clubs that catered to interracial crowds. They were staple features in the slums—"in fact they defined the slums," according to historian Kevin J. Mumford.[109] In the American South, Black and Tan originally referred to a late nineteenth-century coalition of black and white men assembled to defeat a white supremacist party called the Lily Whites. The term evolved from having a purely political association to include social and sexual connotations as well. In these clubs, blacks and whites danced together, an activity that was generally considered immoral because it was assumed that dancing would lead to interracial sex. But it was not only the possibility of interracial sex, both gay and straight, that was considered distasteful, explains Mumford.[110] Interracial coupling in any form was viewed as inherently suspicious by blacks and whites alike. Middle-class blacks disapproved of Black and Tan clubs, and black newspapers characterized the clubs as social menaces that sullied black integrity. Like their white counterparts, many blacks disdained the crossing of racial lines. For black people, the history of white exploitation and the fear of violent racist retribution lay at the root of their contempt. In 1929, a bomb went off in a Chicago nightclub after it went interracial.[111] In no small part, it was because interracial socializing was largely seen as unsavory that Carl Van Vechten and his friends found it appealing, but some of them came to know firsthand the cost of upsetting this particular convention. Actress and dance teacher Rita Romilly, a close friend of Van Vechten's, was disowned by her family, who deplored her interracial social life. She was undaunted by their disapproval, however, and her parties were always heavily populated by the Harlem Renaissance set.

Carl Van Vechten's living room was a veritable Black and Tan. He may have been middle-aged when he threw his first interracial party, but blackness was a central theme in the story of his life.

Yet the author was undeniably white. Carl Van Vechten said that his favorite portrait of himself was an image of him with dark skin and lips even fuller than the set he was born with. Miguel Covarrubias, the artist who drew this image, titled it "A Prediction." But Van Vechten wasn't interested in becoming black. He was no Mezz Mezzrow, a white middle-class jazz musician, son of Russian Jewish immigrants, whose 1946 biography, *Really the Blues,* describes his life as that of a "voluntary Negro" and charts his figurative and literal journey from white to black.[112] It was never Van Vechten's ambition to *become* black. At West 55th Street, Carl Van Vechten lived at the intersection of black and white. He did not want to be black, but he did want blackness. He wanted to know it, to experience it, to represent it, and most of all, to enjoy it.

LOVING THE OTHER

The dynamic of racial sameness and racial difference at the heart of Van Vechten's writing about black art forms describes the essence of primitivism, a concept that emerged in western Europe and reached its apex in the eighteenth century, when transatlantic slavery and colonial expansion were simultaneously at their peak. In *Gone Primitive: Savage Intellects, Modern Lives*, Marianna Torgovnick explains that the primitive world, for those who believed in it, was both exotic and familiar.[113] Exoticism looks a lot like primitivism. They are both portals onto a world of difference. But what is exotic is outside—*out there*, literally and figuratively. In its very etymology, the word refers to that which is considered foreign and strange. What is primitive, however, is already inside, waiting to be set free. In *Civilization and Its Discontents*, Sigmund Freud argued that civilization itself, "the newly-won power over space and time," stood in the way of happiness and could potentially lead to neurosis.[114]

If neurosis was the pathology, primitivism was the antidote. It was a fantasy balm designed for citizens of the modern world who longed for a time and a place free of the confines of industry. Primitivism was an ideal that allowed a retreat into the body and a life before and outside of language. It constituted a sensual awakening to the essential truth of touch, sound, and smell. It was a revival of the self. If the modern city was the product of the mind, then primitivism was the process of the soul.

In 1920s Harlem, the primitive world came alive at night. It was a world of complex texture and brilliant color, spectacular sounds, and fantastic smells. It looked like Josephine Baker,

adorned with bananas and a flapper's spit curls in the Folies
Bergère in 1926–27. It sounded like Duke Ellington, outfitted
in a smart tuxedo at the Cotton Club, where he sat at the piano, pounding out his jungle music. It looked like joy, rhythm,
abandon—like life itself.

To some of us today, it looks like racism. Baker's bananas,
Ellington's jungle rhythms, as well as the Cotton and Plantation
clubs were all inspired by colonialist fantasies that lay at the heart
of the primitive craze. Primitivism upholds immutable distinctions between the teller and the tale. Ultimately, primitivism is
a story about the power of the West to dominate in language as
well as in might. Primitivism is not necessarily racism, however,
as much as they may have in common. Like those of racism, the
roots of primitivism lie in conventional racial imbalances, but
these roots do not necessarily branch out into racist violence.
Primitivists and racists alike believe in fundamental racial differences, but primitivists rejoice in the differences that racists
disdain.

Whether one considers primitivism equivalent to racism, or
even a less pernicious variation of it, it was, irrefutably, a concept central to modernism. Desire for the other defined the
moment. Primitivism *was* the avant-garde; it offered artists in a
variety of media an exciting new way to think about culture.
For instance, Paul Gauguin chose Tahiti for his journey into
darkness because, as he explained to the French painter Odilon,
"Madagascar is too near the civilized world."[115] While Gauguin
crossed continents, Carl Van Vechten and others discovered a
tonic just north of 125th Street. In fact, Van Vechten made a

second career of shepherding others through the Congo of upper Manhattan. "That was almost my fate, for ten years at least: taking people to Harlem," he told William Ingersoll.[116] Harlem was more than a destination; it was his destiny.

"Savages! Savages at heart!" wails Mary Love, a principal character in *Nigger Heaven*. Like her white counterparts of the 1920s, Mary is a victim of the city; in her case, civilization has robbed her of her native racial self. She has lost "her primitive birthright which was so valuable and important an asset, a birthright that all the civilized races were struggling to get back to— this fact explained the art of a Picasso or a Stravinsky."[117] Through no fault of her own, Mary has become unnatural, more white than black. If there is a central lesson in *Nigger Heaven*, it is this: blacks must hold on to their true savage selves or risk something worse than neurosis—annihilation.

When Carl Van Vechten urged black writers and performers to protect their cultural birthright, he was speaking on his own behalf, from the pleasure he took in black difference. He warned against the evils of condescending whites at the same time as he offered up black bodies for the enjoyment of white spectators.

"He loved to twist and squirm with laughter at the oddity of strong contrast," remembered Mabel Dodge Luhan about Carl Van Vechten.[118] Like Van Vechten, Luhan was a patron of the arts, famous for her weekly "Evenings" at her Greenwich Village salon. Van Vechten and Luhan had a tumultuous friendship that included a sixteen-year gap in communication when Van Vechten told her that he didn't like an early draft of her memoirs. "Mabel has her difficult moments, her difficult hours, her difficult days," he wrote of her in his 1955 memoir, "Fragments from an Unwritten Autobiography." But she was worth it. "By her enthusiasm Mabel makes inanimate things live and gives animate beings a more intense life."[119] He modeled a character on Luhan in his 1922 novel *Peter Whiffle*.

Luhan wrote of Carl Van Vechten in *Movers and Shakers*, the third volume of her memoirs, *Intimate Memories*. She explained his attraction to his second wife, Fania Marinoff: "He found he could respond to the exotic small Russian because she was so different." Van Vechten was different looking himself, just as he had been as a child. Luhan described his "large teeth with slits showing between them that jutted out and made him look like a wild boar." Still, "the rest of him looked quite domesticated."[120]

In *Movers and Shakers*, Mabel Dodge Luhan described an "Evening" engineered by Carl, who had promised "two Negro entertainers" for the soirée: "An appalling Negress danced before us in white stockings and black buttoned boots. The man strummed a banjo and sang an embarrassing song while she cavorted. They both leered and rolled their suggestive eyes and made me feel first hot and then cold, for I had never been so near this kind of thing before, but Carl rocked with laughter and little shrieks escaped him as he clapped his pretty hands. His big teeth became wickedly prominent and his eyes rolled in his darkening face, until he grew to somewhat resemble the clattering Negroes before him."[121] Luhan never allowed Carl to bring Negroes to her Evenings again. The scene fascinated and repulsed Luhan, unlike actor and fellow spectator Jack Westley, who found it boring. "It's been done," he yawned, and turned away.[122] But Luhan found the scene compelling, if abhorrent. It is hard to say which scene repulsed—and fascinated—her more: the spectacle of the dancer or of Carl Van Vechten.

Van Vechten's face most likely did not change color, but the pleasure he experienced in the spectacle of blackness was transformative. The transformation began around the same time as that particular Evening, which took place in 1913, the same year Van Vechten reviewed J. Leubrie Hill's show *The Darktown Follies* for the *New York Press*. The audience, he wrote in "The Negro Theatre," an expanded version of his review, "rocked back and forth with low croons; they screamed with delight; they giggled intermittently; they waved their hands; they shrieked, and they pounded their palms vigorously together in an effort, which was availing, to make the entertainers work hard."[123] He admired the dynamic between the actors and the audience. Van Vechten was both within and without this dynamic—in the review, he noted that he was one of the few whites in the theater.

Does race make a difference between the enjoyment taken by the black audience and the enjoyment taken by Van Vechten? To black friends who shared his racial worldview, it did not.

Black artists of the Harlem Renaissance also took pleasure in primitivism for reasons that were as psychological as material. To celebrate that which had been denigrated was to turn negative Old Negro stereotypes on their heads. Langston Hughes, for instance, championed the "low down folks" in his famous essay "The Negro Artist and the Racial Mountain." He defined them as "the people who have their hip of gin on Saturday nights and are not too important to themselves or the community, or too well fed, or too learned to watch the lazy world go around. . . . Their joy runs bang! into ecstasy. Their religion soars to a shout.[124] The black folk described by Hughes were authentic, unconcerned with white opinion. Hughes considered himself one of them, but he was as much an outsider as Van Vechten. During the years of the Harlem Renaissance these two men created a similar story about black authenticity, which was something they both admired from the outside, while looking in and taking notes.

It was important to some black people that white people enjoyed the spectacle of primitivism. For instance, Alain Locke believed that the elevation of the primitive to the world of high art enabled whites to view blacks with appreciation as opposed to denigration, and he applauded the primitivist leanings of white modern artists like Pablo Picasso and Henri Matisse. For Locke and others who glorified Africa, however, the continent was more fantasy than reality.

In his 1940 autobiography, *The Big Sea*, Hughes recalled a life-changing journey to Africa he made in 1923. "My Africa, Motherland of the Negro peoples! And me a Negro! Africa! The real thing, to be touched and seen, not merely read about in a book." But Africa, the real Africa, was disappointing. Hughes was forced to confront the realities of colonialism that dehumanized the people and made them outsiders in their own countries. He would take away an experience of Africa that included "white men with guns at their belts, inns and taverns with signs up, EUROPEANS ONLY, missionary churches with the Negroes in the back seats and the whites who teach Jesus in the front rows." And perhaps even worse, he discovered that he was an outsider to those with whom he felt a kinship. "But there was one thing that hurt me a lot when I talked with the people," he remembered in *The Big Sea*. "The Africans looked at me and would not believe I was a Negro."[125] Hughes discovered that his race did not provide him with organic knowledge of the motherland. In fact, his brown skin did not even make him black in the eyes of the Africans he met.

"Africa!"—the single word accompanied by an exclamation point—provides the rhythm in Hughes's essay "The Negro Artist and the Racial Mountain," which was published three years after his eye-opening journey. It is a celebration of the memory of his childish excitement over the trip, the fantastic exuberance he felt about putting flesh to a dream. "The tom-tom cries and the tom-tom laughs," Hughes wrote. The classic African drum connects modern black identity with a traditional African past that was shunned by those blacks who wanted "to be as little Negro and as much American as possible." When Hughes wrote of "the eternal tom-tom beating in the Negro soul," he was celebrating a blackness that extends across oceans and time, and reinforces the concept of black difference.[126] Like Carl Van Vechten, Hughes believed in black difference as a defense against the internalized racism he saw infecting the lives and imaginations of black people.

At the same time, the connection, however fantasized, that Hughes made between African and black identities has always been central in African American history, and crucial to the psychic survival of black people. As literary critic Robert B. Stepto suggests: "While the 'African' part of 'African American' gives us a place in this world as much as 'American' does, it also teasingly asks us to find it, in a haystack as big as a continent."[127] The struggle to distinguish blackness from Americanness may never be resolved; meaning lies in the struggle itself, the continual and necessary attempt to identify black difference. It provided a link, too, between black and white lovers of Harlem. So it should not be surprising that Hughes and Van Vechten used the same vocabulary to talk about blackness—it is an American vocabulary, after all.

In his attitudes toward primitivism, Hughes changed over the years. In an October 30, 1941, letter to Van Vechten, Hughes wrote: "And I hope (even beg and entreat via letters to the entire Knopf staff) that nobody will, in publicizing my book or writing the blurb, use the words:

childlike
primitive
un-moral
amoral
or
simple

which, aside from being untrue when applied to the American scene, have been quite out-worn in describing Negroes and books by and about Negroes."[128] The concept of primitivism that Hughes and Van Vechten had both championed in the 1920s as an avenue for black artistic freedom had become a straitjacket for Hughes, who had become a character in the story of the primitive—a story that he had in part written. Van Vechten was never similarly constrained; he had always been free to write as he pleased. The difference, of course, was race.

PANSIES AND MARGUERITES TO YOU

Van Vechten's valedictions reflected his fanciful personality. "Turkeys and Cranberries to You!" was how he signed off on a letter to Langston Hughes in November 1925. He volunteered sprigs of larkspur on the eve of 1933. In January 1946 he offered Hughes "four brightcolored roosters to you and a hen to make them happy!" He ended a 1954 letter to Hughes wishing him "18 vestal virgins (housebroken)."[129]

Sometimes they had no direct references, but the last in the litany above refers to an oratorio written by Hughes, "The Five Foolish Virgins." Hughes's libretto was based on a story in the book of Matthew about five wise virgins who waited for their bridegrooms and their foolish counterparts who failed to do so. Hughes often reciprocated Van Vechten's whimsy, but just as often he reverted to "sincerely," which irritated Van Vechten. Once he scolded Hughes: "I wish to GOD you would stop signing yourself 'sincerely.' One is sincere with the butcher."[130] Ten days later, Hughes retorted: "I've been knocking myself out on three (3) very URGENT and long overdue book deadlines, so I reckon *Sincerely* was about the limit of my vocabulary." And then he indulged his friend: "Yours with pomegranates, sequins, gold dust, and melon seed from here on unto the end, Langston."[131] Carl became frustrated when Langston lapsed again. "Appar-

ently I cannot cure you of your business signature of 'sincerely,'"
he wrote Hughes. "So I will take this the way I presume it was
meant. At least it is unique, as no other of my numerous corre-
spondents is so formal."[132] Van Vechten never bothered Langston
about his mode of closing letters again.

When he was feeling creative, Hughes invented unique
closing lines for Van Vechten, as did Van Vechten for his close
friends. There was one, however, that they traded back and forth
in 1925 within a few weeks of the beginning of their correspondence: "Pansies and Marguerites to You." Van Vechten and Hughes
met during an era when gay men were known as pansies or by
the names of other flowers, to the point where collectively they
were sometimes called "horticultural lads." Quite possibly, this
particular farewell was a nod to the popular lexicon of the gay
male world that both Hughes and Van Vechten inhabited. In
Van Vechten's case, his location in that world was literal; at West
55th Street, he lived squarely in the center of what was known
as the "Faggy Fifties."[133]

The black world uptown flourished alongside the burgeoning
gay world of Greenwich Village. The Negro vogue, in fact, gave
way to the "pansy craze," to use a phrase coined by historian
George Chauncey.[134] The most important gay ball in New York
was the Hamilton Lodge Ball, held in Harlem. Langston Hughes
referred to this drag ball in *The Big Sea* in a chapter called "Spectacles in Color."[135] It was a spectacular event, documented in the
black press: "Men Step out in Gorgeous Finery of Other Sex to
Vie for Beauty Prizes," announced a 1930 headline in the *New
York Amsterdam News*. Still, Harlem clubs that were known to

tolerate homosexuality were themselves on the social margins, frequently located in tenement apartments.[136]

The flourishing of a homosexual culture in Harlem was occasioned, in large part, by racism, like the black enclave of Harlem itself. Officials dispatched to squelch vice in other parts of New York looked the other way in Harlem.[137] Harlem residents tolerated homosexuality for the same reason they tolerated white tourists: they had no other choice. Harlem in the 1920s may have been magical, but it was a relatively powerless place in New York, and a substantial number of its residents resented the gay social scene. Still, because of Harlem's "relative openness, and an absence of aggressively enforced codes of conduct, Harlem was an oasis for its own gay population, as well as for white homosexuals who traveled uptown for sanctuary and excitement," explains Kevin Mumford.[138] Certainly, Carl Van Vechten can be counted among gay downtown whites who went uptown in search of sexual recreation.

In 1962, two years before he died, Carl Van Vechten bequeathed to Yale University more than twenty cartons of material: boxes of photographs as well as scrapbooks filled with drawings and newspaper clippings. They arrived in sealed boxes, with instructions not to open them until twenty-five years after his death.

What Van Vechten had bequeathed to Yale was a lasting testament to the breadth of his erotic interests as well as those of some of his friends, like film and theater producer George George, the painter Richard Banks, and others whose unsigned drawings, photographs, and postcards are included in the collection. In many ways, the scrapbooks are "homemade sex books," as art historian Jonathan Weinberg describes them.[139] They document sex in a variety of media: photographs, stories, captions, newspaper clippings, and comics. They are pornographic: the images range from pictures depicting sex between "beautiful boys," as Van Vechten called some young male subjects, to relatively tame drawings of big-muscled sailors that recall adolescent daydream doodling. Some are funny: a photograph of a man hammering a dildo into another man's anus has the caption, "Tom Punches Out." Some tend toward the sophomoric; Van Vechten collected newspaper misspellings: a wife is a fine "cock," not "cook," for instance. There are repeated jokes concerning the number 69; Van Vechten even saved a coat check receipt bearing the number.[140] A few have a somber tone: one article details the murder-suicide of a twenty-nine-year old Boy Scout leader and a fifteen-year old member of his troop. Prior to their deaths, they were "inseparable." Throughout the scrapbooks, scattered images nod to his interest in black primitivism.

Perhaps most important, the scrapbooks are historical. As Jonathan Weinberg puts it, Van Vechten "found homosexuality where homosexuality had been suppressed—the crime reports—and he found homosexuality where it was not supposed to be—the tennis court or the wrestling mat."[141] The crime reports to which Weinberg refers include an article entitled "Sailor Accused of Slaying of Noted Soccer Official." The story includes "vague hints that the victim was homosexual." Another example is a report that the president of the senior class at the University of

Pennsylvania had been arrested on "morals charges." He had been "arrested with a 40-year old man at 52nd and Market Sts. last Monday." Yet another article describes a kidnapping in which the victim was robbed and stripped naked. His four abductors restrained him and drove around for hours. Van Vechten underlined a particular detail: "He said the four forced him to lie on the floor in back and *sat on his head when he* tried to get up." Van Vechten found meaning beyond language, in the invisible interiors of the news being reported. He accompanied the articles and images with ironic captions cut out from newspapers and magazines so that they resemble the cliché of a ransom note. The scrapbook is mostly comprised of articles from the 1950s, but there are earlier ones, including a 1927 article from the *Chicago Defender* about a "dancing party" held at the Renaissance Casino in Harlem, one of the "gayest affairs" in New York.[142]

In their range and detail, these documents are reminders of buried histories, lives that were extinguished under social repression and the general hostility toward homosexuality that even today makes it impossible for many people to live honestly. But the scrapbooks also include stories of progress, as in a 1957 *New York World-Telegram and Sun* report: "A government committee on vice today recommended easing Britain's laws on homosexuality. The committee suggested homosexual behavior in private between consenting adult males 21 years old or older should no longer be a criminal offense." There are articles that detail daring challenges to heterosexism. An example is a 1954 newspaper story about a lesbian couple in Downham, near

"The Village Meets Harlem," *Chicago Defender*, April 16, 1927 (Yale Collection of American Literature, Beinecke Rare Book and Manuscript Library. Courtesy of the Carl Van Vechten Trust.)

Coat check receipt, Carl Van Vechten scrapbooks (Yale Collection of American Literature, Beinecke Rare Book and Manuscript Library. Courtesy of the Carl Van Vechten Trust.)

YOU'LL AGREE
IT'S THE Nth DEGREE!

East African postman carries
special letters in the lobe of his
ear

A MAN'S CHOCOLATE

Good Thing Still A Good Thing

"Good Thing Still a Good Thing," Carl Van Vechten scrapbooks (Yale Collection of American Literature, Beinecke Rare Book and Manuscript Library. Courtesy of the Carl Van Vechten Trust.)

"Yale May Not Think So," Carl Van Vechten scrapbooks (Yale Collection of American Literature, Beinecke Rare Book and Manuscript Library. Courtesy of the Carl Van Vechten Trust.)

London, that successfully married before the vicar discovered the bridegroom was a woman.[143]

The dominant tone is humorous, however. One caption teases: "Yale May Not Think So, But It'll Be Just Jolly."[144] But the scrapbooks constitute more than an elaborate prank. Even as they poke fun at the institution that would house them, the secrecy under which he bequeathed them suggests Van Vechten's certainty that the scrapbooks, had their true nature been revealed, would not have been welcome. Van Vechten's decision to ask Yale librarians to wait twenty-five years after his death to open the boxes reflects his hope that, by that time, the culture would have transformed enough to welcome the historical record the scrapbooks contain.

GAY POET OR NEGRO POET?

The scrapbooks and the collection of nude photographs that were part of Van Vechten's gift to Yale leave no question as to Van Vechten's homosexual desires. Much speculation still swirls around the true story of the sexuality of Langston Hughes. None of his autobiographical writings contain homosexual confessions; unlike Van Vechten, he left no posthumous revelations for scholars to uncover. Added to Hughes's own interest in keeping certain aspects of his life from public view have been the efforts of multiple other people to maintain a portrait of Hughes as heterosexual. These efforts may reflect, in some cases, a response to public pressure, actual or anticipated. In other cases, they may reflect the personal anxieties or prejudices of those who feel the need to quash the question of

Hughes's sexuality. Like any other revered public figure, Hughes is a reflection of his admirers' own desires. He is an invention, what others choose to see.

"In addition to being the best-known, most-read, and most frequently taught African American and, in many cases, American poets, Langston Hughes is also the rare poet for whom one could easily conjure a picture," the poet Elizabeth Alexander has written.[145] Hughes was a defender of the people, an advocate of "the so-called common element."[146] Hughes was a "race man" in the classic sense, much like W. E. B. Du Bois. Carl Van Vechten understood what Hughes symbolized, and wrote to him on November 4, 1941: "I see your name everywhere and I guess you are Garvey, Father Divine, James Weldon Johnson, and James L Ford all rolled into ONE." He had advice about *The Big Sea* and what would eventually become *I Wonder as I Wander*, the second volume of Hughes's autobiography: "Incidentally the history of the race in America can pretty well be read in autobiographies: (1) William Wells Brown (2) Frederick Douglass (3) Booker T Washington (4) W E B Du Bois (5) James Weldon Johnson (6) The Big Sea and its successor."[147]

There were other men, like James Weldon Johnson or W. E. B. Du Bois, for instance, whose work and manner symbolized the ambitions of the Harlem Renaissance. But in his physical beauty, the sensuality of his prose, and his determination to valorize the beat of the tom-tom, jazz, and the "soul-world" of the Negro, Hughes captured the poetry of black life in a way that Du Bois and Johnson did not. If these two men were admired, Hughes was adored. After Hughes swept the *Opportunity* awards dinner in 1925, he continued to find institutional acknowledgment of his talent for the rest of his life. He was the recipient of multiple grants and awards, the subject of abundant positive reviews, and the object of consistent public admiration. Those who recognized his talent early on were ardent in their desire to help and be associated with him.

Not a small amount of that enthusiasm was related to Hughes's charm and good looks. Some people admired him as much for his beauty as for his writing. "Langston is back from his African trip looking like a virile brown god," Countee Cullen wrote to Alain Locke in November 1923.[148] In *The Life of Langston Hughes,* Rampersad describes a romantic triangle involving Hughes, Locke, and Cullen that left Locke hurt and disappointed.[149] Hughes had the same effect on women. His ambiguity frustrated dancer Sylvia Chen, to whom Hughes sent mixed signals for several years before she gave up and married someone else. She wrote to him, "I find I can't be natural with you, because you treat me and most people . . . so artificially."[150]

It was, in part, the ubiquity of his public image that led some people to desire Hughes, as fans imagine they might eventually wind up with the movie star of their dreams. On November 30, 1948, Hampton University's *Hampton Script* promised: "With $$, You Can Marry Hughes." Hughes had visited Hampton on his recent lecture tour. "The handsome traveler contended that the reason he is single today is because he has not found the woman who wished to 'stay on the go.' He continued, 'I do consider myself an "eligible bachelor." However, the woman must meet certain financial specifications.' "[151] This article recalls an item in Van Vechten's scrapbooks, an article whose headline winks: "Noted Men Explain Why They're Single."[152]

Hughes must have known that his appeal served as a kind of social currency. He may have found something useful in remaining elusive. There may have been something productive, materially and otherwise, in creating desire and never fulfilling it, as it is possible to discern from the records of his life that he and others left behind. Langston Hughes was the object of both male and female desire, but in his memoirs he referred only to heterosexual relationships. Yet while he was never as explicit as Van Vechten, according to some critics, there are multiple suggestions in his writing about his sexual interest in men. For others, any portrayal of Hughes as a gay man tarnishes his image as a race man, and there have been multiple efforts to repress public discussions about Hughes's possible homosexuality. One of the most remarkable instances of this repression occurred around the release of the 1989 film *Looking for Langston*. The film, directed by Isaac Julien, is a meditation on gay male culture during the Harlem Renaissance through the prism of the enigmatic sexual identity of Langston Hughes. When Julien and other members of the black British film collective Sankofa showed the film to the Hughes estate, officials there refused to grant permission unless every direct visual and textual reference to Hughes's sexuality was removed from the film.

The panic generated by the suggestion that Hughes may have enjoyed the intimate company of men testifies to the centrality of heterosexuality in the traditional portrait of black male heroism. Ada Griffin, then director of the New York–based Third World

Newsreel, the distributor of *Looking for Langston*, bolstered this argument when she suggested that many of those involved in the production and distribution of the film were simply unaware of the degree of resistance they would encounter from members of the "black bourgeoisie" who consider Hughes "a racial icon."[153] Hughes's status as an icon has depended upon assumptions about his heterosexuality. In no small part, Carl Van Vechten's sexuality has posed a threat to Hughes's iconic status.

George Chauncey Jr., Martin Duberman, and Martha Vicinus remind us in the opening pages of *Hidden from History:* "Homosexuality is not merely a personal characteristic to be alternately ignored or celebrated, as some historians have assumed, but a significant influence on the lives of individuals and on patterns of cultural organizations in ways that historians need to explore."[154] But the question of the importance of sexuality in a writer's life remains, like questions that have historically surrounded the relationship between race and writing, an issue embodied in the essential dilemma captured by Countee Cullen in 1924, when he declared to a reporter for the *Brooklyn Eagle* that he wanted to be known as a "POET and not a NEGRO POET."[155] Gay poet or Negro poet? Which aspects of our identities are essential? Which are contingent? Does a writer have the authority to resolve these dilemmas for himself, or will history always, ultimately, decide for him?

WHAT IS A NEGRO WRITER, ANYHOW?

In March 1926, Du Bois launched "The Negro in Art: How Shall He Be Portrayed?" a symposium published in the *Crisis*.

For seven months, he solicited answers from a racially diverse group of literary figures from all corners of the American literary world. The questionnaire asked:

1. When the artist, black or white, portrays Negro characters is he under any obligations or limitations as to the sort of character he will portray?
2. Can any author be criticized for painting the worst or the best characters of a group?
3. Can publishers be criticized for refusing to handle novels that portray Negroes of education and accomplishment, on the ground that these characters are no different from white folk and therefore not interesting?
4. What are Negroes to do when they are continually painted at their worst and judged by the public as they are painted?
5. Does the situation of the educated Negro in America with its pathos, humiliation, and tragedy call for artistic treatment at least as sincere and sympathetic as *Porgy* received?
6. Is not the continual portrayal of the sordid, foolish, and criminal among Negroes convincing the world that this and this alone is really and essentially Negroid, and preventing white artists from knowing any other types and preventing black artists from daring to paint them?
7. Is there not a danger that young colored writers will be tempted to follow the popular trend in portraying Negro character in the underworld rather than seeking to paint the truth about themselves and their own social class?[156]

In his introduction to the questionnaire, Du Bois discussed the convention of racist portrayals of blacks in literature by whites. He argued, "While the individual portrait may be true and artistic, the net result to American literature to date is to picture twelve million Americans as prostitutes, thieves and fools and that such 'freedom' in art is miserably unfair."[157] Du Bois's remarks concerned white writers who capitalized on racist imagery, but the questionnaire in general reflected anxieties about the effect that the popularization of this imagery would have on black writers. One of Du Bois's fears was that the art of black writers beholden to white philanthropy would be necessarily compromised. Carl Van Vechten led the first round of responders. "I am fully aware of the reasons why Negroes are sensitive in regard to fiction which attempts to picture the lower strata of the race," he began. "The point is that this an attitude completely inimical to art."[158]

In his response to the 1926 *Crisis* questionnaire, Van Vechten rehearsed views on black art that he had been developing since his 1920 essay "The Negro Theatre," but his reply was the first time that he had tried his ideas out on a black readership. Since "The Negro Theatre," Van Vechten had published a series of essays on black culture and performance in *Vanity Fair*, beginning with "Folksongs of the American Negro," a July 1925 treatise on black spirituals. He insisted that "the unpretentious sincerity that inspires them makes them the peer or superior of any folk music the world has ever known."[159] In August he turned his attention to the blues. "Like the Spirituals, the Blues are folksongs and are conceived in the same pentatonic scale, omitting the fourth and seventh tones—although those that have achieved publication or performance under sophisticated auspices have generally passed through a process of transmutation." His tone wavered between scientific and romantic as he described the features of blues music, mainly its "rich idioms, metaphoric phrases, and striking word combinations." He borrowed ideas on the subject from Langston Hughes, with whom he had begun a friendship two weeks before he wrote the article. He had secured Hughes's permission to quote extensively from two letters Hughes had written him. "There seems to be a monotonous melancholy, an animal sadness, running through all Negro jazz that is almost terrible at times," Hughes had reflected in a letter to Van Vechten, who offered these words to the readers of *Vanity Fair*.[160]

Van Vechten discussed black theater in October 1925 in the article "Prescription for the Negro Theatre," whose subtitle ran "Being a Few Reasons Why the Great Colored Show Has Not Yet Been Achieved." By "great colored show," Van Vechten meant a show produced and written by a Negro; apparently, his excitement over *Granny Maumee* in 1914 had waned in retrospect. Van Vechten's ideas on black theater may have evolved from the descriptive to the prescriptive, but they were ultimately the same. Just as he had in "The Negro Theatre," Van Vechten insisted in "Prescription for the Negro Theatre" that authentic black theater would not succeed until black artists began to value what was already theirs, which included "honest-to-God Blues, full of trouble and pain and misery and heartache and tribulation"—not the popular, sanitized blues of Irving Berlin. Even more important, Van Vechten suggested, Negro shows should use chorus girls that reflected the "human palette of color." "Seek beauties who can dance and sing," he suggested," and see that the lightest is about the shade of strong coffee before the cream is poured in, and I guarantee that your show will be a success." If the Negro would only stick to his own material, he would meet the success already achieved by white writers and producers who were not shy to exploit that material, but who lacked the natural ability to truly understand it.[161]

For W. E. B. Du Bois, any advice that the black artist should stick to his own material was an insult. "We can go on the stage; we can be just as funny as white Americans wish us to be; we can play all the sordid parts that America likes to assign to Negroes; but for anything else there is still small place for us," he wrote in "Criteria of Negro Art."[162] Van Vechten understood the dangers of the plantation stereotypes. "The Negro, who has suffered so much, wants to forget the old environment of slavery and broaden out into an imitation of white life," he wrote in "The Negro Theatre."[163] He sympathized with those who wanted the Old Negro to die, but he also held fast to his belief that if the "coon" and "darky" disappeared, the unique quality of black artistry would disappear with them.

However much they clashed, both Van Vechten and Du Bois believed that there was something distinct about black art. "Just as soon as true Art emerges; just as soon as the black artist appears," Du Bois wrote in a 1926 *Crisis* essay, "Criteria of Negro Art," "someone touches the race on the shoulder and says, 'He did that because he was an American, not because he was a Negro; he was born here; he was trained here; he is not a Negro—what is a Negro anyhow? He is just human.'"[164] Du Bois believed that to be a Negro is to be human, but to be a Negro is also to be a Negro, a living repository of the particularities and incongruities of black identity.

Born in 1868, Du Bois was both conservative and forward thinking when it came to the American race problem, and his contradictory views are evident in his criticism of black art, in which he both deplored and advocated black self-consciousness, particularly when it came to writing. His competing perspectives are evident in "Criteria of Negro Art," one of his most famous essays. "The white public today demands from its artists, literary and pictorial, racial pre-judgment which deliberately distorts Truth and Justice, as far as colored races are concerned," Du Bois reasoned. He believed strongly that African American art should serve as a vehicle to better black social and political lives. Therefore, black art must present black people in a manner that made obvious their respectability according to bourgeois norms. "We are bound by all sorts of customs that have come down as second-hand soul clothes of white patrons," he explained. "We are ashamed of sex and we lower our eyes when people will talk of it. Our religion holds us in superstition. Our worst side has been so shamelessly emphasized that we are denying we have or ever had a worst side. In all sorts of ways we are hemmed in and our new young artists have got to fight their way to freedom."[165] Du Bois did not believe in self-censorship, but he was certain that black artists had a responsibility to reckon honestly and fully with the implications of their work. Nothing less than the future of the race was in their hands.

Du Bois and Van Vechten fundamentally disagreed on the nature and purpose of black art, but they were similarly concerned with the attitudes of whites toward blacks, as were most Harlem Renaissance writers, by necessity. In 1922, James Weldon Johnson published *The Book of American Negro Poetry*, the first anthology of African American literature. The collection was more than a repository of black verse. Its purpose was to establish the humanity of black people. Johnson explained in his introduction: "A people may become great through many means, but there is only one measure by which its greatness is recognized or acknowledged": art. Literature, painting, poetry, and other fine arts were means through which to prove that blacks deserved a role on the national stage. Black artists themselves never doubted their merit. But like it or not, Johnson explained, white opinion necessarily counted the most. The black artist had no choice but to keep white readers in mind. "The public, generally speaking," Johnson wrote, "does not know that there are American Negro poets."[166] It does not need to be said that "the public" to which he refers—and which he means to educate—is white. It is this audience whose sympathies all black writers were forced to solicit in order to have a respectable public existence.

Six years later, Johnson believed the problem had improved dramatically. "The Negro author—the creative author—has arrived," he proclaimed in his 1928 essay "The Dilemma of the Negro Author," published in *American Mercury*. "America is aware today that there are such things as Negro authors," he wrote.[167] Like Du Bois's "public," Johnson's "America" was white. In his

duty as an agent for larger changes, the black artist had succeeded, Johnson concluded in another essay, "Race Prejudice
and the Negro Artist," published in *Harper's* a month prior to his
American Mercury essay.[168] Yet the Negro author was still confronted with an age-old dilemma. Unlike the "plain American
author," Johnson explained, the "Aframerican" author was faced
with the problem of a divided audience. "The moment a Negro
writer takes up his pen or sits down to his typewriter he is
immediately called upon to solve, consciously or unconsciously,
this problem of the double audience."[169]

Would black readerships solve the problem? No, answered
Johnson. When they did exist, they exerted their own particular pressure on the African American writer. He explained: "When
he turns from the conventions of white America he runs afoul
of the taboos of black America. He has no more absolute freedom to speak as he pleases addressing black America than he
has in addressing white America. There are certain phases of
life that he dare not touch, certain subjects that he dare not
critically discuss, certain manners of treatment that he dare not
use—except at the risk of rousing bitter resentment."[170]

Langston Hughes was willing to risk both the resentment of
black readers and the disappointment of white readers. In 1926,
he announced he was finished with looking over his shoulder
and guessing at possible reactions to his work. He threw off the
shackles of white *and* black spectatorship alike with the famous
lines: "We younger Negro artists who create now intend to
express our individual dark-skinned selves without fear or
shame. If white people are pleased we are glad. If they are not,

it doesn't matter. We know we are beautiful. And ugly too. The tom-tom cries and the tom-tom laughs. If colored people are pleased we are glad. If they are not, their displeasure doesn't matter either. We build our temples for tomorrow, strong as we know how, and we stand on top of the mountain, free within ourselves."[171]

Hughes began "The Negro Artist and the Racial Mountain" by citing an unnamed fellow black poet (Countee Cullen), who wanted to be known as "a poet—not a Negro poet." The description was accurate, but James Weldon Johnson, for one, believed that Cullen was a racial poet—more of a racial poet than Hughes—whatever his ambitions. Cullen acceded to the characterization in a letter to Harold Jackman: "James Weldon Johnson may be perfectly right about my being more of a racial artist than Langston, and about my being at my best in racial poems. Even so, if that is the truth, I find it [a] bitter and unfortunate truth, and were I criticising my own work, I should condemn myself from that standpoint."[172]

Cullen published a mixed review of *The Weary Blues*, Hughes's first book and the winner in the poetry category of the first *Opportunity* awards contest (Cullen placed second). "I regard the jazz poems as interlopers in the company of the truly beautiful poems in other sections of the book," he wrote. "In the light of reflection I wonder if jazz poems really belong to that dignified company, that select austere circle of high literary expression which we call poetry."[173] Cullen, son of the premier African Methodist Episcopal minister in Harlem, was deeply religious, and he characterized Hughes's poetry as a "storm" that prevented true communion with God. Cullen sent the review to Van Vechten before he published it. Cullen warned him, "I am sure you will disagree with me terribly in a number of things that I have said, but that is inevitable, and I would rather quarrel with you than most people."[174]

To Hughes, Cullen's ambition to be a poet and not a Negro poet was a sign of racial self-hatred. The poet's failure to hear the "eternal tom-tom beating in the Negro soul" was evidence that he had been vanquished by whiteness. For Hughes, racial integrity for the black artist meant embracing the divide decried by Du Bois and Johnson, the eternal and intractable distinction between black and white. Like Carl Van Vechten, Hughes believed in, and celebrated, black difference. But he also believed that a Negro poet was already a poet, and the connection between blackness and Americanness did not have to be insisted upon—it already existed. Hughes and Van Vechten both embraced the paradox of the simultaneity of black sameness and difference.

Johnson's "Dilemma of the Negro Writer," written two years after "The Negro Artist and the Racial Mountain," contains a cautionary tale for writers like Hughes. "I have sometimes thought it would be a way out," Johnson wrote, "that the Negro author would be on surer ground and truer to himself, if he could disregard white America; if he could say to white America, 'What I have written, I have written. I hope you'll be interested and like it. If not, I can't help it.' But it is impossible for a sane American Negro to write with total disregard for nine-tenths of the people of the United States. Situated as his own race is amidst and amongst them, their influence is irresistible."[175]

That influence was also destructive. Like Du Bois's concept of "double-consciousness," Johnson's "dilemma" caused a rupture in the black self. Conflicting desires to write without constraints and to produce work that might "have some effect on the white world for the good of his [the black writer's] race," in Johnson's words, engendered a kind of schizophrenia in black writing, Johnson argued: "On one page black America is his whole or main audience, and on the very next page white America."[176] The obligations of race uplift and the "irresistible" nature of white influence wreaked havoc on black creativity. Hughes's claims of freedom amounted only to wishful thinking.

But Johnson believed that the black artist's predicament would change, and that it was up to the artists themselves to change it. In the concluding paragraph of his essay, Johnson advised the Negro author to "fashion something that rises above race, and reaches out to the universal in truth and beauty."[177] His diagnosis raises a serious question: even if it were possible, would it ever be desirable for the black writer to "rise above race"? When we wish away race, what is it exactly that we are trying to make disappear?

A PECULIAR ART

Hughes used "The Negro Artist and the Racial Mountain" to bash not only Countee Cullen but everyone—readers and writers alike—who shared Du Bois's view that black writers should remember their racial duty every time they took pen to paper. Ostensibly, however, Hughes crafted the essay as a direct response to "The Negro-Art Hokum" by George Schuyler, which had been published in the *Nation* the week before. In his essay, Schuyler characterized any belief in an African American art form distinct from a white, or "mainstream," American art form as a foolish myth.[178] "As for the literature, painting, and sculpture of Aframericans—such as there is—it is identical in kind with the literature, painting, and sculpture of white Americans," Schuyler insisted.[179]

Schuyler pulled no punches in "The Negro-Art Hokum." He described the African American as a "lampblacked Anglo-Saxon" and insisted that all arguments concerning the singular quality of black identity had been concocted by "Negrophobists" who subscribed to the myth "that there are 'fundamental, eternal, and inescapable differences' between white and black Americans." He continued: "On this baseless premise, so flattering to the white mob, that the blackamoor is inferior and fundamentally different, is erected the postulate that he must needs be peculiar; and when he attempts to portray life through the medium of art, it must of necessity be a peculiar art. While such reasoning may seem conclusive to the majority of Americans, it must be rejected with a loud guffaw by intelligent people."[180]

George Schuyler thrived on the controversy he attracted throughout his career. He was a rebel, a socialist in the 1920s and a rabid anticommunist in the 1960s. He often ridiculed the self-seriousness of Harlem Renaissance writers. But beneath the provocative barbs of "The Negro-Art Hokum," Schuyler issued a serious challenge to the logic of Du Bois and Johnson, who believed that America was composed of two distinct halves, one black and one white. Schuyler contended that a common national identity united black and white Americans that superseded racial or ethnic allegiances. To him, the division between American and Negro was a fiction, one that had never existed at all. He did not believe in racial homogeneity; he believed in national diversity.

Carl Van Vechten liked Schuyler very much, and when Isak Dinesen, author of the 1937 memoir *Out of Africa,* asked a Negro escort to a book party, he chose George Schuyler for the task. "It's in doing things like that that I forwarded the Negro's cause, not by writing propaganda," Van Vechten told oral historian William Ingersoll in 1960.[181]

Van Vechten, Schuyler, and Hughes were similar in their disdain for propaganda, humorless advertisements for race pride and black uplift in the guise of art. For these three men, and the rest of their cohort, real black art should refuse, even contradict, the careful approach advocated by Du Bois. Van Vechten and Hughes wrote with reverence about "the squalor of Negro life, the vice of Negro life."[182] Both Hughes and Van Vechten defended the black artist's right to paint the world and its citizens as he saw them. "The true artist speaks out fearlessly," Van Vechten believed. If the true artist is black and declines to represent "the sordid but fantastic experience of Lenox Avenue," then he effectively "delivers his great gifts to the exploitation of the white man," wrote Van Vechten.[183] In reality, few black artists were in a position to "deliver" anything to whites, and the story of white appropriation of black artistic gifts is, in essence, the story of African American experience in this country. In his essays and reviews, Van Vechten revealed that he understood the complex and historically unjust dynamic between whiteness and blackness, but when it didn't suit his purposes, he simply refused to recognize it.

Van Vechten had one message when it came to race and the arts, and he hammered it home with the conviction of a missionary: black artists should manipulate white stereotypes, fears, and fantasies about black people for their own benefit. In "Moanin' wid a Sword in Mah Han'," his final *Vanity Fair* essay, Van Vechten urged black writers to take advantage of white interest in black life. That single theme echoed throughout his writing about black literature, theater, and music. "It is a foregone conclusion," he wrote in "Moanin'" about black spirituals, "that with the craving to hear these songs that is known to exist on the part of the public, it will not be long before white singers have taken them over and made them enough their own so that the public will be surfeited sooner or later with opportunities to enjoy them, and—when the Negro tardily offers to sing them in public—it will perhaps be too late to stir the interest which now lies latent in the breast of every music lover."[184]

Van Vechten's advice to black artists was simple, consistent, and unsentimental to the point of being crass. Like an evangelist, he warned of the particular hell awaiting those who failed to heed his admonition: if black artists failed to exploit the "wealth of novel, exotic, picturesque material" at their finger-tips, some enterprising white artist would do it.[185]

And just as he predicted, one particularly enterprising white writer did. Carl Van Vechten published "Moanin' wid a Sword in Mah Han'" in June 1926. *Nigger Heaven* would be released in August.

2 *NIGGER HEAVEN*

A STUDENT OF THE COLORED RACE

"Title of 'Nigger Heaven' comes to me today," wrote Carl Van Vechten in his August 14, 1925, daybook entry. Like a prophecy, the title announced itself on an otherwise typical day that ended with a trip to the upscale Renaissance Casino and Ballroom in Harlem. There, Van Vechten joined Walter White, Rudolph Fisher, Eric Walrond, Langston Hughes, Bruce Nugent, W. E. B. Du Bois, Jesse Fauset, Countee Cullen, and others for the announcement of the first round of *Crisis* magazine awards. On the same day, Van Vechten's *Firecrackers* was released. It was the last in a quartet of novels that began with *Peter Whiffle* (1922) and was followed by *The Blind Bow-Boy* (1923) and *The Tattooed Countess* (1924). In *Firecrackers*, Gareth Johns, the protagonist of *The Tattooed Countess*, explains the title of the book: "Explosions which create relationships are sporadic and terminating, but if you avoid the explosions you perdurably avoid intercourse."[1]

An exercise in avoidance *Nigger Heaven* was not. It quickly became the key ingredient in the pot of turbulence that had begun to simmer between the old and new literary guard of the Negro Renaissance. The conflict concerned one of the most contested issues during the Negro Renaissance: the relationship between race and art. *Nigger Heaven* took the disturbance to a boil and brought to the fore one of the most pressing questions for readers and writers of African American literature: does a white person, any white person, have the authority to tell a black story? In particular a story called "nigger"?

The title came suddenly, but it took Van Vechten several months to begin writing *Nigger Heaven*. In May 1925 he had made his first attempts to write his "Negro novel," as he referred to it in those early days, but illness, work, and parties and other pleasures kept getting in the way. He drank—and he worried. "I hope soon to start work on my Negro novel, but I feel rather alarmed," he confided to Hughes in early June of that year. "It would be comparatively easy for me to write it before I knew as much as I know now, enough to know that I am thoroughly ignorant!"[2] A visit from Nora Holt failed to restore his confidence. He described a rousing evening spent in her company in mid-August: "She stays till 4. I get very drunk & drink six cups of very black coffee. Go nearly mad with nerves."[3] September came and went. "Something seems to hold me back," he reported to Hughes.[4] In mid-October, he decided against a trip to Paris so that he could begin the novel. Finally, on the morning of November 3, he sat down to work and completed a draft of the first chapter before lunch. But the project continued to rattle him. In a November 30 letter to H. L. Mencken, he predicted that his anguish would only worsen. "At present I am in the midst of labor on a new novel which I expect will lay me low," he wrote. "I wish you'd give me an hour or two when you next come up: I need your optimistic Americanism. Ain't it hell to be a Nordic when you're struggling with Ethiopian psychology?"[5]

He was in the same state of mind when he wrote to Hughes a week later. "I get too emotional when writing it," he confessed, "and what one needs is a calm, cold eye. Perhaps future revisions may be made in that spirit. If not, I am become a Harold Bell Wright."[6] Wright's melodramatic novels were best sellers. One of them became a feature film that launched the career of Gary Cooper; another starred John Wayne. Van Vechten himself was known for his fanciful prose, which reviewers described as being more stylish than substantive. His intentions for *Nigger Heaven* were earnest, however. Despite the fact that W. E. B. Du Bois would dismiss it as "cheap melodrama," and even a fan like Wallace Thurman would question its literary merit, Van Vechten would always refer to *Nigger Heaven* as his only serious novel. A glossary of "Negro Words and Phrases," which takes up the final pages of the book, contains some of the literary fancy for which Van Vechten had become famous. One entry—"boody: see hootchie pap"—leads readers to the definition of hootchie pap: "see boody." Overall, the glossary was meant to translate black idiom for white readers unfamiliar with it, and also lend respect to its internal logic. But, like the book as a whole, the glossary was also designed to show off Van Vechten's own fluency with that idiom.

Once Van Vechten committed to the novel, he threw himself into its composition. "This will not be a novel about Negroes in the South or white contacts or lynchings," he announced to Gertrude Stein in late June. "It will be about NEGROES, as they live now in the new city of Harlem (which is part of New York). About 400,000 of them live here now, rich and poor, fast and slow, intellectual and ignorant. I hope it will be a good book."[7] Despite his initial troubles and distractions, Van Vechten whizzed through the first draft; in one week, he wrote the first four chapters and the prologue. By late December, he had finished the manuscript.

Along the way, Carl conducted research. He read the folk tales of turn-of-the-century fiction writer Charles Chesnutt and James Weldon Johnson's 1912 novel *The Autobiography of an Ex-Coloured Man*, a story about a black man who passes for white. He turned an ethnographic ear to the blues music that he loved, gleaning its syntax and rhythm. In a letter to Gertrude Stein, he revealed that he had treated some of his ribald evenings with black friends as opportunities for research as well. "I have passed practically my whole winter in company with Negroes and have succeeded in getting into most of the most important *sets*," he wrote.[8] Like Truman Capote, whom Van Vechten would photograph in 1948, he developed a reputation for utilizing others in the service of his art. "'Careful!'" cautioned a writer in a 1932 editorial for the *Saturday Review*. "If you happen to meet Carl Van Vechten at a cocktail tea, or a dinner, or supper, watch your manners and your conversation. For Mr. Van Vechten is writing a novel to be entitled 'Parties,' and for all you know you may be serving as copy for it."[9] *Parties* would be Van Vechten's final novel.

Some black reviewers of *Nigger Heaven* found no humor in Van Vechten's propensity for using his friends in his work. Several months after *Nigger Heaven* was published, the radical black newspaper *Chicago Whip* reported: "Van Vechten makes no secret of the fact that he is gathering 'mattah' for a much more sensational book to be published in the future."[10] Reviewers at the *Whip* and other black news outlets chastised the black writers in Van Vechten's circle for providing him with material. At the same time, Van Vechten wondered if he had lost his ability to write. His one idea for a new novel, about "a colored girl in love with a white boy & her family forces her to marry a black," was fueled by alcohol. "This seems good at 10 p.m. after some cocktails."[11] He would never write this novel, or any other novel about black life after *Nigger Heaven*.

It was true that Van Vechten had used some of his friends for copy—to their pleasure. Nora Holt enjoyed the scandal that accompanied her role in the novel as the seductress Lasca Sartoris. True to her name, Lasca Sartoris is famous for her lascivious appetite and sartorial elegance in *Nigger Heaven*. When Mary Love, another central character in the novel, studies a photograph of Sartoris, she is arrested by her smart mode of dress and "the abundant sex-appeal in this lithe creature's body."[12] Van Vechten had captured Holt to a tee, according to her friends, who pestered her: "My God Nora you have broken out again—This time in Carl Van Vechten's new novel. What will you do next?" She feared her next adventure would be dull by comparison unless Carl intervened. "Invent something for me," she demanded of him from Paris.[13] Holt had quit New York eight months earlier when she made the front page of the *Inter-state Tattler,* Harlem's gossip weekly, after detectives caught her in bed with a well-known married lawyer, William Patterson, who would play a crucial role in the famous Scottsboro trial of 1931, and become the husband of Louise Thompson (former Godchild of Charlotte Mason) in 1940. Reporters at the *Tattler* hungrily catalogued developments of what they called "by far the most sordid episode of her colorful career." At the time, Holt was in the middle of her fifth divorce, which had proved to be another Harlem sensation. The caption that accompanied her photograph read: "She can't behave."[14] While she was touring in Paris, Van Vechten arranged for her to meet Gertrude Stein. "I am sending you Nigger Heaven today, and I am sending you several people, all of whom matter more or less, but the most is Nora Ray, who is slightly mulatto, terribly amusing, adorable, rich, chic, et autres choses aussi. Get her to sing for you if you can."[15] (Holt wouldn't officially divorce her fifth husband until the fall, when she ended a letter to Carl with "Love, Nora Holt Ray," with the Ray crossed out, and "Ha Ha!" in hand next to it.)[16] Van Vechten predicted that Stein and Holt would adore each other and they did. "I like Nora a lot and she is tender and I like her postal cards."[17]

Tall and handsome, Harold Jackman served as the physical model for the main character, Byron Kasson, but he wished Van Vechten had incorporated more of his true personality into the character (a charming, successful public school teacher in Harlem, Jackman was nothing like the perpetually unhappy and aimless Kasson), and he confided his disappointment to Coun-

Nora Holt: "She Can't Behave," *Inter-state Tattler*, January 22, 1926
(Yale Collection of American Literature, Beinecke Rare Book and
Manuscript Library. Courtesy of the Carl Van Vechten Trust.)

tee Cullen, who called Van Vechten "mean" for having hurt
Jackman's feelings.[18]

Harold Jackman admired Van Vechten, not only as a writer
but also as a person—a white person in whose company racial
difference dissolved. In a 1925 letter to Van Vechten, Jackman
confessed: "Do you know I have been wanting to tell you—so I

think I'll do it now and get it out of my system—that you are the first white man with whom I have felt perfectly at ease. You are just like a colored man! I don't know if you will consider this a compliment or not, but that's the only way I can put it."[19]

Van Vechten spent two months revising *Nigger Heaven,* enlisting black friends and fellow writers, such as Rudolph Fisher and James Weldon Johnson, to help him with language and character. And then, over lunch on March 18, 1926, he and Alfred Knopf agreed to send the manuscript off to the printer. *Variety* was the first of many newspapers to get wind of it. A May 19 item in the newspaper read: "Carl Van Vechten is writing a two-volume story to be called 'Nigger Heaven.' Carl has been spending a lot of time absorbing atmosphere and is said to have been royally entertained by many of the highbloods in New York's Negro sections." The *Philadelphia Inquirer* confirmed the news in June: "Mr. Carl Van Vechten, who has long been a student of the colored race, is the author of 'Nigger Heaven,' a novel Alfred A. Knopf will publish August 20."[20]

Carl had concerns about how the book would be promoted, writing to his publisher: "Ordinarily . . . books should not be advertised so long in advance, but this book is different. It is necessary to prepare the mind not only of my own public, but of the new public which this book may possibly reach . . . so that the kind of life I am writing about will not come as an actual shock."[21] Provocative ads aimed at bookstores were featured prominently in *Publishers Weekly.* "Between the covers of this unusual novel you will be selling your customers a new world," promised one. A notice in the *New Yorker* addressed readers who

Aaron Douglas, *New Yorker* ad for *Nigger Heaven*, August 27, 1926 (Manuscripts, Archives and Rare Books Division, Schomburg Center for Research in Black Culture, The New York Public Library, Astor, Lenox and Tilden Foundations. Courtesy of the Carl Van Vechten Trust.)

had not made their own journeys to the black mecca: "Why go to HARLEM CABARETS when you can READ NIGGER HEAVEN?" Ads directed at black readers promised a different story. The radical *Messenger*, to which George Schuyler was a regular contributor, advertised *Nigger Heaven* as "a story of two lovers, climbing Jacob's ladder under the shadows of Harlem."[22] The advertising— and the sensational title—worked. The book went into its sixth printing within two months of its release. *Nigger Heaven* was, by far, the best-selling novel of the Harlem Renaissance.

Van Vechten began to vet the title a few weeks after he started the novel. "Do you like the title?" he asked Gertrude Stein. Apparently, she did, or at least she posed no objection.[23] From there, he moved on to the James Weldon Johnsons. "I spring my title on Grace Johnson, etc.," he wrote in a November 25, 1925, daybook entry. Grace Nail Johnson, the wife of James Weldon Johnson, warned him that his title would be "hated."[24] James Weldon Johnson suggested "Black Man's Heab'n" as an alternate title, but Van Vechten would not be deterred. He rejected Johnson's alternative on the grounds that it "unfortunately omits to suggest the ironic symbolism of the title actually used," as he reasoned in a note scribbled on the same slip of paper on which Johnson had written his suggestion.[25]

Johnson's suggestion was not easy on the ear, but *Nigger Heaven* was not easy on the emotions, as Countee Cullen's reaction revealed. Two days after his visit to Grace Johnson, Van Vechten tried the title out on Cullen. He turned "white with hurt & I talk to him," Van Vechen wrote in his daybook.[26] The two men had radically different artistic temperaments. The

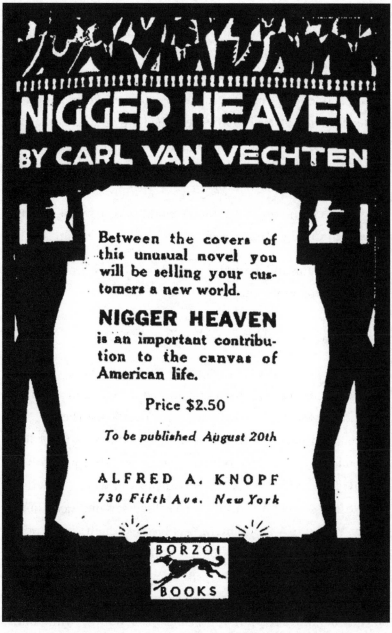

Aaron Douglas, *Publishers Weekly* ad for *Nigger Heaven*, June 26, 1926 (Manuscripts, Archives and Rare Books Division, Schomburg Center for Research in Black Culture, The New York Public Library, Astor, Lenox and Tilden Foundations. Courtesy of the Carl Van Vechten Trust.)

sensual blues poetry of Langston Hughes that Van Vechten had championed had left the conservative Cullen cold. ("I am not at all a democratic person," he once wrote to Harold Jackman. "I believe in an aristocracy of the soul.")[27] Predictably, Van Vechten's title offended him. But his respect for Van Vechten brought Cullen back to 150 West 55th Street the following day to resume the discussion, which amounted to "another long argument about the sensitiveness of Negroes," as Van Vechten described their exchange.[28]

Van Vechten admired Cullen's work, of course, and he used lines from Cullen's 1925 poem *Heritage* as his epigraph:

> All day long and all night through
> One thing only I must do:
> Quench my pride and cool my blood,
> Lest I perish in the flood.

Heritage begins with the prophetic question "What is Africa to me?"[29] Carl Van Vechten considered Africa metaphorically in his own writing. In his 1920 essay "The Negro Theatre," Van Vechten had declared that the genius of the artistry of black minstrel performer Bert Williams lay in his ability to collapse the divide between Africa and Broadway. But where Cullen saw a philosophical conundrum, Van Vechten saw financial opportunity. *Africa,* to Van Vechten, was black authenticity, a primitive birthright that Negroes must reclaim if they wanted to make commercially viable art.

Cullen was grateful for Van Vechten's work on his behalf, but he had long been nursing suspicions about the white man's enthusiasm for black art. In an exchange with Alain Locke in May 1925, Cullen called Van Vechten's choice of title for Hughes's *The Weary Blues*, "a sore spot": "That is just the title to suit him, and many other white people who want us to do only Negro things, and those not necessarily of the finest type."[30] He felt certain that the title was a mistake, but he did not feel himself in a position to advise Hughes on the matter.

And then in October, several weeks before his argument with Van Vechten, Harold Jackman encouraged Cullen to read the current *Vanity Fair*, which contained "Prescription for the Negro Theatre." At the time, Cullen was pursuing a master's degree at Harvard, which he would receive the following year. "'Vanity Fair' is not taken by the University library," he informed Jackman, "and I'm not rich enough to buy it; still, without reading the article, I know Carl is coining money out of niggers."[31]

In his 1932 novel, *One Way to Heaven*, Cullen fashioned a scene of retribution. The novel's protagonist, an eccentric, well-to-do black woman called Constancia Brandon, encourages Mattie, her maid, to invite Walter Derwent, a white novelist based on Carl Van Vechten, to her wedding. Derwent is Constancia's friend; Mattie has not even met him. Mattie's reluctance has to do with race, in particular her discomfort with whites. Constancia persists: "You are missing a splendid material opportunity, for Walter Derwent has coined enough money on his articles about us to afford a handsome donation to the gift-table."[32] In *One Way to Heaven*, the gift-table is turned, and it is blacks who profit from Van Vechten, not the other way around.

At least symbolically, this is exactly what happened with *Nigger Heaven*.

Walter Derwent is a sympathetic character in *One Way to Heaven*. The relationship between him and Constancia is more than a friendship; it is an alliance, sustained by mutual respect and at least some semblance of equity. Their friendship resembles the textured and intricate relationship between Van Vechten and black artists during the Negro Renaissance and is certainly no less substantial than the friendship between Cullen and Van Vechten itself. For instance, Cullen may have objected to the title of *Nigger Heaven*, and harbored suspicions of Van Vechten in general, but he was enthusiastic about the novel prior to its publication. "You spoke of the possibility of letting me have *proofs* of *Nigger Heaven* to take away with me," he wrote to Van Vechten in late June 1926. "If *you can* do this easily, nothing would contribute more to my pleasure going over." Van Vechten was unable to deliver the proofs in time before Cullen left on a trip to Jerusalem. "Keep my copy of *Nigger Heaven* until I return," Cullen instructed on July 1. Once the novel was published, he sent his best wishes to Van Vechten from Jerusalem: "I hope your book is out and doing well."[33] No more letters passed between them for fifteen years.

"Altho we never had any kind of quarrel after Nigger Heaven appeared," Van Vechten remembered many years later, "there was a break in our relationship (it is probable that Countee was shocked by the book) which continued until 1941 when we began again where we left off."[34] For the next five years, they exchanged letters about work, parties, and gossip about mutual friends. When Cullen died in 1946, Van Vechten sent to his widow, Ida, a set of photographs he had taken of her late husband.

Van Vechten may have been moved by Cullen's reaction to the title, but his determination to use it outweighed his sympathy. He proved no less intractable when it came to the passionate objections of his own father, who had not been shy in expressing his assessments of Van Vechten's previous books, either. Charles Duane Van Vechten was frank about his opinions of *The Blind Bow-Boy*: "A *very well written* picture of depravity." He held a relatively kinder view of *Peter Whiffle*: "To tell the truth I am not particularly interested though there are many (for me) good things in the book—have been trying to answer a question— what message did you wish to give your readers?" About *Nigger Heaven*, he was definite: "Your 'Nigger Heaven' is a title I don't like . . . I have myself never spoken of a colored man as a 'nigger.' If you are trying to help the race, as I am assured you are, I think every word you write should be a respectful one towards the black."[35]

A week later, the elder Van Vechten wrote again: "I note what you have to say about the title to your new book, including that statement that some of your negro friends agree with me— You are accustomed to 'get away' with what you undertake to do: but you do not *always* succeed; and my belief is that this will be another failure, *if* you persist in your '*I shall use it nevertheless.*' Whatever you may be compelled to say *in* the book, your present title will not be understood & I feel certain you should change it." He began this second letter with the sadly predictive line: "Please bear in mind what I am about to have the courage to say to you—It is the *last* word I shall ever say to you on the subject."[36] Charles Van Vechten died seven months before the novel was published. He did not live long enough to see whether his prediction that the title would be misunderstood came true—which in large part, it did.

The elder Van Vechten knew his son well. "I have a very strong will, and I'm not deterred by temptation," Carl said in 1960.[37] Van Vechten certainly understood the power of his title and its ability to wound even friends and family, but true to his father's characterization of him, he persisted nevertheless. He had his reasons.

Van Vechten's explicit intentions in *Nigger Heaven* were to celebrate Harlem, to advertise, literally, its virtues and vices to white readers unfamiliar with but curious about the black mecca. On a deeper level, he was probably just as motivated by a desire to celebrate himself. Ultimately, *Nigger Heaven* was a stage on which Van Vechten exhibited himself as a white insider to black culture. He used *nigger* in the title and in the body of the book to establish his privileged status as an honorary white among blacks. A footnote accompanies the first appearance of the word: "While this informal epithet is freely used by Negroes among themselves not only as a term of opprobrium, but also actually as a term of endearment, its employment by a white person is always fiercely resented. The word Negress is forbidden under all circumstances" (26). Van Vechten used *nigger* in his title to proclaim his authority to use it; it was an authority that a number of black artists and intellectuals did not dispute. To them, Van Vechten was an exception to the rule of white racism, and his black supporters predicted that the positive effects of his title would outweigh the negative in the long run. "I might make a stir about your title and be a good 'race man' but fundamentally I am too anxious to have the sting of the term extracted in the fashion that such employment promises to do it," wrote Charles S. Johnson to Van Vechten.[38] Walter White, Van Vechten's dogged defender since 1924, not only approved of the title, he confessed to Van Vechten his wish that he had thought of it first.

Carl had considered other titles, among them "The Great Black Walled City," "White Tar," and "Rest Yo Coat." But "Nigger Heaven" was irresistible. He found justification to use it in *Folk Beliefs of the Southern Negro*, a study published in 1925 by a white folklorist, Newbell Niles Puckett. Van Vechten quoted from the book in his notes: "Nigger Heaven is an American slang expression for the topmost gallery of a theatre, so classed because in certain of the United States, Negroes are arbitrarily forced to sit in these cheap seats." A handwritten note next to the phrase "arbitrarily forced" reads: "The title of the novel derives from this fact."[39] These galleries went by the equally sardonic terms "buzzard's roosts" and "coon's hill." All three expressions were bitter commentary on the nature of black public lives lived under Jim Crow segregation. Van Vechten was no stranger to these terms; he had used the term *nigger heaven* in his novel *The Tattooed Countess*, published in 1924, to describe shabby seating areas in a

Cedar Rapids opera house.[40] *The Tattooed Countess* contains no black characters.

Van Vechten did not invent the phrase *nigger heaven,* nor was he the first white writer to use *nigger* in the title of a book. He was preceded in 1922 by Clement Wood, who published *Nigger: A Novel,* a story in which the term is used to evoke the pathos of its main character's life in the Deep South during the era of Reconstruction, a life characterized by an endless cycle of defeat. In Wood's novel, *nigger* is the wound that will never heal. When Van Vechten finally read the book, he wasn't impressed. "I read Clement Wood's *Nigger* & didn't think much of it," he wrote in a July 1926 daybook entry, less than three weeks before *Nigger Heaven* was released.[41] Born in Alabama, Wood was highly regarded as a writer among Harlem Renaissance intellectuals. Wood and Du Bois were friendly and traveled in the same political circles, and Wood had served as a judge for literary contests sponsored by the *Crisis* and *Opportunity.* His novel did not incur Du Bois's wrath, although some black reviewers took exception to the title.

Prancing Nigger, a 1924 novel by Ronald Firbank, concerns the travails of a socially ambitious black family in a fictitious Caribbean country as they move from the city to the capital and into black high society. Its original title was *Sorrow in Sunlight*— until Carl Van Vechten encouraged him to change it for commercial reasons. "Prancing Nigger" is the nickname one of the main characters in the novel bestows upon her husband, who is first seen dozing under a tree, "gently nodding, beneath a straw-hat, beautifully browned."[42] The title was Van Vechten's suggestion, but the novel was a product of its author's imagination. "Firbank's treatment of the Negro is his own," wrote Van Vechen in his introduction to the book.[43] It was unique, he said, and owed nothing to the white authors of black life who preceded him, such as Harriet Beecher Stowe, author of *Uncle Tom's Cabin*, or T. S. Stribling, author of the 1921 novel *Birthright*. Both works were well received in black literary circles. In fact, some black writers were encouraged by the attention garnered by these novels, taking it as a sign that black writers of black stories were on the verge of a similar kind of success.[44]

Even W. E. B. Du Bois liked *Prancing Nigger*. He called it a "delicious book," though he predicted that most black people would condemn it outright because of its title. "In it the writer is unbound by convention, white or black," Du Bois wrote.[45] He could have been describing *Nigger Heaven*. Du Bois applauded Firbank's rendering of "black" dialect, a dialect that looks and sounds very much like the dialect spoken by some black characters in Van Vechten's novel. Yet the very features Du Bois admired in *Prancing Nigger* he found repulsive in *Nigger Heaven*. Perhaps Du Bois simply considered *Prancing Nigger* a better novel than *Nigger Heaven*. Maybe he found Firbank's novel more acceptable because its setting is a fictional country, outside the realm of American race relations. Decorated with cotton trees, twilight, and cane fields, *Prancing Nigger*, like Wood's *Nigger*, is a sentimental story that posed no threat to the modern black identity the architects of the New Negro movement were trying to build. Unlike Clement Wood and Ronald Firbank, however, Van Vechten claimed to represent a modern black city—*the* modern black city, the promised land of Harlem. In his version of this city, Du Bois claimed, Van Vechten had not managed to find any citizens worthy of sympathy.

The characters in *Nigger Heaven* are wooden, Du Bois said, and the book contains an offensive amount of debauchery. In the prologue to the novel, Harlem's garish, high-living Scarlet Creeper (a footnote next to his name directs readers to the glossary, where "Creeper" is defined as "a man who invades another's marital rights") takes Ruby, a luscious "golden brown," to a Lenox Avenue nightclub, where men and women dance "in such close proximity that their bodies melted together as they swayed and rocked to the tormented howling of the brass, the barbaric beating of the drum" (12). Toward the end of the novel, Byron and Lasca snort cocaine and attend a "Black Mass," where a naked black voodoo priestess performs "evil rites" (256). Scenes like these make up only a fraction of the novel, but Du Bois's reaction was emotional, of course, not mathematical.

The difference between his assessments of *Nigger, Prancing Nigger,* and *Nigger Heaven* had to do as much with their authors as the novels themselves. What made Van Vechten's novel "an affront to the hospitality of black folk," as Du Bois described it, was that Van Vechten had been an honored guest inside Harlem's interiors.[46] Unlike Firbank and Wood, Van Vechten and his novel had hit too close to home.

Du Bois was not alone in his conviction that Van Vechten had abused black hospitality, that he had been accepted behind closed doors, welcomed to the table, and then insulted his hosts with exceptionally bad manners. Reviewers who had never met

Van Vechten perceived the book as a personal transgression. A critic for the *Chicago Whip* advised "the black people of New York" to "politely hang the unwelcome sign in his face and direct him back to Greenwich Village where the New York neurotics revel."[47] Even Charles S. Johnson believed he had given away family secrets, although he cited this as one of the successes of the book, undeniable evidence of its authenticity.[48] But to those who felt wounded by the title, it appeared that Carl had broken bread with blacks, and instead of thank you, he had said *nigger*.

To some critics, the story as much as the title revealed Van Vechten's truly sinister intentions toward black people. But in truth, the story unveils nothing new about Van Vechten. Ultimately, it is simply a portrait of the miserable fate he had predicted for black artists in his essays for *Vanity Fair*. The central player in this literary nightmare is a young man called Byron Kasson.

WATER, WATER, EVERYWHERE

Byron Kasson is a writer who can't write. What he lacks in ability he makes up for in looks, at least according to the other main character, Mary Love. Her first glimpse of him reveals "the symmetrical proportions of his body, the exquisite form of his head, emphasized by his closely cropped, curly black hair" (24). At the time, he is mid-dive, plunging into a pool at the home of a mutual acquaintance, Adora Boniface.

The plot of *Nigger Heaven* turns on Byron's singular lack of imagination despite the fact that the world continually presents him with remarkable stories that would keep another writer, a *real* writer, glued to his typewriter. "The worst difficulty of all was to find a subject: there was so little to write about," he sighs. He tries, but even he must concede that his stories are "spineless" (175). He has a gift, though, as his college writing instructors had assured him. Ultimately, Byron's greatest problem has little to do with skill, which can be learned, or ambition, of which he has plenty. Instead Byron's problems are personal and of his own creation. By the book's end, he has been the author of only his own misery. His misery has to do with race.

Van Vechten was fond of the writer-who-can't-write conceit. It animates the plot of *Peter Whiffle,* which is a fictional biography of the eponymous character, a man who made an art out of never producing any art.[49] By the end of his life, Whiffle has come to understand his lack of productivity: "I have tried to do too much and that is why, perhaps, I have done nothing. I wanted to write a new Comédie Humaine. Instead, I have lived it." But Whiffle views his life "more like a success than a failure" because he has left behind no bad work (244). Even though his death "awakened no comment" (1), the novel is a testament to the singular artfulness of the life lived by Whiffle, the author who never published a book.

By contrast, there is no artfulness behind Byron's lack of productivity in *Nigger Heaven.* Whereas Whiffle waxes philosophical on the problem, Byron's paralysis is pathological. He suffers from a case of metaphorical blindness that is nearly biblical. Outside his window, next to him on a trolley car, at his elevator-operating job, and even in his living room, poignant, gorgeous, and tragic stories, black stories, offer themselves up to Byron. He cannot see them because he cannot *see* black people. "What could he write about? What was there interesting to write about?" he sighs, just after a close friend announces that he is going to pass for white (185). In 1926, there was no story more compelling than the story of a black person who passes for white, and conflicts over racial identity in general provided the drama for the entire Negro Renaissance. But from Byron's perspective, race itself is only a burden, something to be agonized over and, when possible, avoided. He cannot see the beauty in blackness, nor can he see the material advantages of writing about race. Byron is the black writer Carl Van Vechten warned about in his 1926 essay "Moanin' wid a Sword in Mah Han'," he who would abandon the wealth of material that was part of his heritage, and therefore make of it a "free gift" to white writers to exploit for their own ends.

Carl Van Vechten assigned himself the task of showing his main character the error of his ways. In the novel, Van Vechten appears as Gareth Johns, and he and Byron find themselves seated next to each other at a dinner party in Harlem. Johns is a famous white author who has never before been inside a Negro home. He marvels at the sophisticated décor, the clever conversation, and the cosmopolitan guests. "So you know Wallace Stevens!" (100) Johns exults after Byron's girlfriend, Mary Love, recites from memory "Cy est Pourtraicte, Madame Ste Ursule, et les Unze Mille Vierge," a poem from Stevens's first book, *Harmonium*, published in 1923, which Van Vechten had persuaded Alfred Knopf to publish. Gareth Johns is Carl Van Vechten before he mastered the Walter White hustle.

Byron admires Johns's enthusiasm as well as his literary success, and confesses his own ambitions to become an author. "How does one go about writing?" he asks Johns. The answer, Johns tells him, is simply to start writing. He seems baffled by Byron's dilemma. "The low life of your people is exotic," Johns replies. "It has a splendid, fantastic quality. And the humor! How vital it is, how rich in idiom!" Byron turns cold. "I'm afraid I don't know very much about the low life of my people," he says. Well, then why not write about the dinner party taking place around them, or Negro college life? Johns offers. "I went to a white college," Byron says, and turns away (106–7). He will pay for rejecting Johns's advice.

Nigger Heaven is a roman à clef; most of the principal characters have a real-life counterpart. Adora Boniface, at whose party Mary admires Byron as he dives into the pool, is modeled on A'Lelia Walker, daughter of Madame C. J. Walker, who made a fortune designing products for black hair and skin. Walker was a popular Harlem hostess and Van Vechten was a staple on her guest list. In an unpublished eulogy, Van Vechten described Walker: "She looked like a Queen and frequently acted like a tyrant. She was tall and black and extremely handsome in her African manner. She often dressed in black. When she assumed more regal habiliments, she was a magnificent spectacle."[50] In "Those Were the Fabulous Days!" a 1952 profile of Harold Jackman, he remembered her parties—"big, private formal affairs"— held at the "Dark Tower," Walker's Harlem townhouse, which got its name from a column written by Countee Cullen in *Opportunity*. Regular guests who didn't need invitations included Cullen, Langston Hughes, and Van Vechten. At these affairs, Jackman met the eccentric English writer Osbert Sitwell, British politician John Strachey, lately of the British cabinet, and the French princess Violette Murat. In those fabulous days, Jackman counted Lord Peter Churchill as one of his closest friends.[51]

Like Walker, Adora Boniface in *Nigger Heaven* is rich, lovely, and crude. In a private exchange with Mary at her own party, Adora confesses to being "tired to death of all those Niggers downstairs" (26). Van Vechten's footnote appears at this point in the book, where Adora uses the word as a term of both opprobrium and endearment. It is a gesture of intimacy between Mary and herself. Mary, who is hopelessly uptight, agrees with Adora silently—she would never speak such an impolite word aloud.

Van Vechten based the demure and beautiful Mary Love very loosely on his glamorous close friend and frequent correspondent Dorothy Peterson, an actress and public school teacher of French and Spanish. Langston Hughes once described Peterson as "a charming colored girl who had grown up mostly in Puerto Rico, and who moved with such poise among these colorful celebrities that I thought when I first met her she was a white girl of the grande monde, slightly sun-tanned."[52] The acerbic "Sage of Baltimore," Henry Louis Mencken, appears as Russett Durwood, who struggles with Ethiopian psychology, just as Mencken did. Durwood edits *American Mars,* a play on *American Mercury,* the journal from whose perch Mencken launched his wicked satires of American life and culture. A pivotal encounter with Durwood seals Byron's fate.

Durwood summons Byron to his office after reading a story that Byron submitted to *American Mars*. Byron discovers that Durwood has only advice to offer him, not a promise of publication. "Why in the hell don't you write about something you know about?" Durwood asks, and then embarks upon an impassioned monologue on the wealth of material in Harlem (222). In *Nigger Heaven*, white characters are able to see and celebrate the variety in blackness, while many black characters cannot. The only exception is Mary Love, who offers Byron the same advice as Durwood and Johns. Byron resents her for it, but in the novel it is only his resentment toward would-be helpful whites that matters. Byron is steaming when he leaves *American Mars*. "He treated me that way because I am a Negro!" he burns. Byron is paranoid and can only see Durwood as another player in a cosmic plot to destroy him. "He hated them all, black and white. All conspiring to effect his downfall" (230). His paranoia costs him dearly.

Lasca Sartoris, the resident femme fatale in *Nigger Heaven*, finishes Byron off. Her carnivorous sexuality undoes him, and when Lasca spurns him, Byron kills the man who has replaced him in her affections. In the final scene, a white policeman removes Byron's gun from his grip.

By the end of the novel, Byron's biblical curse of blindness has been lifted. In the final pages, he realizes "he had only himself to blame." (272) He comes to his senses and realizes that Durwood had been right. Unfortunately, it's too late for this revelation to do him any good. It is finally neither the cop nor Durwood nor Lasca who does him in, but his own miserable attitude. Like Countee Cullen, like every black person that did not agree with Van Vechten, Byron is simply too sensitive.

Langston Hughes saw something authentic in the character of Byron Kasson. In *The Big Sea*, he would describe the main character of *Nigger Heaven* as a perfect reflection of the "bitterness and frustration of literary Harlem" that lay beneath the glamorous façade of the "so-called Negro Renaissance."[53]

SENSITIVE

The word *sensitive* has more than one meaning. It can mean "highly responsive or susceptible" or "delicately aware of the attitudes or feelings of others." Carl Van Vechten believed that sensitivity, in both these senses, was the Achilles' heel of the black artist. Sensitivity that functioned as touchiness or a concern with external opinion led to self-censorship and stood in the way of truth and freedom. In his answer to the *Crisis* questionnaire "The Negro in Art: How Shall He Be Portrayed?" he expressed sympathy for those who were ticklish about negative portrayals of black people. But as much as he sympathized, he believed ardently that to surrender to sensitivity—whether one's own or that of others—was to sacrifice creativity. This is the message of *Nigger Heaven*.

As the human incarnation of sensitivity itself, Byron Kasson is trapped in a prison of his emotions, which appear to have no relationship to reality. But isn't it possible to imagine that Byron's touchiness comes from somewhere, that it results as much from his history as his distorted psychology, something imprinted as deeply as his birthright? According to the logic of the novel, Byron alone is responsible for the downward spiral of his life. But Byron is a young black man living in the United States of the 1920s. Lynching is legal; segregation is the law of the land. Byron may have grown up in a comfortable, middle-class home in Philadelphia, but his privileged background does not render him immune to the racism that structures the world around him. More than sensitivity, Byron represents the paradox that is black life in the modern world. He is the New Negro, powerless to extricate himself from the Old.

For example, shortly after Byron begins his romance with Mary Love, the two of them spend an afternoon in the park. A white couple on horseback appears, and Mary reflects sympathetically on the woman's appearance. Her reverie is interrupted when the white woman exclaims to her husband: "Disgusting . . . that they should permit Niggers in the park!" (147) Both Mary and Byron crumple under the verbal assault; their romantic afternoon is spoiled. There will be no recourse or vindication. In the 1920s, hate speech, as a category, did not exist. In a novel burdened with seemingly unending discussions about "the race problem," and nightlife scenes that are typically more bizarre than salacious, this scene subtly and effectively communicates the painful impact of *nigger* on the most mundane level. There is no winking irony here, no coy delight. In this scene, the word is meant to wound. And it does.

Van Vechten intended his title to be ironic. Because they were sensitive, Negroes could not appreciate irony, Van Vechten insisted. "Irony is not anything that most Negroes understand, especially the ones who write for the papers," he groused in 1960, when he was still prickly, thirty-four years later, over negative black reaction to the book.[54] To him, the fault lay exclusively with black readers and critics who simply didn't get it. Like Byron Kasson, like Countee Cullen, they were too sensitive, and maybe too obtuse to understand that Van Vechten was entitled to use the title. He was an insider, after all, but to black readers and critics outside of his inner circle, Van Vechten's status was irrelevant. These blacks found it offensive that Van Vechten would use his cultural standing as a justification or excuse for his title or his novel. Whether Van Vechten meant to offend was irrelevant; his title was an offense. Whether his book revealed the truth about black life in Harlem, as some claimed, was also irrelevant. For those who were alienated by the novel, there was only one relevant truth about *Nigger Heaven:* it was a black book written by a white man with the word *nigger* in the title. Defenders of the novel considered this reasoning simplistic, given all that Van Vechten had achieved for "the race." To them, the degree of outrage over the book was out of proportion; it was just a book, after all. Carl Van Vechten certainly believed the outcry was extreme and unfair. It hurt his feelings. He was sensitive.

NEGRO DREAMS

"A flock of reviews, some good, some bad, all stupid," Van Vechten wrote in an August 26, 1926, daybook entry. "I am fairly discouraged about *Nigger Heaven.*" The reviews ran from raves to violent condemnations from black critics and readers.

Van Vechten paid little attention to white reactions to the book, probably because they were generally positive, often tepid, sometimes silly, and generally missed the point, like the reviewer in *Time* magazine who saw the book as evidence that Van Vechten had "sickened" of Negroes.[55] Four years after the book was published, Van Vechten received a letter from a white reader who asked if it had "aroused animosity against you from certain quarters as being too friendly towards the Negro?" He described her attitude as being typical of whites in a letter to James Weldon Johnson, and in his reply informed her that the novel had never "aroused anything but curiosity and interest from white readers. On the other hand," he told her, "some Negroes have objected that it presents too sordid a picture of their life."[56]

Van Vechten was crushed by the wave of denunciation from black critics. He pretended otherwise in an upbeat letter he sent to Johnson in early September, in which he enclosed a blistering review ("a vivid report") by Hubert Harrison of the *Amsterdam News* that he thought Johnson would find amusing. "Harlem, it appears, is seething in controversy," he told Johnson. "Langston, the other night at Craig's, suggested to a few of the knockers that they might read the book before expressing their opinion, but this advice seems to be regarded as superogatory."[57]

"I fairly revel in public condemnation," Countee Cullen bragged to Harold Jackman in a May 6, 1926, letter.[58] On this issue, Carl Van Vechten proved to be the sensitive one. The criticism devastated him, and in his daybooks, he described the *Amsterdam News* review as an attack. He was pained by the suggestion that he had betrayed the people he loved—*his* people.

Black people. He recorded his dismay and bruised ego in his daybooks. "At 4 Langston appears & later Jim Harris with a list of questions regarding Nigger Heaven, as apparently he is being pestered by people who say I have betrayed the race! All this upsets me as much as usual," he wrote in September 1926. He slept badly that night and sought comfort from his wife: "Before dawn crept into Marinoff's bed." His distress generated vivid, violent dreams. "I go to bed about one & dream I am a Negro being chased in riots," he recorded in one entry. Even good reviews and breathtaking sales could not cure his anxiety. "I dream I am a Negro & being pursued," he wrote four days after the first set of bad dreams.[59]

Later that month, Van Vechten learned that he had been barred from the popular nightclub Small's Paradise. "We don't care when we get written about, but not when we get exaggerated about," a representative from the club told Lewis Baer, an editor at Albert & Charles Boni Publishers and a friend of Carl's.[60] Baer had been trying to arrange a party in honor of the musician W. C. Handy at Small's, a party that he wanted Van Vechten to attend, so Baer asked him to smooth over the situation. "A letter from Lewis Baer informs me that the management of Small's doesn't want me at W. C. Handy's party!" Van Vechten wrote in his daybook. "I am cross & distant."[61] Van Vechten had been welcome at Small's just a week earlier, when he had attended a party given by Langston Hughes and three of his classmates from Lincoln University in Pennsylvania, where Hughes was a senior, to raise money for their tuition. Two days after receiving Baer's letter, Van Vechten ventured to Small's flanked by

Zora Neale Hurston and Walter White. He was greeted with his usual welcome. The subject of his ostracism never came up again.

Real trouble lay ahead, however. In late October, as the sixth printing of *Nigger Heaven* was ready to go to press, Van Vechten learned that Shapiro Bernstein Co. had initiated a lawsuit against him for using lyrics from two of its popular songs, "Shake That Thing" and "If You Hadn't Gone Away," in his novel without permission. "The penalty, Alfred says, of success," he wrote in his daybook.[62] Van Vechten called Hughes at Lincoln and asked him for help. At 7 p.m. the following day, a Saturday, Hughes arrived at West 55th Street and began to replace the original verses with his own material (for example, "Yes sir, that's my baby" became "Oh how I'm aching for love!") to appear in the sixth printing of the book. He completed drafts of all the verses that night and left for Lincoln late the next evening. Van Vechten was still forced to settle with Bernstein in the amount of twenty-five hundred dollars. He sent the check in early November, he recorded in his daybook, and then went home and drowned his frustrations: "I come home & proceed to get drunk."[63]

Langston Hughes saved Van Vechten from a lawsuit, but his public image in Harlem took a beating. His novel was denounced at a gathering at the Harlem Public Library, where the crowd turned on a "large white-haired old gentleman" sitting in the back, remembered Langston Hughes fourteen years later. As the crowd raged, the man stood and, "stammering in amazement," announced: "Why, I'm not Carl Van Vechten."[64]

A professor from Wilberforce University in Ohio set fire to two pages of the book at a December Harlem gathering. "Burn 'em up!" shouted the crowd, four hundred strong, as S. R. Williams lit the pages. The exercise proved so effective, so cathartic, that Williams suggested that another ceremony be held to burn the entire book.[65]

The purpose of the gathering was to protest three recent lynchings in South Carolina. The group had assembled to appoint delegates to request President Coolidge to enforce the Fourteenth Amendment, which recognized slaves and their descendants as U.S. citizens, as rigorously as he enforced the Eighteenth Amendment, Prohibition. The equation of *Nigger Heaven* to the lynching of black people is not extreme within the logic of the New Negro movement, which held that there was a clear connection between negative racial representation and racist acts. Witness the passionate denunciation of *Birth of a Nation* by the NAACP, which was based wholly on a conviction that the film, with its racist revisionist history and outright endorsement of the Ku Klux Klan, would lead to racial violence. And it did; several lynchings were directly attributed to the film, which the Klan used as a recruitment tool.

Some black writers tried to stem the effects of *Nigger Heaven* by directly confronting those who praised it. Aubrey Bowser, a teacher and writer in Harlem, sent a four-page, single-spaced letter to Carl Van Doren, criticizing a favorable review Van Doren had written of the book for the *New York Herald Tribune*. Van Doren had spoken movingly about the particular gifts the Negro had to offer to American culture at the March 21, 1924, "coming-out" ceremony for the Harlem Renaissance. "You are a liberal thinker," Bowser conceded, "but your review of 'Nigger Heaven' in the Sunday Tribune of August 22nd shows the white critic's usual failure to catch the Negro's viewpoint." Bowser had mixed up Van Doren's review with one written by Edwin Clark, which was published on the same day in the *New York Times Book Review*, in which Clark quoted from Russett Durwood's speech to Byron about the need for black artists to utilize their own material before a white writer did so. Bowser took offense. Black writers were hemmed in by these very expectations on the part of white editors, he contended. Until black writers had true literary vehicles—not the sociological *Crisis* and *Opportunity*, he said, or the *Messenger*, which was "merely polemic"—they would not be able to portray Negro life as it should be. "As it should be, I repeat," wrote Bowser, "not in the morbid manner of Van Vechten, who wallows in a sewer and calls it Harlem."[66]

Bowser found a public platform for his outrage in early November at the inaugural "book evenings" discussion at the Harlem branch of the New York Public Library at 135th Street. The topic was *Nigger Heaven;* the room was packed. Along with Harlem journalist Cleveland Allen, Bowser denounced the book and wondered aloud where the Society for the Suppression of Vice had been when the book was published. "Nobody praised the book," the *Pittsburgh Courier* reporter noted, "but few made weak apologies because they thought the author was sincere and meant no offense."[67] Ernestine Rose, who was white and the head librarian and host of the book evening, had invited

Van Vechten to come and defend his book. "Why not take this occasion to find out the truth about the Library, which you have used in your book quite freely, and, forgive me for saying so,— with almost complete unaccuracy," she wrote.[68] Van Vechten declined.

George Schuyler, who was also present at the library that night, proved to be no friend to the book. According to the *Courier* report, Schuyler "ridiculed the work and said the characters did not have any common sense." In a late November review for the *Pittsburgh Courier*, Schuyler explained: "Mr. Van Vechten knows Harlem pretty well, but I know it better. He omitted a great deal from his book." Surprisingly, Schuyler, who months before had written an essay about the meaninglessness of racial difference, chalked up the weaknesses of the book to race. "Of course, it is written by a white man," he allowed, "and once in a while one comes across the usual bad breaks," especially in matters having to do with Negro psychology and character.[69]

Schuyler's public position on the novel changed over time. In a 1955 *Courier* column devoted, in part, to Van Vechten's seventy-fifth birthday, he remembered the book differently: "He presented an entirely new picture of the contemporary Negro in his fine novel of Harlem, 'Nigger Heaven,' a book which can stand re-reading." The favorable mention, tucked into much longer praise concerning Van Vechten's "outstanding contributions to American civilization," was perhaps less a testament to the strength of the book than a demonstration of Schuyler's enduring fondness for its author, a man whose contributions to black progress were much more substantial than the novel.[70]

But in fact the novel itself *was* outstanding, as outstanding as its author. *Nigger Heaven* may have had a simple message—that sensitivity kills artistic freedom—but it provoked complex reactions from its reading public. Van Vechten himself, in "A Note by the Author" included with the 1951 edition of the novel, described the plot as "the oldest story in the world, the story of the Prodigal Son, without the happy ending of that Biblical history" (188). But *Nigger Heaven* was unique, at least insofar as it generated some of the most remarkable writing of the Harlem Renaissance: the reviews.

A BRUTAL AND BUNGLING BOOK

"There is one thing that Carl Van Vechten's 'Nigger Heaven' has done, if it has done nothing else," wrote Alice Dunbar-Nelson, a *Pittsburgh Courier* columnist, poet, activist, and the widow of poet Paul Laurence Dunbar. "It has released the largest, most vivid, devastating, complete, powerful, biting, scathing, prolific, asbestos-lined, vituperative, picturesque flood of adjectival vehemence spread over the pages of the 'Race' papers that has been turned loose since the 'Birth of a Nation.' "[71] There were dozens of reviews. Then there were reviews of the reviews. In histrionic hyperbole, *Nigger Heaven* was condemned and glorified, as was its author. To some, the book was nothing less than sober—and tedious—propaganda for the black race. To others, it was nothing more than contemptible dross. It was forward thinking. It was a step backward. Van Vechten kept track of all of the reviews, passing choice ones along to his friends. Hubert Harrison's review in the September *Amsterdam News* especially caught his attention.

Hubert Harrison was born in St. Croix, Danish West Indies, and immigrated to New York in 1900. He was a friend of Claude McKay, who described him as having a "large sugary black African way," a voice that when he was upset "sounded like the rustling of dry bamboo leaves agitated by the wind."[72] He had a fan in Henry Miller, who called Harrison his "quondam idol." In *Plexus,* the second volume of *The Rosy Crucifixion,* his memoirs, Miller remembered Harrison's physical presence ("the great sculptured head which he carried on his shoulders like a lion") and oratorical genius ("with a few well-directed words he had the ability to demolish any opponent").[73]

Harrison's voice on the page was no less profound. He was largely self-educated, and he was fearless. His politics were radical. A published criticism of Booker T. Washington got him fired from the Post Office in Harlem. An attack on the Socialist Party, of which he was then a member, led to his suspension from the party (from which he ultimately resigned). Marcus Garvey admired him, and invited him to lead a delegation of the United Negro Improvement Association to Liberia. Shortly afterward, he broke with Garvey. From his perches at various media outlets, including the *Amsterdam News,* the *Pittsburgh Courier,* the *Chicago Defender,* the *New Republic,* and the *New York Times,* he lobbed criticisms of the Ku Klux Klan and the Negro Renaissance; the latter, he claimed, didn't really exist, but was merely an invention of "Greenwich Village neurotics"—like Carl Van Vechten.[74]

Harrison's review of *Nigger Heaven* was peppered with homophobia embedded in false compliments. "He can describe furniture and its accessories, female clothes and fripperies with all the ecstatic abandon of a maiden lady at a wedding and the self-satisfaction of a man-milliner toying with a pink powder-puff. In that domain, I think, he hasn't an equal—among men."[75] He aimed his deepest digs at those blacks who counted themselves among Van Vechten's friends, describing them, in words he borrowed from John Milton's *Paradise Lost,* as a " 'crowd of timorous and flocking birds,' who hover around in Harlem dreaming that they are writing 'Negro' literature, because Van Vechten's kind has coddled them at pink-tea literary contests. May this brutal and bungling book serve as a spur to make them leap over the wall of weakness with which they are surrounded."[76] Harrison's review itself was brutal. He took the novel apart, section by section, in precise and trenchant prose.

Harrison didn't stop there. Six weeks later he published " 'Nigger Heaven'—A Review of the Reviews," in which he dissected arguments made in defense of the novel written by anonymous reviewers as well as well-known black writers like James Weldon Johnson, whom he accused of never having actually read the book. Otherwise, how could he praise it? Harrison insisted that his dislike for *Nigger Heaven* had nothing to do with its title, and scoffed at reviewers who took the book down on those grounds alone. Again, he blamed Van Vechten's circle of friends for the book, the "dusky hosts—and hostesses—over whose bottles he imbibed the conception of Harlem, which is here exhibited."[77]

But it wasn't Van Vechten as an author per se that Harrison resented. *Peter Whiffle, The Tattooed Countess,* and *The Blind Bow-Boy* were all "worthwhile," he wrote. In particular, he praised *The Tattooed Countess* for its character and atmosphere. It wasn't

Van Vechten, and it wasn't the title either, Harrison insisted. It was the content. "I condemned Van Vechten's book as a poor specimen of literary craftsmanship," Harrison wrote.[78]

Hubert Harrison may have found *Nigger Heaven* repellent but he also found it useful. It offered him a prime example of all he considered noxious about the so-called Negro Renaissance. (In 1927, he would write an article for the *Pittsburgh Courier* entitled "No Negro Literary Renaissance," in which he likened the validity of the Negro literary renaissance to the existence of snakes in Ireland—"there isn't any.")[79] Like other critics, Harrison used the book as Command Central from which to launch stylish missiles at uptown literary pretenders and downtown deviants. In doing so, he proved Alice Dunbar-Nelson right. *Nigger Heaven* made good copy—even for the reviewers who despised it. The offensive white-authored book that distorted black life proved to be a gold mine. To use Van Vechten's words, the novel provided for Harrison and others a "wealth of material" that played a central role in a passionate, public, and interracial discussion about race.

NEGROES ARE PEOPLE

Nora Holt found Hubert Harrison's reviews "disgusting and crude." "I happen to know him," she wrote to Van Vechten. "Always makes a desperate attempt at cynicism." She reassured him that several Harlemites who were at first antagonistic to the novel's title were "quite *mad* over" the book after reading it.[80]

Indeed, the congratulations were as effusive as the vituperation. A telegram from Eric Walrond rang with applause for the book and its accurate and glamorous depiction of Harlem. A telegram sent by Paul Robeson praised the novel for its "absolute understanding and deep sympathy." Walter White crowed on August 19: "As one race author to another I send you my warmest congratulations on the natal day of Nigger Heaven." Alain Locke sent a letter from Berlin in which he cited *Nigger Heaven,* and the excitement surrounding it, as a central reason for his imminent return to the United States. Gertrude Stein wrote from France to say that the novel was the best thing Van Vechten had ever written.[81] Stein had played a crucial role in *Nigger Heaven.* After an evening spent at a rent party, Mary Love, hopelessly cerebral and out of touch with her racial birthright, is reminded of a conversation in "Melanctha," Stein's "Negro story," recalling by heart a long passage that takes up two pages of the novel (57–58).

Anita Loos, author of the best-selling *Gentlemen Prefer Blondes,* agreed with Stein: "It is by far your best," read her telegram. Harold Jackman told Van Vechten that he preferred *Peter Whiffle,* but still he applauded Van Vechten for having "shown many of the colored writers a thing or two." Ellen Glasgow, a white southern novelist, called it "grand, barbaric, and so alive it bleeds."[82] As a person, Ellen Glasgow sometimes turned his stomach, Van Vechten once wrote in his daybook, but he respected her as a writer; he asked to use her letter in his collection of endorsements for *Nigger Heaven,* and she agreed. In return he endorsed her books as well.

Charles S. Johnson wrote a formal letter in support of the novel on *Opportunity* letterhead. He called *Nigger Heaven* "the first achievement of a novel of Negro life." He saw it as epoch-making work, much like *Granny Maumee* of 1917. He hoped it would have an encouraging effect on black writers, and open the door for a black author to write such a dynamic story about his own life. *Nigger Heaven* pointed the way toward the future, Johnson believed. He suggested James Weldon Johnson for the job of writing a review in *Opportunity*. Van Vechten was more than flattered by the support from black friends—he needed it. He asked Johnson for permission to publish the letter. Johnson granted it, asking for one change—replacing the phrase "the first achievement of a novel of Negro life" with the fleshier but less absolute phrase "the first achievement of a novel embracing the broad pattern of Negro life."[83] If indeed there was one definitive story of Negro life, suggested Johnson in his revision, Van Vechten had only embraced its contours, not captured it. Johnson's revision was more precise but also more ambiguous, in that it allowed for more than one interpretation of what he considered Van Vechten's achievement. Charles S. Johnson believed the greatest tribute he could offer the book was his regret that a Negro had not written it. Van Vechten's close friend, novelist Nella Larsen, shared the sentiment. "Why, oh why, couldn't we have done something as big for ourselves?" she lamented to Van Vechten.[84]

James Weldon Johnson did write a review of *Nigger Heaven*, just as Charles S. Johnson had suggested. "It was inevitable that the colorful life of Harlem would sooner or later claim the pen of Carl Van Vechten," he began. "He has taken the material it offered him and achieved the most revealing, significant and powerful novel based exclusively on Negro life yet written." It was brilliant, absorbing, and real, claimed Johnson. As opposed to the satire for which Van Vechten had become famous, *Nigger Heaven* was serious, just as Van Vechten himself claimed. "He does not moralize, he does not over-emphasize, there are no mock heroics, there are no martyrdoms," Johnson wrote, and then praised Van Vechten by calling the book, of all things, a piece of pro-Negro propaganda. "If the book has a thesis it is: Negroes are people; they have the same emotions, the same passions, the same shortcomings, the same aspirations, the same graduations of social strata of other people."[85]

The disagreement over *Nigger Heaven* that divided black readers and critics came down to this: those who saw *Nigger Heaven* as having depicted black people as alien and strange, and those who valued the novel for its representation of blacks as everyday human beings, complex and flawed—just like white people. Alice Dunbar-Nelson appreciated the book and its author for this simple triumph: "It is a relief to find him describing a cultured woman, like Mary, without patronizing her. As far as I know, this is absolutely the first time such a thing has been done by a white man. . . . Just a plain acceptance of a cultivated brown woman." To black supporters, it was baffling that detractors could not see this straightforward fact. *Nigger Heaven* was a black book, true to the complex nature of black experience. Van Vechten had successfully proved that a white man could produce such a book. "And does he know the 'Race'? Through and through he does," Dunbar-Nelson concluded.[86] Nella Larsen, too, hoped the book would answer skeptics, like one white friend of

Van Vechten's who had asked him, in "shocked horror," if it was true that Van Vechten knew a Negro? "What will she say when she reads this sly story, with its air of deceptive simplicity and discovers that Carl Van Vechten knows the Negroe?"[87] To Larsen and others who supported the book, its greatest achievement was that it dramatized the paradox at the core of black American identity, a paradox that shaped the lives of Van Vechten and his close friends, which was that the line between blacks and whites was both fact and fiction. *Nigger Heaven* may have required different kinds of ads for black and white readerships, but it offered to both the same fleshy contradiction. The novel both upheld and upended fantasies about racial difference; and it established and undermined ideas about racial sameness. In the novel Negroes are people, but they are also Negroes, with a distinct cultural sensibility, a characteristic set of concerns, and a particular worldview. Van Vechten captured the dissonance of the world in which he moved in *Nigger Heaven*, which was, from the day it was conceived, a unique and undeniable progeny of the Negro Renaissance.

W. E. B. Du Bois saw no virtues in either *Nigger Heaven* or its author upon the publication of the book, as he revealed in a withering review in the December issue of the *Crisis*. "Carl Van Vechten's 'Nigger Heaven' is a blow in the face," Du Bois began. He addressed the title promptly: " 'Nigger Heaven' does not mean, as Van Vechten once or twice intimates, a haven for Negroes—a city of refuge for dark and tired souls; it means in common parlance, a nasty, sordid corner into which black folk are herded, and yet a place which they in crass ignorance are fools enough to enjoy." Du Bois, who had passed the evening with Van Vechten on the day that the title of *Nigger Heaven* had presented itself, felt that Van Vechten had deliberately misused the phrase that served as the title of his book. "Harlem is no such place as that," he wrote, "and no one knows this better than Carl Van Vechten."[88]

Du Bois felt that Van Vechten had misled readers. Nightclubs were only a marginal feature of life in Harlem, he claimed. "The average colored man in Harlem," he contended, "is an everyday laborer, attending church, lodge and movie and as conservative and as conventional as ordinary working folk everywhere."[89] In other words, black people were just like white people—a fact that black fans of the book felt that *Nigger Heaven* established irrefutably.

Du Bois wanted the white reading public to know exactly the same thing that Van Vechten wanted the white reading public to know—that blacks and whites were alike, and different, too. There *was* such a thing as black difference, "something distinctively Negroid," Du Bois contended, but "it is expressed by subtle, almost delicate nuance, and not by the wildly, barbaric drunken orgy in whose details Van Vechten revels." Van Vechten had cheapened the Harlem that he loved, and revealed a base attitude more pathetic than that of his main character: "Life to him is just one damned orgy after another, with hate, hurt, gin and sadism." Readers inclined toward such titillating rot should dispose of the book in the sewer, Du Bois advised, and pick up the *Police Gazette* instead.[90]

"That was a very hot crack that Du Bois handed to you in the December 'Crisis.' I think it was quite severe, even from his viewpoint," wrote author Charles Chesnutt in a letter to Van Vechten. "Walter White was here the other night, and he tells me that he wrote Du Bois a letter criticizing his review." A turn-of-the century writer, Chesnutt wrote fiction about the "color line" and passing, among other topics. Van Vechten was impressed by his skill and had consulted his work as he embarked on *Nigger Heaven*. He used Chesnutt as an example for Byron, who in reading Chesnutt's 1899 short story collection, *A Wife of His Youth*, realizes that his obsession with "the Negro problem" has rendered him unable to develop the literary skills that Chesnutt possessed. In their correspondence, Chesnutt told Van Vechten that he had come around to *Nigger Heaven* after first having reservations about the book. "Your title gave me a shock at first."[91]

Van Vechten had become enchanted with Chesnutt over the course of his baptism into blackness. He wrote excitedly about *A Wife of His Youth* in a review of *The New Negro*. Chesnutt's facility with irony left him gaping with astonishment, he said, and it was clear to him why Negroes, being "no lovers of irony," hadn't taken to his work. "They do not, for the most part, even comprehend it and are likely to read literalness where it is not intended."[92]

Walter White did write a letter to W. E. B. Du Bois about *Nigger Heaven*, just as he had promised Chesnutt he would. "Dear Dr. Du Bois," he began. "I would like to bring to your attention and that of the readers of The Crisis a factor in consideration of this novel which most of its colored readers seem to have missed." He used an anecdote to illustrate his point:

I recently had an experience which demonstrated to me anew how many sympathetically-minded but uninformed white people there are who are wholly unaware of the various strata of Negroes. The experience to which I refer came about through "Nigger Heaven." A certain white man of New York read the book and wrote a letter to Mr. Van Vechten saying that it opened up an entirely new field to him and his friends, vis., that there were these different classes of colored people. This man asked Mr. Van Vechten if he would agree to talk informally to a group of his friends at his home. Mr. Van Vechten was reluctant to do so and suggested that I should be asked, which suggestion was followed.

Just a few days ago, Mrs. White and I dined with this man and his wife and some other friends and later I spoke to a group of about twenty-five people belonging to one of the most socially exclusive and wealthy groups in New York. Later I found out that of the twenty-five people present, fifteen were millionaires.

I spoke of the Negro's cultural contributions, reading some of the poetry of Countee Cullen, Langston Hughes, James Weldon Johnson, and others; telling of the rise in the world of music of Negroes like Roland Hayes, Paul Robeson, Marian Anderson, Julius Bledsoe, Rosamond Johnson and Taylor Gordon; of your own contributions to literature, and of other phases of the Negro's cultural contributions.

Following my talk, the opportunity was given for questions. One man whose name is one of the most prominent in American life, asked this question. "Is it really true that there are educated negroes in Harlem as Mr. Van Vechten shows in his 'Nigger Heaven'? If so, how many are there?" The things that I said are commonplace to those of us who, being Negroes, know about them but to this group it was of amazing newness. Not one of the questions asked intimated any degree of shock or disgust at the characters in "Nigger Heaven" which have given greatest offense to some of the Negro critics of that book. Instead, the amazement was the same as that expressed in many reviews of "Nigger Heaven" in the Southern press— not that there are low Negroes *but that there are so many intellectual and aspiring ones!* After the questions were ended, two men of wide influence said this to me, "Prejudice against Negroes exists because the average white person knows nothing about the things which you have said here tonight which are set forth in 'Nigger Heaven.' What can I do to help spread this information to white people who do not know the facts?"

I have no quarrel with any Negro who objects to "Nigger Heaven" either because of its content or its title. Every person who has read the book has, of course, full right to his own opinion concerning it. It does seem to me unfortunate, however, that when a book which is being read and will be read by people who will never read a line of what you or I or other Negroes may write and who through such reading will learn of the various things which are going on in Negro life, that so many Negroes should reveal themselves as so narrow-minded as to resent a frank and honest picture of [them] whether they like this picture or not.

I do not agree with you that "Nigger Heaven" is an affront "to the intelligence of white people" for my observations have been precisely to the contrary. And as for its being "an affront to the hospitality of black folk," is such a dictum literary criticism or is it a matter solely for the consideration of those who have shown hospitality to Mr. Van Vechten?[93]

It could have been a scene in *Nigger Heaven*. The book—and Walter White—managed to convert twenty-five whites like Gareth Johns, Van Vechten's double in *Nigger Heaven*, to the cause of the Negro. The novel had sold to these rich whites the new world promised by the ads in the book—but it was not the world of cabarets. Instead it looked much like their own worlds. The revelation of black-white sameness would only create more racial understanding on the part of whites, White suggested to Du Bois.

Du Bois's review stung Van Vechten for months. At least some semblance of civility between them survived. In November Van Vechten ran into Du Bois at an event at the Dark Tower, the name of A'Lelia Walker's salon. "Swell Harlem was there & a great many from down town," he recorded in his daybook. "I ran into Dr. Du Bois for the first time since his attack in *The Crisis* & we chatted amiably."[94]

Ultimately, White's letter failed to achieve its purpose. Nothing would ever convince Du Bois that the effect of *Nigger Heaven* could be anything but detrimental to black people. Perhaps most of all, Du Bois feared the impact *Nigger Heaven* would have on black writers. And in fact, *Nigger Heaven* did cast a shadow over at least two New Negro writers: Langston Hughes and Claude McKay.

THE BADDEST NEW NEGRO

No writer suffered from allegations that he had lost himself under Van Vechten's influence more than Langston Hughes. According to Harlem Renaissance watchdogs, and even some of his own fans, when it came to Carl Van Vechten, Langston Hughes did not know his own mind.

Suspicions that had been brewing about the influence of Van Vechten over Hughes peaked with *Fine Clothes to the Jew,* Hughes's second book of poems, published in 1927, just a year after *The Weary Blues.* Hughes explained the title in *The Big Sea.* "I called it *Fine Clothes to the Jew,* because the first poem, 'Hard Luck,' a blues, was about a man who was often so broke he had no recourse but to pawn his clothes—to take them, as the Negroes say, to 'the Jew's' or to 'Uncle's.'" Hughes came to regret the title: "It was confusing and many Jewish people did not like it. I do not know why the Knopfs let me use it, since they were very helpful in their advice about sorting out the bad poems from the good, but they said nothing about the title."[95]

The Knopfs may not have expressed their objections to Hughes directly, but Blanche did alert Van Vechten to the disapproval of her father-in-law, Samuel Knopf, who served as treasurer at the publishing house. "Blanche tells me that Sam Knopf insists that Langston Hughes change the name of *Fine Clothes to the Jew,* a pretty piece of impertinence, this," he recorded in his November 5, 1926, daybook entry. Van Vechten had a great deal of influence with the Knopfs. They had been close friends for many years, and Van Vechten had been one of their most successful authors since the publication of *Peter*

Whiffle in 1922. Blanche Knopf in particular deferred to Van Vechten, not only on matters concerning Hughes's career, but also on issues concerning black writers in general, as Van Vechten represented to her a white expert on black art. Samuel Knopf held some sway over his daughter-in-law, but Van Vechten's influence was greater, at least in this respect. He put his foot down, and there was no more discussion about an alternate title.

The book had Jewish supporters, including Arthur and Amy Spingarn, both of whom admired *Fine Clothes,* declaring the book even finer than *The Weary Blues.* Arnold Rampersad, author of *The Life of Langston Hughes,* has equated *Fine Clothes* to *Leaves of Grass* by Walt Whitman in terms of their significance within the Western canon. Even more than *The Weary Blues,* Rampersad has written, *Fine Clothes to the Jew* perfectly captures the blues idiom.[96]

It was perhaps because *Fine Clothes* rendered the blues so precisely that some critics despised it. Hughes remembered in *The Big Sea:* "The Pittsburgh Courier ran a big headline across the top of the page, LANGSTON HUGHES' BOOK OF POEMS TRASH. The headline in the New York *Amsterdam News* was LANGSTON HUGHES—THE SEWER DWELLER. The Chicago *Whip* characterized me as 'The poet lowrate of Harlem.' "[97] The same reviewers who had condemned *Nigger Heaven* condemned *Fine Clothes to the Jew.* Ultimately, the trouble with *Fine Clothes,* the trouble with Hughes, and the trouble with the Negro Renaissance in general was Carl Van Vechten, to whom Hughes had dedicated *Fine Clothes.* This fact the *Whip* found particularly obscene, as did Floyd Calvin of the *Pittsburgh Courier,* who summed up his review of *Fine Clothes* in two sentences: "The author dedicates the volume to Carl Van Vechten. 'Nuff sed."[98]

Indeed, the dedication spoke volumes, representing much more than a personal tribute. This single act of affiliation set in type the position Hughes had taken in the current debate about black art. It was a public acknowledgment of his creative bond with Van Vechten, and it was also a personal proclamation of disagreement with the older guard of New Negroes, who faulted the younger generation for having encouraged Van Vechten to write *Nigger Heaven*. If Van Vechten intended *Nigger Heaven* to serve as a public dedication to Harlem, then Hughes used *Fine Clothes to the Jew* to affirm, literally, his dedication to Carl Van Vechten.

Fine Clothes was considered a vulgar example of race betrayal among some writers of the New Negro era. But in its failure the book was a success, in that it added yet another layer to the ongoing conversation about black art. Apparently, even a well-regarded black artist, a darling of the black community, could fail to produce respectable black art, too.

The *Courier* offered Hughes an opportunity to defend himself and his work, which he did in a two-part article entitled "Those Bad New Negroes: A Critique on Critics," which was published on April 9 and April 16 of 1927. Hughes cited reasons for the "definite but rather uncritical aversion to much of the work of the younger Negro writers" on the part of the Negro press. First, the "best Negroes" suffered from internalized racism and rejected anything "black" in black art that made it different from art produced by whites. They were interested only in images of themselves that would not reveal them to be any different from whites. These best Negroes believed that "what white people think about Negroes is more important than what Negroes think about themselves." The best Negroes were not really cultured anyway, he went on, and couldn't appreciate the subtleties in art. They were pseudo-intellectuals, pretenders. An accurate story about the "best" colored people "would be more wrathfully damned than NIGGER HEAVEN."[99]

"Young Author Calls Van Vechten Friend of Negro," ran the headline for the next installment in the *Courier* published the following week. Hughes continued his statement on behalf of the bad New Negroes (he assumed he was considered the "baddest") first by chastising the black press for its "hysterical and absurd" condemnation of *Nigger Heaven*. "Certainly the book is true to the life it pictures. There are cabarets in Harlem and both white and colored people who are nationally known and respected can be found almost any night at Small's. I've seen ministers there—nobody considers cabaret-going indecent any longer." Overall, he applauded Van Vechten for his "sincerely, friendly, and helpful interest in things Negro."[100]

Hughes did not speak for every young writer of the New Negro generation. Allison Davis, an anthropologist and educator, was born, like Hughes, in 1902, but he shared the older generation's opinion of the Negro Renaissance. With degrees from Harvard, the University of Chicago, and the London School of Economics, Davis spent his career dissecting the patterns of institutional bias that crippled African American educational, social, and economic progress until his death in 1982. He received posthumous recognition when the U.S. Postal Service issued a stamp bearing his likeness in 1994. Davis was a model of black achievement, a stellar representative of Du Bois's Talented Tenth. Much like Du Bois, he was zealous in his conviction that the self-styled "New Negroes" were reinforcing the very stereotypes he had made it his life's mission to undo.

Davis upbraided the entire cohort of New Negro writers in "Our Negro 'Intellectuals,'" an August 1928 essay published in the *Crisis*. "For nearly ten years," he began, "our Negro writers have been 'confessing' the distinctive sordidness and triviality of Negro life, and making an exhibition of their own unhealthy imagination, in the name of frankness and sincerity." Davis chose his words carefully; "sincerity" was the word that circulated among black writers in reference to Carl Van Vechten. "A dog or savage is 'sincere' about his bestialities, but he is not therefore raised above them." Milton, Fielding, and James Weldon Johnson were truly, authentically sincere artists. Langston Hughes, like fiction writer Rudolph Fisher, Claude McKay, and even Countee Cullen, had become an exhibitionist, or "sincerely bestial."[101] Underneath his article runs a selection of photographs of *real* intellectuals—valedictorians, salutatorians, M.A. students, and members of Phi Beta Kappa.

Who was most responsible for the depravity among New Negro writers? Carl Van Vechten, declared Davis. In *Nigger Heaven*, Carl Van Vechten had "warped Negro life into a fantastic barbarism." Most dangerous was the spell Van Vechten had cast over

Langston Hughes. "I think the severest charge one can make against Mr. Van Vechten is that he misdirected a genuine poet."[102] Davis had grown up in the bosom of the Washington elite, whose pretensions Hughes had exposed in "Our Wonderful Society: Washington," an essay that appeared in the August 1927 issue of *Opportunity*, no doubt to Davis's displeasure.

Hughes reeled from Davis's jabs, and defended himself in a letter to the *Crisis*. "I do not know what facts Mr. Davis himself may possess as to how, where, or when I have been misdirected by Mr. Van Vechten, but since I happen to be the person who wrote the material comprising FINE CLOTHES TO THE JEW, I would like herewith to state and declare that many of the poems in said book were written before I made the acquaintance of Mr. Van Vechten." He insisted that none of the poems in the book had anything to do with Van Vechten, and were certainly not influenced by him.[103] Hughes sent a copy of his *Crisis* rebuttal to Van Vechten, who praised it and thanked Hughes for representing him favorably. He was disturbed that the article had found its way to the pages of the *Crisis* in the first place. "What can you think of Du Bois printing such rubbish?" he asked Hughes.[104]

Allison Davis didn't believe Hughes, and his suspicions were in large part correct. Concrete evidence of Van Vechten's influence on Hughes's latest collection of poetry lay in a source to which Davis was not privy: Van Vechten's daybooks. Van Vechten recorded two visits from Hughes during which they discussed the manuscript of what would become *Fine Clothes to the Jew*. Just as he had done with *The Weary Blues*, Van Vechten delivered to Knopf the final version of *Fine Clothes*, for which he had most likely played the role of informal editor. Davis's allegation that Hughes had been corrupted by Van Vechten revealed more about his own personality and anxieties than about either object of his scorn, of course, but that Van Vechten did influence the career of Langston Hughes is undeniable. This fact was certainly clear to Alain Locke, who thanked Van Vechten on more than one occasion for his nurturance of Hughes's career, which he called Van Vechten's most significant contribution to the Harlem Renaissance.

Twenty years older than Hughes, Benjamin Brawley was a contemporary of Carl Van Vechten's. Like Allison Davis, he was a serious and accomplished man, an educator and a scholar, who committed much energy to monitoring the state of black art. In an essay called "The Negro Literary Renaissance," Brawley described the postwar surge in black creativity as having sunk to "hedonism and paganism." Jazz and blues were symptoms of black cultural and moral degradation, and *Fine Clothes to the Jew* was a perfect embodiment of the new preference for "sordid, unpleasant, or forbidden themes." Brawley pitied Hughes, and saw in *Fine Clothes* evidence of the corruption of a real talent. "About Langston Hughes the only thing to observe is that here we have the sad case of a young man of ability who has gone off on the wrong track altogether," he sighed. He blamed Hughes for his own artistic and moral decline; his view of Van Vechten was favorable. "When Mr. Hughes came under the influence of Mr. Carl Van Vechten and 'The Weary Blues' was given to the world, the public was given to understand that a new and genuine poet had appeared on the horizon," he wrote.[105] To Brawley's thinking, Van Vechten had not corrupted Hughes. Instead, he had actually opened the door for the poet, who then failed to fulfill his promise due to his own bad choices.

But Van Vechten objected even to this favorable mention. Like Hughes, he resisted any suggestion, positive or negative, that he had had any influence over Hughes, and corrected Brawley in a personal letter. "The Weary Blues had won a prize before I had read a poem by Mr. Hughes or knew him personally. The volume, of which this was the title poem, was brought to me complete before Mr. Hughes and I had ever exchanged two sentences. I am unaware even to this day, although we are the warmest friends and see each other frequently, that I have had the slightest influence on Mr. Hughes in any direction. The influence, if one exists, flows from the other side, as any one might see who read my first paper on the Blues, published in Vanity Fair for August 1925, a full year before Nigger Heaven appeared, before, indeed, a line of it had been written. In this paper I have quoted freely Mr. Hughes's opinions on the subject of Negro folksong, opinions which to my knowledge have not changed in the slightest."[106]

It was true, of course, that Hughes had enlarged Van Vechten's understanding of the blues, but Van Vechten's assertion that he had not in any way influenced Hughes was simply false. Well into the 1940s, Van Vechten continued to influence Hughes's career. Would Hughes have become the "poet of the Negro race" if it weren't for Carl Van Vechten? This is the question at the heart of the controversy over the relationship between Hughes and

Van Vechten. The charge of corruption had less to do with Hughes's poetry per se, and more to do with his integrity as a *black* poet. But it is simply true that without this white man, Hughes may not have emerged as the celebrated black poet he came to be.

Van Vechten sent Hughes a copy of his rebuttal to Brawley, in which he chastised the critic for his lack of "meticulous niceness in regard to matters of fact."[107] One expected more from a college professor, he concluded. Van Vechten meant to rankle Brawley. He knew that what Brawley hated most about the New Negro writers was the lack of formal structure (like proper grammar) in their work, their refusal to master the technique of a poet like Tennyson, who he felt should serve as an "example to the young writers of the Negro race."[108] Brawley despised jazz and blues for their stylistic freedom. What Hughes and Van Vechten called authentic black art, Brawley saw as simple vulgarity.

THE DIRTIER PARTS

Like Langston Hughes, Jamaican-born novelist Claude McKay felt forced to defend himself from accusations involving Carl Van Vechten; in his case that his 1928 novel *Home to Harlem* was nothing more than a black version of *Nigger Heaven*. "Many persons imagine that I wrote *Home to Harlem* because Carl Van Vechten wrote *Nigger Heaven*," he wrote in his 1937 autobiography *A Long Way from Home*. It wasn't true, he claimed. "I never saw the book until the late spring of 1927."[109] By that time *Home to Harlem*, his first novel, was nearly complete; it would be published in 1928. Like *Nigger Heaven* and *Fine Clothes to the Jew*, *Home to Harlem* shook the foundation of the black literary community.

Critics asked of this book the same questions they had asked of its predecessors: what role did white expectations play in the creation of black stories? Could black art exist within a white-controlled publishing industry? At what cost did black writers exercise literary freedom?

Readers of *Home to Harlem,* like readers of *Nigger Heaven,* follow its characters into the underworld of Harlem. Jake and Ray, the two main characters, represent the sensual and the intellectual, respectively: the body and the mind. The story begins when Jake arrives in Harlem after deserting from the army. He had enlisted eagerly, but because of his race, found himself assigned only menial duties. After two years in the service, he begins to long for Harlem—in particular, the women of Harlem: "Fifth Avenue, Lenox Avenue, and One Hundred and Thirty-fifth Street, with their chocolate-brown and walnut-brown girls, were calling him." Upon arriving in Harlem, he meets a prostitute named Felice and spends the night with her. The next morning, he discovers that she has disappeared, but left his money behind. Jake and Felice are reunited at the end of the novel ("O my Gawd! It's my heartbreaking daddy! Where was you all this time?"). In between there are poolrooms and dance halls; there is fighting and gambling and eating and sex. Like Van Vechten, McKay attempted to capture the atmosphere of Harlem nightclubs. At the Congo, two dancers "reared and pranced together, smacking palm against palm, working knee to knee, grinning with real joy."[110]

Eventually, Harlem proves too much for Jake, and he takes a job on the railroad to free himself from the city's hold on him. There he meets Ray, a Haitian-born waiter who spends his leisure time reading Sappho. Like the cerebral Mary Love in *Nigger Heaven,* Ray feels hampered by his education. "I wonder sometimes if I could get rid of it and go and lose myself in some savage culture in the jungles of Africa," he says to Jake, who, in turn, envies Ray's intellect.[111] *Home to Harlem,* like *Nigger Heaven,* is more than a portrait of the black mecca, it is a meditation on the question of racial difference: whether it resides in the body or the mind, whether "blackness" is a consequence of biology or experience.

W. E. B. Du Bois thought the book was trash. "I have just read the last two novels of Negro America," began Du Bois in the June 1928 issue of the *Crisis.* "The one I liked; the other I distinctly did not." He described Nella Larsen's *Quicksand,* with its beautiful but perpetually unhappy and restless mixed-race heroine, as "fine, thoughtful and courageous." *Home to Harlem,* on the other hand, nauseated him: "After the dirtier parts of its filth I feel distinctly like taking a bath."[112]

But unlike *Nigger Heaven,* Du Bois conceded, *Home to Harlem* had some redeeming qualities, in particular the range of descriptions of the "beauty of colored skins" ("low-brown, high-brown, nut-brown, lemon, maroon, olive, mauve, and gold," read one of the novel's several paeans).[113] But ultimately, he concluded, "McKay has set out to cater to that prurient demand on the part of white folk for a portrayal in Negroes of that utter licentiousness which conventional civilization holds white folk back from enjoying—if enjoyment it can be called."[114] Du Bois did not remark upon the fact that there is a nigger heaven, literally, in *Home to Harlem.* Once Jake and Felice take in a movie downtown, where from the "nigger heaven" section, "they watched high-class people make luxurious love on the screen. They enjoyed the exhibition. There is no better angle from which one can look down on a motion picture that that of the nigger heaven."[115]

The review infuriated McKay, and he fired back an immediate response. He accused Du Bois of lacking any feeling for art: "Nowhere in your writings do you reveal any comprehension of esthetics and therefore you are not competent or qualified to pass judgment upon any work of art." He pitied Du Bois for his limitations: "You have been forced from a normal career to enter a special field of racial propaganda and, honorable though that field may be, it has precluded you from contact with real life, for propaganda is fundamentally but a one-sided idea of life. Therefore I should not be surprised when you mistake the art of life for nonsense and try to pass off propaganda as life in art!"[116]

Claude McKay was a latecomer to the Harlem Renaissance. He was traveling in Morocco when he received a letter from James Weldon Johnson in January 1928, not long before *Home to Harlem* was released, urging him to return to Harlem and become part of the Negro Renaissance. "My dear Mr. McKay," the letter began, "I have been wanting to write you for some time. I should like very much if you were back in the states, in fact, right in New York. You ought to be here to take full advantage of the great wave of opportunity that Negro literary and other artists are now enjoying. In addition—we need you to give more strength and solidity to the whole movement. I wish you would think about coming back, and if I can in any way be of assistance whatever, please do not hesitate to call on me." Johnson tried again five years later. "I feel very strongly that you ought to come and stay," he wrote. "New York is your market, and the United States is your field. Furthermore, we, the Negro writers, need you here."[117] Eventually, Johnson used his influence at the U. S. State Department to smooth the way for McKay's return. McKay finally arrived in New York in February 1934.

McKay was anxious about returning to Harlem. The pile of mail that included Johnson's letter also contained clippings of nasty reviews of *Home to Harlem* from the black press that confirmed his suspicions that negative feelings about the novel persisted. He balanced this against reports from friends in the States that the Harlem social scene had grown and taken on spectacular dimensions since he left in 1922. But the prospect of coming face-to-face with the Negro elite unsettled him. In addition, he had become disillusioned by the white leftists whom he had once counted among his closest friends, like Max Eastman, his champion and the editor of *New Masses*. They had not understood *Home to Harlem*, either. "I consider the book a real proletarian novel," McKay explained to Johnson in May, "but I don't expect the nice radicals to see that it is, because they know very little about proletarian life and what they want of proletarian art is not proletarian life, truthfully, realistically, and artistically portrayed, but their own false, soft-headed and wine-watered notions of the proletariat."[118] Ultimately, there was only one home for him in Harlem, and that was among the black intelligentsia. When McKay returned to New York, he found that, in the end, the commercial success of his novel had made more of an impression than the novel itself.

Claude McKay and Carl Van Vechten met in Paris during the summer of 1929. "One of Mr. Van Vechten's Harlem sheiks introduced us after midnight at the Café de la Paix." Van Vechten also recorded the meeting, identifying the "sheik" in his August 9, 1929, daybook entry: "Meet Harold Jackman at the Café de la Paix who introduces me to Claude McKay. I am very soused by now & stagger in around midnight."[119]

McKay's reputation had preceded him. Four years earlier, Alain Locke had entertained Van Vechten with gossip about McKay. At that time, Locke and McKay were in the middle of a battle over McKay's poems. In his position as editor of the Harlem edition of the *Survey Graphic* and *The New Negro,* Locke had been too timid to publish one of McKay's radical poems, and had changed the title of another from "The White House" to the more oblique "White Houses" for publication in *The New Negro* without consulting McKay. McKay was still furious with Locke twelve years later when he recounted the episode in his autobiography. Locke claimed that he made the change out of concern for McKay. With its original title, Locke explained, the poem might be mistaken for an indictment of the American presidential residence, and could therefore create problems for McKay when he returned to the United States. McKay suspected that Locke was looking out for his own interests, deeming him a right-wing coward, unworthy of leadership in the Negro Renaissance. In McKay's diagnosis, that unworthiness had something to do with Locke's aesthetic limitations and "effete" European pretensions.[120]

Locke wrote a crushing review of *A Long Way from Home* for the radical magazine *New Challenge*, in which he ridiculed McKay for portraying himself in his memoir as the "playboy of the Negro Renaissance." He pronounced McKay a "spiritual truant," whose memoir confirmed his lack of fidelity to any movement or ideology: "Surely this career is not one of cosmopolitan experiment or innocent vagabondage, but, as I have already implied, one of chronic and perverse truancy." McKay represented to Locke what Hughes represented to his own critics: the failures of the Negro Renaissance itself. Locke had become disappointed in the New Negro movement he had several years before exalted. He urged young black writers to reverse the current trend in black writing, to "purge this flippant exhibitionism, this posy but not too sincere radicalism, this care-free and irresponsible individualism." Black artists had turned away from their noble purpose, and now addressed themselves primarily "to the gallery of faddist Negrophiles."[121] Locke may or may not have exempted his friend Carl Van Vechten from the unit of Negrophiles that had managed to compromise black art, but catering to white demands was exactly what Van Vechten encouraged black artists to do.

Despite his controversial and colorful background, his stubborn opinions and considerable temper—features he shared with Van Vechten—McKay failed to hold Van Vechten's interest when they met, largely because Van Vechten was drunk. "I am afraid that as a soft drinker I bored him," McKay remembered. "The white author and the black author of books about Harlem could not find much of anything to make conversation."[122]

To make matters worse, Van Vechten became obsessed with a truckload of enormous carrots he saw passing by during their meal together. "Perhaps carrots were more interesting than conversation," McKay reflected. "But I did not feel in any way carroty." Van Vechten excused himself from the table and never came back. Later, he relayed a message to McKay through Jackman—the "precious, hesitating sheik," as McKay described him. "The message said that Mr. Van Vechten was sorry for not returning, but he was so high that, after leaving us, he discovered himself running along the avenue after a truck load of carrots."[123]

But overall, somehow McKay was left with a good impression of Van Vechten, even though he had met some of Van Vechten's erstwhile black friends who warned him against the white author. And at least one white "non-admirer of Mr. Van Vechten" told McKay that he would not like him "because he patronized Negroes in a subtle way, to which the Harlem élite were blind because they were just learning sophistication! I thought it would be a new experience to meet a white man who was subtly patronizing to a black; the majority of them were so naïvely crude about it. But I found Mr. Van Vechten not a bit patronizing, and quite all right."[124]

McKay insisted in his autobiography that *Home to Harlem* was already under way when he heard about Carl Van Vechten's novel, but McKay did not reveal to his readers how determined he was for his novel to appear first. He was an insider, he said, and the fact that he was black meant that his would be the more authentic portrait of Harlem. And in fact, some reviewers felt that because he was an insider, he had done more damage to Harlem's reputation than Van Vechten. McKay felt vindicated by a "lovely lady in Harlem" who spoke to him about the novel upon his return to the United States: "Why all this nigger-row if a colored writer can exploit his own people and money and a name?" she asked. "White writers have been exploiting us long enough without any credit to our race."[125]

Regardless of his intentions and explanations, McKay could not shake the yoking of his novel with *Nigger Heaven*. After his book came out, both favorable and negative reviews of *Home to Harlem* in influential periodicals began with reviews of *Nigger Heaven*. "With due respect to Carl Van Vechten's aims and intentions in 'Nigger Heaven' I did not like the book overmuch," wrote Herschel Brickell in *Opportunity*. "But I do like Claude McKay's 'Home to Harlem.'"[126] Dewey Jones in the *Chicago Defender* also used *Nigger Heaven* as a standard and decided that McKay had not measured up to it. "'Home to Harlem' is 'Nigger Heaven' in a larger and more violent dose," he wrote. "Where Mr. Van Vechten hesitated to delve too deeply into the morass of filth with which we all know Harlem abounds, Mr. McKay comes 'full steam ahead' and 'shoots the whole works.'"[127] McKay was annoyed by the implication that he was not truly the author of his own work, that his take on Harlem was merely a version, good or bad, of Van Vechten's Harlem. He wrestled with the shadow of *Nigger Heaven* and, as had been the case with Hughes, his struggle with the book was ultimately a war to maintain both his artistic and his racial integrity.

Even James Weldon Johnson, who had insisted that McKay throw his hat into the New Negro literary ring, compared *Home to Harlem* with *Nigger Heaven*—and judged *Nigger Heaven* the superior black story. "The lusty primitive life in *Home to Harlem* was based on truth, as were the dissolute modes of life in *Nigger Heaven*," he began. But McKay had sunk lower, portraying a lustier life than readers found in *Nigger Heaven*. Van Vechten had treated his educated black characters with respect, Johnson wrote, unlike McKay, who "made no attempt to hold in check or disguise his abiding contempt for the Negro bourgeoisie and 'upper class.'"[128] Van Vechten excerpted these paragraphs, which appeared in Johnson's autobiography, and published them in the afterword of the 1951 edition of *Nigger Heaven*, when the debate ignited by the novel had not yet been resolved.

MAKE IT HOT!

Amid the acidic reviews, accusations of race betrayal, and intermittent book burnings, Wallace Thurman, Langston Hughes, Zora Neale Hurston, Eric Walrond, Aaron Douglas, and others decided to fight fire with *Fire!!* a journal they dedicated "to younger Negro artists"—themselves, essentially.

These younger Negro artists, a single-minded entity named by Hughes in "The Negro Artist and the Racial Mountain," took their protests to the page and began to hatch *Fire!!* in the summer of 1926, before the publication of *Nigger Heaven*. Wallace Thurman was elected to light the match. "You're the only possible choice for editor," insisted Langston Hughes in a letter on *Fire!!* letterhead. "It's a great chance to do something worthwhile. I'll help all I can," Hughes offered and urged Thurman to include "some really good poetry."[129] Hughes suggested Aaron Douglas for the artwork and advised Thurman that the covers should be done in black on red. Perhaps it went without saying that Van Vechten would serve as a patron.

In the foreword to *Fire!!* the younger Negro artists announced the ambitions of the magazine: "*FIRE . . . melting steel and iron bars, poking livid tongues between stone apertures and burning wooden opposition with a cackling chuckle of contempt.*"[130]

The editors of *Fire!!* aimed their livid tongues at W. E. B. Du Bois and the rest of the conservative old guard. They showed their contempt in prose about sex and drawings of nude black bodies. The journal opens with a pen-and-ink drawing of a shapely black woman with natural hair leaning against a palm tree. Opposite, a story by Wallace Thurman, "Cordelia the Crude," chronicles the travails of a sixteen-year-old "potential" Harlem prostitute, who was "quite blasé and bountiful in the matter of bestowing sexual favors upon persuasive and likely young men."[131] "Smoke, Lillies and Jade," a prose poem by the young aspiring artist Bruce Nugent, depicts a love story between two men, Alex and Beauty: "Beauty's breath was hot and short. . . . Alex ran his hand through Beauty's hair. . . . Beauty's lips pressed hard against his teeth. . . . Alex trembled."[132] Du Bois, who had lamented in his 1926 *Crisis* essay "Criteria of Negro Art" that black people had become "ashamed of sex" because of the way black sexuality had been distorted and overemphasized in white media, was bound to take offense—or so hoped the editors of *Fire!!*

"Wish we could get a good personal estimate of some leading Negro," Hughes wrote to Thurman, "sort of a sharp, keen biographical sketch, say of Du Bois." Du Bois was among a short list of contenders, among them Alain Locke, whom Thurman would not allow to participate in the composition of the magazine, as well as "Morton," which was most likely a misspelling of Robert Moton, an educator and protégé of Booker T. Washington. Moton had contributed an essay to Alain Locke's 1925 anthology *The New Negro* entitled "Hampton-Tuskegee: Missioners of the Masses." Thurman held a particular contempt for Locke and Du Bois, and liked the idea of using the sketch, as well as the entire magazine, to punish the old guard for being the old guard. Eventually, Thurman decided against including a sketch of a specific person. Instead he chose Arthur Huff Fauset, an educator, folklorist, and half brother to Jessie, to create a general portrait of the enemies of black creative freedom, "if he's not afraid."[133] In his essay, entitled "Intelligenstia," Fauset proved himself to be fearless.

"The average member of the Intelligentsia," Fauset claimed, "comes as near being a true intellectual as the proverbial hot water in which resides a cabbage leaf comes to being stew." Fauset attacked the intellectual elite, "snobbish sycophantic highbrow hero-worshippers," for its host of pretenses and failure to accomplish anything meaningful. He condemned the so-called intelligentsia for the threat it posed to true creativity. "They simply give art and artists a black eye with their snobbery and stupidity; and their false interpretations and hypocritical evaluations do more to heighten suspicion against the real artist on the part of the ordinary citizen than perhaps any other single factor in the clash of art and provincialism."[134] (Many years later, Fauset would develop an equal amount of antipathy toward Carl Van Vechten. In 1982, a year before he died, Fauset remembered Van Vechten as an "ogre," a Machiavelli with the "power to promote the interests of aspiring young Blacks willing to pay him homage.")[135]

"Intelligentsia" was a call to arms, vicious—but vague. Who were these contemptible snobs whose contributions to society were as "negligible as gin at a Methodist picnic"?[136] What crimes had they committed, exactly? The answer lay in the reactions of black people to *Nigger Heaven*, as Wallace Thurman revealed in the final section of the magazine, "Fire Burns."

" '*Fire Burns*,' should really be kept burning," Hughes advised Thurman, who was always a supporter of Van Vechten's, although they never became friends. The section ought to serve as "a department of clever, satirical comment on the vices and virtues of the race. Make it hot!"[137]

The heat in "Fire Burns" emanates courtesy of Carl Van Vechten. In his opening paragraph, Thurman reminded readers of a review of *Nigger Heaven* that he had published a couple of months earlier in the *Messenger,* where he was then serving as managing editor, in which he predicted that black people would erect a statue in Van Vechten's honor at the corner of 135th and Seventh Avenue, the heart of Harlem, once they got past the sting of the title. Instead, Thurman reported, Van Vechten faced a figurative lynching. Still, he defended his prophecy. Overall, his point was not to "endow Mr. Van Vechten's novel (?)

with immortality," but to comment upon the fickle and superficial nature of black critical response to the novel and its author.[138]

Ultimately, however, the book itself was beside the point. Thurman used *Nigger Heaven* as a weapon to attack the old guard. Nothing "could be more ridiculous," he wrote, "than the wholesale condemnation of a book which only one-tenth of the condemnators have or will read." In their criticisms of *Nigger Heaven*, "the so-called intelligentsia of Harlem has exposed its inherent stupidity."[139] The novel had thus served a greater purpose than Van Vechten had ever intended. In fact, for Thurman and others, the book had done more for them than it had done for its author. It enabled members of the younger generation to distinguish themselves from their predecessors. It had become their cackling chuckle of contempt.

Like Langston Hughes, Thurman resented the assumption that he and other New Negroes had somehow been duped by Van Vechten. Hopefully, the future would vindicate him, and Thurman imagined that "a few years hence Mr. Van Vechten will be spoken of as a kindly gent rather than as a moral leper exploiting people who had believed him to be a sincere friend." In "Fire Burns," Thurman insisted that those who believed that Van Vechten had "ingratiated himself with Harlem folk" in order to write his book were implicitly suggesting that he and other black friends of Van Vechten's were gullible fools.[140] Thurman and his staff used *Fire!!* as an opportunity to exhibit both their independence from Van Vechten and their identification with him.

In "Fire Burns" Thurman responded to critics who maintained that *Nigger Heaven* perpetuated racist assumptions about black people. Van Vechten's novel should not be blamed for the inevitability of white racism. Black people who feared that *Nigger Heaven* would confirm racist ideas should realize that "any white person who would believe such poppy-cock probably believes it anyway, without any additional aid from Mr. Van Vechten."[141]

Like Langston Hughes and Carl Van Vechten, Thurman believed that all forms of censorship hurt black artists. In his view, any writer "preparing to write about Negroes in Harlem or anywhere else . . . should take whatever phases of their life that seem the most interesting to him and develop them as he pleases."[142] *Nigger Heaven* provided, for Wallace Thurman, an occasion to argue against racial parochialism in general, particularly in the arena of literary production. Whites should be able to write about blacks, and blacks should be able to write about whatever they pleased. White freedom, in essence, was black freedom.

Six months later, in an interview with Marxist literary critic Granville Hicks, Thurman described the dynamic between the older and younger generation of New Negroes: "They tolerate us, and we laugh at them. They don't help us very much, and we feel we've done more for the race in five or six years than they have accomplished in a generation." He allowed that the NAACP had not been completely useless, but younger artists had no use for it any longer: "It has had its day, and we are going to have ours."[143] Of course, to the younger generation, the line between foes and friends was not as neat as Thurman presented it to Hicks. Just as much as Thurman and Hughes, Du Bois and Locke obsessed over the relationship between race and creative freedom; they devoted their professional lives to the question of how the Negro should be represented in art. The issue of race and representation actually braided the two generations; and the younger generation would not have recognized itself without the old. It was so important to the younger artists that the old guard disapprove of them that they invented discord where it did not exist. In *The Big Sea,* Langston Hughes wrote about the older generation's impression of *Fire!!* "None of the older intellectuals would have anything to do with *Fire.* Du Bois in the *Crisis* roasted it."[144] Du Bois did no such thing. His applause was faint—he called it "a beautiful piece of printing" and complimented Aaron Douglas on his illustrations—but he hardly pulled out the carving knives he had used to slice *Nigger Heaven,* although Hughes gave the impression that he did.[145]

Real opposition to *Fire!!* came from Rean Graves, a critic for the *Baltimore Afro-American,* in a review entitled "Writer Brands Fire as Effeminate Tommyrot." Graves called Aaron Douglas's pen-and-ink drawings "hudge pudge." A contribution by Countee Cullen was marred by "superfluous sentences." As for Langston Hughes, he had "displayed his usual ability to say nothing in many words."[146] Graves gave the contributors the censure that they were after, but *Fire!!* was supposed to be hated by the powerful, inviolable W. E. B. Du Bois. In "Criteria of Negro Art," Du Bois had mourned the sad fact that black writers were "bound by all sorts of customs that have come down as second-hand soul clothes of white patrons."[147] The members of the self-named younger generation believed that they had inherited the creative strait-jacket of their soul clothes from Du Bois himself. They used *Fire!!* to break free, and freedom looked like *Nigger Heaven*. On the other hand, Carl Van Vechten had not set out to antagonize anyone. He had intended his novel to serve as a bridge between black and white, not a means to deepen the chasm between the older and younger generations.

Whether they despised it or exalted it, every black person who wrote about *Nigger Heaven* agreed on one thing: the title was important. Each and every critic had to concede, whether he or she liked it or not, that it was at least noteworthy that a white man had published a book with the word *nigger* in the title, particularly a white man so deeply imbedded in black culture. It was important, if for no other reason, because black people believed it was important.

Radical journalist Hubert Harrison, W. E. B. Du Bois, and James Weldon Johnson all thought the title was noteworthy, even though each said otherwise in his review. But it was the title, not the story, that motivated crowds of people to gather in Harlem to condemn the book. Black people "got mad as soon as they heard of it," Langston Hughes remembered in *The Big Sea*. "And after that, many of them never did read it at all."[148] Fair or not, it is the *nigger* in *Nigger Heaven* that stung, and Van Vechten knew it. When William Ingersoll asked him in 1960 if the word had fewer ugly connotations in 1926, he responded, "It had more,

I'd say."[149] It continues to sting today as much as it did in every preceding generation.

THE DIRTIEST WORD

In 2007, the New York City Council passed a resolution to ban the word *nigger* from public usage. It was a symbolic gesture, of course, but a step that reflects the desire of a good many who would like the word erased from the American vocabulary—the legal historian Randall Kennedy calls them "eradicationists."[150] "Forwards, never backwards!" chanted the supporters of the ban on the steps of city hall. But maybe their victory was no victory at all.

What is this word?

The journalist Farai Chideya has called it the "nuclear bomb of racial epithets."[151] Prosecutor Christopher Darden calls it "the filthiest, dirtiest, nastiest word in the English language."[152] It is a word that has cost people their reputations and careers. It has motivated lawsuits and ended relationships. But it will probably never disappear because of the essential paradox that it represents. For *nigger* is *both* backwards and forwards, in many ways a container of the fundamental unity and disunity between black and white—just like *Nigger Heaven*.

First and foremost, *nigger* is history. Kennedy explains that *nigger*, which derives from *niger*, the Latin word for black, did not begin its life as a racial slur. Jabari Asim, editor of the *Washington Post Book World*, argues that the word has never been neutral as a name for blacks. Both agree that it entered the American vocabulary as early as 1619, when English settler John Rolfe recorded the first shipment of "negars" to Virginia. Two hundred years later, *nigger* had achieved full-fledged status as a racial epithet. In *The N Word*, Asim charts the progression of American history, and the progression of the history of *nigger*, and finds they are one and the same.[153] It is perhaps an uncomfortable truth that those who would eradicate the word want to wish away history. To erase *nigger* would be to erase a central feature in the story of blackness as it has been lived in this country. *Nigger* is the signpost at the intersection where African American and American history meet.

Langston Hughes explained what the word meant to those who had negative feelings about *Nigger Heaven*: "The word *nigger*, you see, sums up for us who are colored all the bitter years of insult and struggle in America: the slave-beatings of yesterday, the lynchings of today, the Jim Crow cars, the only movie show in town with its sign up FOR WHITES ONLY, the restaurants where you may not eat, the jobs you may not have. The unions you cannot join. The word *nigger* in the mouths of little white boys at school, the word *nigger* in the mouths of foremen on the job, the word *nigger* across the whole face of America!"[154] *Nigger* was everything the New Negro was trying to leave behind.

But for Hughes personally, as well as for many of his contemporaries, *nigger* was also the way forward. James Weldon Johnson tried to encourage his readers to see Van Vechten's title as a sign of hope. "There are those who will prejudge the book unfavorably on account of the title," he wrote. "This attitude is natural, but it is probable that the reaction against the title of the novel will not be so strong as it was against the title of the play which was produced sixteen years ago," he said, most likely referring to a 1909 play *The Nigger* by Edward Sheldon, whose story amounted to a sympathetic look at miscegenation. "Indeed," Johnson continued, "one gauge of the Negro's rise and development may be found in the degrees in which a race epithet loses its power to sting and hurt him."[155] Johnson stood behind the title because of the principle it represented. The principle was progress. For progress to be achieved, the conventions of the past must be gutted.

Walter White believed that the sting of *nigger* had already been extracted. As he announced in his *Courier* column two months before the book was released: "An interesting advance we have made as a race in overcoming too great sensitiveness is seen in the reception of the announcement of the title of this new book. . . . One can judge how far we have progressed when one notes the calmness with which the title of Mr. Van Vechten's book has been received. Intelligent Negroes simply say, 'We will wait and see what is in the story, and let it go at that.' "[156] White was a victim of wishful thinking, and for many people even today the wound represented by Van Vechten's title has not yet healed.

Contemporary philosopher and critic Judith Butler says that we must not hide from words like *nigger* and *spic*. Otherwise, their meanings will never change. But she concedes that to use them at all—even to write them—necessarily recirculates the wounds they represent.[157]

Mos Def, a phenomenon of music and screen, explains a popular variation of the word: "When we call each other 'nigga,' we take a word that has been historically used by whites to degrade and oppress us, a word that has so many negative connotations, and turn it into something beautiful, something we can call our own."[158] In contemporary hip-hop and rap music, language is a blunt instrument used by lyricists to menace the bogeymen of past respectability. Conservative censors are conjured and mocked; each *nigga* is a nose thumbed at bourgeois pretensions. In this way, *nigga*, like *nigger*, is power. *Nigga* is to Mof Def what *nigger* is to Judith Butler, and before her, Walter White, James Weldon Johnson, and Charles Johnson: hope. A common belief bridges a divide between them that is eighty years wide, which is that to use the word *nigger* (without rancor, of course) is to communicate a belief in change.

As an emblem of the past as well as a sign of aspiration, *nigger* continues to be meaningful, even useful. Carl Van Vechten always maintained that pleasure was more important to him than pedagogy, but for me, his novel has served as an irresistible invitation for instruction.

WORD AND WOUND

"Judith Butler would say that *nigga* represents 'an ironic hopefulness that the conventional relation between word and wound might become tenuous and even broken over time,'" I told my students, quoting from her book *Excitable Speech: A Politics of the Performative*. Dutifully, they nodded their heads. It was the spring semester of 2005 at the University of Vermont. Our topic was *Nigger Heaven*. The course was "The Harlem Renaissance," and all of my students were in the English department's master's program. I had believed that the theoretical lessons of Judith Butler would allow us some distance between the title and our experience of it. But there was no vigorous discussion, only painful, impenetrable silence. The experience led me to consider how great the divide has become, in academic circles, between heart and head.

After class, I returned to my office and waited for e-mails from my students, but there was only one, from a black student who described how his internal alarms went off every time anyone (including me) used the word *nigger*, even if only to pronounce the title of the book, and particularly when it came out of the mouths of white students. He said it was instinct, his heart and not his head. But in actuality, most students, regardless of race, seemed to find themselves unable to say *nigger* in class. A few followed my lead and said it, but not before embarking on an elaborate mea culpa. For the most part, students resorted to the popular cushion: "the n-word." The phrase in heaviest circulation that day in our discussion was "n-word heaven." Each use was accompanied by finger quotation marks. As for me, I avoided these phrases, but whenever I could avoid saying *nigger*, I did, too.

Both "the n-word" and "n-word heaven" sounded awkward, without rhythm. Not to mention that "N-word Heaven" is simply not the title of the book. I recalled a story about a Harlem Renaissance conference during which a prominent black scholar of African American literature refused to say *nigger* or *nigger heaven*, using instead the same roundabout phrases that we were using. At the time I heard the story his verbal acrobatics seemed silly. They seemed silly during our discussion, too, but I couldn't see any way out of them. How could I possibly insist that my students say the word *nigger*? What would be gained by such a demand? But our awkward sidestepping solved nothing; quite the contrary, it kept the word in the center of the table, glowing in neon.

My students and I did not invent the trap that had us in its grips, of course. We were enacting a now-common modern ritual made perhaps most public in the 1995 murder trial *The People v. Orenthal James Simpson,* in which former American football star O. J. Simpson was tried and acquitted on two counts of murder following the deaths of Nicole Brown Simpson, his ex-wife, and her friend Ronald Goldman. It has been called the most publicized murder trial in history. As Ann duCille explains, the "quintessentially American word 'nigger' was recreated in the public imagination as the unspeakable thing never spoken—a word so extraordinary, so far outside common usage, so rabidly racist and un-American that it could be only alluded to as the 'N word.' He who would say 'nigger' would also plant evidence to frame an innocent black man."[159]

Ann duCille refers to the revelation during the trial that the prosecution's star witness, Los Angeles police detective Mark Fuhrman, had perjured himself on the witness stand when he testified that he had not used the word *nigger* in ten years, when he had actually been taped using it forty-two times, "repeatedly and with relish," in the words of Randall Kennedy.[160] Amid allegations of racially motivated malevolent police work, what branded Mark Fuhrman an irrecoverable racist in the imagination of the American public was his articulation of *nigger,* a word whose very expression was considered such an act of rhetorical violence that it could not even be uttered in the courtroom of the Simpson trial—instead everyone resorted to "the n-word," the same clumsy phrase we used in my class. Looking back at the trial, considering, once again, its impression on the American psyche, it is no wonder that my students were anxious about saying *nigger* out loud. The wound they feared opening was much bigger and older than they were.

For years I did not teach *Nigger Heaven* because I did not want to subject my students to the wound that is the title of the book. I could not get past specific images: a student at the checkout desk at a bookstore or a library, the title begging to be called out by anyone, with any kind of motive. Then there was the classroom to consider, and what the repetition of the word *nigger* would recall for each student, whatever his or her race. Cultural historian John Gennari has said, "When sound enters the body and vibrates its chambers—not just in the ganglia of the eardrum but throughout the skeleton and its attached muscle, tissue, and sinew—that body changes. We hear through our bodies as well as through our ears, and what we hear collapses distinctions between subject and object, public and private."[161] As an auditory experience, *nigger* recalls a host of personal and historical memories and images that the listener cannot control. To experience the wound of *nigger* is to be human, and a living repository of American history.

But if *nigger* represents a public pain, then perhaps it can also engender a private pleasure, because there is enjoyment in saying the thing that should not be said, maybe even more so between people who should not be saying it to each other. Sounds engender "familiarity and intimacy; they remind us of what we have in common."[162] The pleasure was mutual between Van Vechten and black friends like Langston Hughes when they tossed the word back and forth in correspondence. Intimacy inspires a common vocabulary—in this case, a vocabulary that included the word *nigger*.

EASY TO EXPLAIN

It is spring and I am in New York. I am walking down Broadway, headed toward the Columbus Circle subway station. Two black men are talking on the corner in front of me. One of them wears a hat, a fedora—tan, with a dark brown band. He has one hand in his pocket; he gestures with the other. His companion wears a leather jacket; his gray beard is neat and spare. The man with the fedora stretches out his arm to make a point. He says something that causes the man in the leather jacket to bend forward and dip his head in laughter. Then he straightens and crosses his arms over his chest, still laughing.

I reach the corner and hear the man with the tan fedora say it: *nigger.* He is talking about someone he knows; the word seems to serve as a kind of affectionate critique of something this someone has done. He is still gesturing as I pass. He smiles, and I smile back. It is spring in New York, and the sun is shining.

Sometimes I get pleasure, transgressive pleasure, when I hear black people speak the word among themselves. I like to hear it when it's stolen—when I'm eavesdropping, catching just a beat of a private conversation. In the language of the man with the fedora was a southern rhythm, and the word was a beat in the rhythm of talk between intimates. That hint of the black South always so pleasing to my ear, particularly when I'm so far away, here in New England.

Two black men on a street corner, talking, listening, and laughing; the scene is a story in itself. What I am witnessing—through sight and sound—are black people staking out a place in time, in history—right here, on this sidewalk. To stand in public and tell a story that the world doesn't necessarily honor—to speak a complex and contradictory story about identity—this is the ambition of African American narrative since its inception, and it has been, historically speaking, no small feat. There is history here in the story unfolding in front of me; the history that these men are enacting is a moment of triumph *over* history, but it is also a gesture of intimacy between two individuals.

"The situation is easy to explain," wrote Van Vechten to Langston Hughes. "You and I are the only colored people who really love niggers."[163] Van Vechten wrote these lines during the controversy over *Fine Clothes,* specifically upon receiving Hughes's response to Benjamin Brawley. The critics were right about Van Vechten and Hughes. They did love what Du Bois called the "sordid" and Brawley called the "low down." They loved all the aspects of blackness that those who were aesthetically conservative, more concerned with uplift than freedom, wanted to chase down and hide behind locked doors. They took pleasure in these things; they loved blackness without condition or reservation. Like the men on the street corner, they did not particularly care who was watching.

But a book jacket is not a street corner, and a title is not a conversation. The pleasure and humor and irony Van Vechten intended when he used his title did not translate to the larger black world, still damaged by the wound and trying to find a way out of *nigger,* not a way back into it. But as one critic wrote, "Many agree that had the novel been written for no other reason than to start Harlem thinking, it has accomplished its purpose to a marvelous degree."[164] In my classroom, *Nigger Heaven* still accomplishes this purpose more than any other book I teach.

As sound, *nigger* is a psychological and physical experience, and it is more than this, too. It is artifice and integrity, regression and progression, Old Negro and New. Inside its phonetics lie the rhythm of history, American and African American. As a name for black, *nigger* is a lie. But it also says something true about the lives black people have lived within the borders of the United States. Blackness is language, and language is a territory. Africa survived the Middle Passage in stories. The enduring wealth and legacy of blackness lie in these stories. "Language is the only homeland," the poet Czeslaw Milosz has said. For black Americans, language, not Africa, is the motherland, and *nigger* is its frontier.

The paradox of *nigger* is at the heart of the paradox of black American experience. Somewhere in that heart is a chamber made of whiteness. Without that white chamber, the heart of blackness would not beat. During the Harlem Renaissance, Carl Van Vechten was that chamber. *Nigger Heaven* was its blood.

3 LETTERS FROM BLACKS

THE ONLY WHITE MAN HERE

"Heaven forbid that I should ever be bitten by the desire to write another novel! Except, perhaps, one to dedicate to you," Nella Larsen wrote to Carl Van Vechten in March 1927. "For, why should Langston Hughes be the only one to enjoy notoriety for the sake of his convictions?"[1] Larsen had just completed *Quicksand*, her first novel, and was hoping to make a name for herself in the black literary world of New York. She had set her sights on the vanguard, the cohort of writers and artists who had collaborated on *Fire!!* and whose intentions Hughes had declared in "The Negro Artist and the Racial Mountain." Larsen was intrigued and inspired by the reaction Hughes had set off with *Fine Clothes to the Jew*, in particular his decision to dedicate the book to Van Vechten, and she wanted to make a similar kind of stink. After *Nigger Heaven*, the surest way for her to get the kind of attention she wanted was to make public her private friendship with Carl Van Vechten who, at the time of her letter, had been her close friend for two years.

Van Vechten had been coaxing Larsen to try her hand at fiction since they met in late March 1925. At the time, Nella was working as a librarian at the Harlem Branch of the New York Public

Library. Nella and Carl became close quickly, and he encouraged her to write about the black cultural and social world with which he had recently fallen in love. He sent her books and praised her talent when she experienced one of her frequent bouts of insecurity. He spoke flatteringly of Nella in a letter to Gertrude Stein, calling her "one of the most intelligent people I know." Larsen admired Stein greatly, and was inspired by "Melanctha." Van Vechten urged Larsen to write to Stein and tell her so. Stein treasured the letter, telling Van Vechten that Larsen's letter had "pleased me the most of any of the letters I have ever seen about Melanctha."[2]

Close though they were, Larsen didn't tell Van Vechten that she was already in the middle of a draft of her first novel. When he found out and asked her about it, she responded with her characteristic self-deprecation: "When I first started, I honestly thought it was really good, now, something more than half-way, I'm afraid it's frightfully bad. Too, I'm getting rather bored with it. I wonder how many half-finished novels there are knocking about in the world."[3]

When she completed her manuscript, Larsen brought it directly to Van Vechten, who read it in one sitting and called it "remarkable" in his daybook. He offered to take the book to Knopf, just as he had done with Langston Hughes's first book. But first he wanted her to make some changes. It was too short, he said, and he didn't like the title. Larsen revised the book according to Van Vechten's suggestions, and she changed its title from *Cloudy Amber* to *Quicksand*. The novel was published by Knopf in March 1928.

Nella Larsen and Carl Van Vechten had met at the home of Dorothy Peterson, a mutual friend. Van Vechten was accompanied by Eric Walrond and Donald Angus, Van Vechten's onetime lover and constant companion in Harlem. Larsen was acquainted with Van Vechten's reputation. He had been a celebrity in New York long before he began writing about black music and culture, but his recent publications in *Vanity Fair* had given him a particular status in black social circles. He and Larsen were drawn to each other immediately. He was hard to miss. He was then forty-five, but Van Vechten's taste in fashion had not changed since he was a young man who was most comfortable in pointed patent-leather boots. Van Vechten's friend Lawrence Langner, codirector of the Theatre Guild, compared the adult Van Vechten's style to "the dowager Chinese empress gone berserk" when Van Vechten showed up at a party draped in red and gold Oriental robes.[4] Van Vechten and Larsen both enjoyed testing social conventions. Not only did their social worlds overlap, they shared the same taste for ribaldry and the same impatience with priggishness. Larsen was in her thirties when she met Van Vechten, established in her librarian career, and she felt a little out of place among the legion of New Negro writers, whose credos consistently emphasized youth. Her friendship with Van Vechten boosted her self-confidence, and he quickly gained her trust, which she did not give easily.

Within a few months of their meeting, Larsen and Van Vechten were seeing each other, with or without their spouses, several times a month, and by 1927, they often met several times a week. It was an intense connection, romantic but not sexual,

Langston
fun
Carl
august 31 - 1927
[signature]

Carl Van Vechten, 1927 (Photograph by James Allen. Yale Collection of American Literature, Beinecke Rare Book and Manuscript Library. Courtesy of the Carl Van Vechten Trust.)

similar to the bonds between Van Vechten and his other close female friends, like Nora Holt and Ethel Waters (the latter addressed him in letters as her "Nordic Lover" and "My Primitive Passion").[5] Carl sent Nella flowers every year to commemorate the day of their first meeting, and hosted birthday parties for her, as he did for other friends. Nella appreciated his frank expressions of affection and admiration, which extended to the page: while Dorothy Peterson served as the physical inspiration for Mary Love, the heroine of *Nigger Heaven*, Larsen biographer George Hutchinson has pointed out that it was Larsen's eclectic and erudite personal library that Van Vechten replicated on Mary's bookshelves. Larsen equally admired Van Vechten; in a biographical statement she wrote for Knopf to use for publicity, she listed bridge and "collecting Van Vechteniana" as her only two hobbies.[6] Larsen admired Van Vechten's daring and also the excitement still surrounding *Nigger Heaven*. (In 1927 Van Vechten traveled to Los Angeles to meet with Cecil B. DeMille to discuss the possibility of making a film out of the novel, but the project never materialized.)

Quicksand is a novel about Helga Crane, a beautiful, light-skinned young woman with a black American father and a white Danish mother, just like Nella Larsen. Helga is consumed by internal conflicts over race and sex that send her all over the country and abroad in search of emotional and psychological peace and a sense of belonging. Her existential quest is framed by the language of race, and she is misinterpreted and rejected by both blacks and whites who, in turn, find her difficult to read as she consistently acts out of violent, contradictory emotions that even she doesn't understand.

Helga wants to be admired as an object of desire and she wants to be seen as a human being, but she finds it impossible to have both at the same time. When she travels to Denmark, the birthplace of her mother, she is treated as an exotic creature, more fantastic than human. Helga has ambivalent feelings toward the community of elite blacks in New York. They ignite in her an emotional cocktail of longing, disgust, and shame. But the author of *Quicksand* was not ambivalent in her attitude toward the black bourgeoisie. Larsen portrays the "best" black people of New York—race women and men like Jessie Fauset and W. E. B. Du Bois—as hypocritical and small-minded, concerned only with living safe and segregated lives.

Interracial socializing may have been de rigueur for New Negro artists and writers, but there were other black New Yorkers who found it abhorrent, particularly when it involved black women. "It is a most disgusting thing to see," declaimed Terrence Williams in his 1927 *Pittsburgh Courier* article "Writer Scores Best Girls Who Entertain 'Nordics.'" Williams found disgusting the sight of black women of "poise and finesse" spending time with "Nordics"—"'queer' folks from Greenwich Village," specifically—instead of black men. "While our men are showing what fine mettle they are made of, in every possible endeavor," Williams wrote, "these indiscreet females of the species are out there in the cabarets, these big fashion balls, escorted by the Nordics." The only Nordic Williams named in the article was

Carl Van Vechten, who had deceived the "dear, lovely creatures" who had opened their homes to him, said Williams, and then been rewarded with the slap of *Nigger Heaven*—a slap he felt they roundly deserved.[7]

Unfortunately for her, Larsen's efforts to ruffle black critics and establish herself among the rank of black literary iconoclasts escaped the notice of the people she wanted to irritate. W. E. B. Du Bois, for instance, described *Quicksand* as a beacon of decency and taste in the current sea of amorality in Negro literature. In his review for the *Crisis*, he set *Quicksand* in opposition to *Home to Harlem*, the ignoble story that Claude McKay had forced upon the world. Du Bois wrote that Larsen had created "an interesting character" in Helga, and composed "a close yet delicately woven plot."[8] He saw in the novel echoes of the work of Jessie Fauset, which must have annoyed Larsen, since the tidy, sentimental fiction for which Fauset was known represented precisely what Larsen was writing against. But in his review, Du Bois kept the focus mainly on *Home to Harlem*. Ultimately, he praised *Quicksand* not as much for what it was as for what it wasn't—and it wasn't *Home to Harlem* or, by implication, *Nigger Heaven*.

Larsen upped the ante with *Passing*, her second novel, which she initially wanted to call *Nig*, but the Knopfs, bewildered by the outrage over the title of Van Vechten's novel, were not interested in courting more controversy. Nella changed the title without a fuss, but she did dedicate *Passing* to Carl (and to Fania, with whom she had also become close), just as she had threatened to do in her March 1927 letter to Van Vechten. But the dedication failed to set off an explosion like the one Hughes had triggered with *Fine Clothes to the Jew*. In fact, no one really seemed to notice. Hughes wrote *Fine Clothes* when he was only twenty-five, still very much the literary wunderkind who had published his most famous poem at the age of eighteen. Nella would never be a literary darling like Hughes, although *Quicksand* would earn her a bronze medal from the Harmon Foundation, and both *Quicksand* and *Passing* received favorable reviews and garnered the respect of her New Negro peers.

On the other hand, Taylor Gordon, a singer, vaudeville performer, and yet another black artist whom Van Vechten admired and encouraged, would experience the kind of wrath that Du Bois was famous for—and that Larsen had hoped for—when he made public his close relationship with Van Vechten by including a foreword written by Van Vechten in his memoir *Born to Be*. "Taylor Gordon's autobiography is another product of the Van Vechten school of Negro literature," began Du Bois's review in the *Crisis*. He resented the involvement of Muriel Draper, a society hostess, interior designer, and writer, and Miguel Covarrubias as well. "I am frank to say, however, that I think I could exist quite happily if Covarrubias had never been born," wrote Du Bois. The book revealed Gordon as a representative of all the New Negro was trying to leave behind, Du Bois believed. "I may be wrong, but in this book I get the impression that Taylor is 'cutting up' for the white folk. I can see Carl and Muriel splitting their sides with laughter while he jigs and 'yah-yahs!'"[9] Nella found Du Bois's reaction to *Born to Be* both entertaining and dispiriting. "The dunning of Taylor Gordon's book is very amusing what with you, Muriel and Miguel all included. I should

Carl Van Vechten, Fania Marinoff, and Taylor Gordon, cover illustration by Miguel Covarrubias for Gordon's *Born to Be*, 1929

hazard that it will be a howling success, though I am beginning to feel that the reading public is getting rather bored with Negro books."[10]

Nella finished *Passing* in August 1928. She alerted Carl immediately: "I have this day completed your novel 'Nig.' That is, it has only to be copied. Thank God, Glory Halleluja Amen!"[11] *Passing* does indeed bear the unmistakable imprint of Carl Van Vechten. George Hutchinson has noted the similarities between the descriptors Larsen used for one of her main characters, Clare Kendry, and the language Van Vechten used to describe cats, a species that fascinated him and to which he had devoted an entire book, *The Tiger in the House* (1920), which is still considered one of the most masterful books about cats ever written. Clare is "catlike," agrees literary scholar Kathy Pfeiffer, who also sees significance in the similarity between the names Clare and Carl.[12] Clare Kendry and Carl Van Vechten are alike, too, in that they both live among white people but delight in the company of black people. Clare, whose skin is light enough for her to pass for white, describes her urgent desire "to see Negroes, to be with them again, to talk with them, to hear them laugh."[13] Clare's naked, urgent longing for blackness turns another character, Irene Redfield, an already cold woman, even colder.

Both *Quicksand* and *Passing* are novels about desire and repulsion—black for white and vice versa and, in the case of *Passing*, one woman for another woman. Irene is fixated on Clare. She speaks of her with disdain, but when she is in Clare's presence, Irene is confounded by her beauty, her "tempting mouth," "arresting eyes," and the luster of her skin. At one point she is seized by emotions out of her control and grasps Clare's hands, blurting, "Dear God! But aren't you lovely, Clare!!" (194) All the scenes between the two women vibrate with a sexual tension that Irene cannot acknowledge, so she entertains a fantasy that Clare is having an affair with her husband, Brian. Most scholars today agree that her suspicion of her spouse's infidelity is only a ruse that Irene concocts to protect herself from her own homosexual longings.

Van Vechten adored *Passing*. He read it the same night that he received his copy, interrupted only by a dinner obligation. He liked it so much he could barely sleep, as he recorded in his daybook. The next morning, Carl brought the book with him to the Knopf offices. "I stir Blanche & Alfred up about Nella Larsen's *Passing*, making quite a scene."[14] He stopped at a florist to have flowers sent to Nella. Several days later, the marketing department at Knopf called him into a meeting with Larsen, and together they developed a strategy for selling the book that would showcase Van Vechten's enthusiasm.[15]

Just as Larsen finished *Passing*, her marriage fell apart. She was a private person, and Van Vechten was one of very few people in whom she confided about her personal life. Her husband, Elmer Imes, did, too, and Van Vechten recorded visits from both distraught parties in his daybooks. The couple was in some financial trouble, and Elmer, a physicist and research engineer, soon moved to Nashville to take a position at Fisk University, where Larsen had attended school for one year before being dismissed, probably for her refusal to adhere to the conservative dress code. Soon, Elmer would break his wife's heart by falling in love with another woman, the director of publicity and finance at Fisk, who was white and a very beloved member of the university community. Nella still loved her husband and held on to the hope that they might reconcile, even as the strain of his affair affected her health. When the couple decided to separate, Elmer wrote to Van Vechten immediately, asking that he counsel his soon-to-be ex-wife.

In the midst of her personal misfortune, and at the same time as she began to be recognized as a literary force among New Negro writers, Larsen was confronted with charges of plagiarism. A short story she had published in the *Forum*, "Sanctuary," bore unmistakable similarities to "Mrs. Adis," a story published eight years earlier by British writer Sheila Kaye-Smith. Larsen published a defense of her work as an original piece of fiction, but the shame of the accusations devastated her. Fortunately, Van Vechten took her side. He was, in fact, one of her only friends to defend her character while gossip about her spread throughout the black literary world.

About six years after the plagiarism scandal, and three years after the salacious details of her divorce from Imes made the front page of the *Baltimore Afro-American*, Larsen disappeared from the social world to which she had once longed for entry. No one was more devastated than Carl Van Vechten, who received his last letter from Nella in 1937, on his fifty-seventh birthday. For the rest of his life, Carl tried to reach Nella, to discover some news about her through mutual friends (whom she had also cut off), but he never heard from her again. Larsen died in 1964, the same year as Van Vechten. She was seventy-two and had spent her post–Harlem Renaissance years working as a nurse in New York.

SUCH EXTRAORDINARY PEOPLE

Wallace Thurman didn't like *Passing* any more than he liked *Quicksand.* In a letter to Hughes, he described the novel as evidence of its author's inability "to invest her characters with any life like possibilities."[16] Still, he invited Larsen to join the masthead of *Harlem,* the successor to *Fire!!* She declined, she told Van Vechten, because Wallie, as his friends called him, could not afford to pay his contributors.

Thurman had scathing opinions of much of the work of prominent New Negro writers, which he revealed to Hughes. Eric Walrond should finish the novel he was working on "or destroy it."[17] Walrond, who had been among the first to congratulate Van Vechten on the publication of *Nigger Heaven,* would never finish *The Big Ditch,* the book to which Thurman referred. But his 1926 short story collection, *Tropic Death,* is regarded as one of the most successful works of the Harlem Renaissance.

Claude McKay's second novel, *Banjo,* Thurman said, was "turgid and tiresome." Jessie Fauset, who had recently published her second novel, *Plum Bun,* should be returned to Philadelphia, the city where she had grown up, "and cremated." Rudolph Fisher, who had published *Walls of Jericho,* his first novel, in 1928, "should stick to short stories." As for Zora Neale Hurston, who gave *Fire!!* its name—she ought to "learn craftsmanship and surprise the world and outstrip her contemporaries as well." His prescription for the young *Fire!!* contributor Bruce Nugent was first a spanking, then a trip to a monastery where he should be "made to concentrate on writing." Thurman had a prescription for Hughes, too: "You should write a book." And for himself: "I should commit suicide."[18]

Hughes did, of course, write more books. The next one would be his first and only novel, *Not without Laughter*, published in 1930, and written with much encouragement and critical advice from Carl Van Vechten. Wallace Thurman did not commit suicide, although he did try. He fought depression his entire life. "He almost always felt bad," Hughes remembered of him in his 1940 autobiography, *The Big Sea*. According to Hughes, Wallie was "a strange kind of fellow, who liked to drink gin, but *didn't* like to drink gin; who liked being a Negro, but felt it a great handicap; who adored bohemianism, but thought it wrong to be a bohemian. He liked to waste a lot of time, but he always felt guilty wasting time." When he drank too much at parties, Hughes wrote, Thurman would threaten to throw himself out of a window.[19] Thurman's depression may have been a consequence of health problems that had plagued him from childhood. His close friend Dorothy West, who had won second place in the 1926 Opportunity awards contest for her short story "The Typewriter" at the age of nineteen, remembered him as slight and frail, but possessing "the most agreeable smile in Harlem and a rich infectious laugh."[20] Thurman married Louise Thompson Patterson in 1928. The marriage lasted for a few months until Patterson could no longer abide Thurman's sexual ambivalence. He wouldn't "admit that he was a homosexual," Patterson told Arnold Rampersad years later. She said he never took anything seriously.[21]

Thurman found the controversy over *Nigger Heaven* extremely amusing. The novel inspired him, as it had Nella Larsen, and it played a role in much of his own writing during the 1920s. More than any other black Harlem Renaissance writer, Thurman saw an opportunity in *Nigger Heaven,* and used the novel and its author as anchors to establish his own position in the debate over race, writing, and freedom. Van Vechten and his novel played crucial roles in *The Blacker the Berry,* Thurman's 1929 novel about intraracial prejudice, whose main character is a young woman called Emma Lou Morgan.

"Why *had* her mother married a black man? Surely there had been some eligible brown-skinned men around."[22] Since childhood, Emma Lou has been derided by playmates, and her mother, Jane, has tried various painful remedies purporting to blunt the blackness of her daughter's skin. "Try some lye, Jane, it may eat it out. She can't look any worse" (32). Color is the issue, not race: "Not that she minded being black, being a Negro necessitated having a colored skin, but she did mind being too black" (21). Wallace Thurman himself was intimately familiar with the issue of intraracial color prejudice, having experienced it his entire life. Bruce Nugent admitted to feelings of disgust when he first met Thurman, as he recounted in his autobiographical novel, *Gentleman Jigger,* in which he appears as Stuartt Brennan and Wallace Thurman as Raymond Pellman. Meeting Pellman was "a distinctly unpleasant shock" for Brennan; Pellman was "too black." He had admired Pellman/Thurman from the accounts he had heard from mutual friends, but he could not help his instincts. "Stuartt had been taught by precept not to trust black people—that they were evil."[23] Eventually, the two men became close friends.

In *The Blacker the Berry*, Emma Lou is also a victim of the color prejudice practiced by everyone around her, including her family. Even her one source of comfort, her Uncle Joe, displays a picture on his bedroom wall of a "pickanniny" splayed out "like a fly in a pan of milk amid a white expanse of bedclothes" (22). But Emma Lou is as much a perpetrator of intraracial prejudice as she is a victim, and the plot of the novel turns on the question of whether she will be able to overcome her own self-hatred as well as her pedestrian views on interracial relations. On a night out with a group of Harlem Renaissance writers, Emma Lou is unhinged by the sense of interracial fraternity among them. "Such extraordinary people—saying 'nigger' in front of a white man! Didn't they have any race pride or proper bringing up? Didn't they have any common sense?" (143)

Her transformation is occasioned by her friendship with Campbell Kitchen, a character modeled on Carl Van Vechten. She meets Kitchen through a former employer who has arranged for Emma to work for Kitchen's wife, Clere Sloane, while she is in Europe. Sloane, like Fania Marinoff, is "a former stage beauty who had married a famous American writer and retired from public life" (185). Kitchen and Van Vechten have similar profiles. "Campbell Kitchen, along with Carl Van Vechten, was one of the leading spirits in this 'Explore Harlem: Know the Negro' crusade," the narrator explains. But Kitchen is "sincere," and he uses his cultural capital to champion spirituals in the mainstream press, to publicize unknown blues singers, and to promote young black writers, even personally shepherding their work to publishers and editors (186). Like Carl Van Vechten, Kitchen has written a book about Harlem that, in Thurman's assessment, "had been a literary failure because the author presumed that its subject matter demanded serious treatment" (187).

When Emma Lou meets Kitchen, she expects "a sneering, obscene cynic, intent upon ravaging every Negro woman and insulting every Negro man." Instead, she finds him to be harmless and entirely likable. Emma Lou becomes not only a fan but also something of Kitchen's disciple, and he inspires her to take stock of herself: "Was she supersensitive about her color?" (187) Kitchen invites Emma Lou to use his library and supplies her with tickets to musical concerts and the theater. After some time, and much more personal drama, Emma begins to share Kitchen's belief that "every one must find salvation within one's self." With more life experience, and through her friendship with Kitchen, Emma Lou is ready to release the demons that have long plagued her. Kitchen helps her to see that she has been the main source of her own unhappiness, although she has been heretofore "too obtuse to accept it" (216).

Campbell Kitchen accomplishes a lot in *The Blacker the Berry*, and yet he never says a word of dialogue. He is less a character than a collection of aphorisms, a white canvas onto which Emma Lou fashions a new, complete sense of self—a black self. As for Kitchen's real-life counterpart, Van Vechten found *The Blacker the Berry* "a good book but lacking in tenderness."[24]

In *The Blacker the Berry*, black characters are each other's worst enemies, and intraracial cruelty poses by far a greater threat to black personal integrity than white racism. But for all its dark wit and bold condemnations, the novel ends on a note of hope. By the time Thurman published his last novel, *Infants of the Spring,* in 1932, all that hope had evaporated.

Infants of the Spring is a portrait of its author's own disillusionment with the Negro Renaissance. The sort of Harlem party Thurman had described in *The Blacker the Berry,* in which black people moved in unison with delirious abandon, had deteriorated in *Infants* into an interracial setting of counterfeit harmony. Raymond, the main character, based on Thurman himself, is repulsed as he wanders through a party at Niggerati Manor, where he lives along with the rest of his friends, a group of bohemian artists. All around him, whites and blacks are locked in a desperate embrace. Such scenes used to delight him, but now "the drunken revelry began to sicken him. The insanity of the party, the insanity of its implications, threatened his own sanity." The New Negro movement had failed because it was built on a façade, Thurman believed, and he used his novel to drive his point home. In the end, Paul, a would-be writer, commits suicide by slitting his wrist in a bathtub at the manor. Unable to publish a novel in life, Paul thinks that his suicide will lead to posthumous literary success. Unfortunately, his novel, written in pencil, is obliterated by the water that overflows from the "crimson streaked tub."[25] Langston Hughes called *Infants of the Spring* "a bitter, but superb, portrayal of the bohemian fringe of Harlem's literary and artistic life."[26]

Wallace Thurman died of tuberculosis in 1934 at the age of thirty-two, two years after *Infants* was published. By that time, he had survived two suicide attempts. Thurman deliberately accelerated his own death, according to Dorothy West. He was living in California at the time, having become a successful screenwriter in Hollywood, when his health began to fail. He knew he was going to die, so he returned to New York, "determined that his end should be spectacular," West wrote. Ignoring his doctor's advice, Wallie got drunk and "stayed drunk," she remembered.[27]

Two years earlier, the same year he published *Infants*, Thurman had coauthored a novel with white author Abraham Furman that they called *Interne*. It was an exposé of the horrid conditions at the City Hospital on Welfare Island (now called Roosevelt Island) in New York. Inspiration for the book came from a visit he made to the hospital that pierced through his sardonic exterior and left him "shocked and horrified."[28] In a terrible ironic twist, Thurman died in the same hospital. It was a prolonged and painful death. For six months he lay wasted, terrified, and alone, abandoned by most of his friends. He wrote to William Jourdan Rapp: "All of my Harlem friends have evidently already consigned me to the grave so conspicuous are they by their absence (which, however, is no surprise me.)"[29] He died bravely, turning his stay at the hospital into a nonfiction essay that was never published.

Dorothy West thought that *Interne*, like the rest of Thurman's fiction, was beneath him. Both *The Blacker the Berry* and *Infants of the Spring*, she wrote, demonstrated his artistic immaturity. At best they were simply incomplete. West diagnosed Thurman and his entire generation of Negro writers as having fallen victim to "overpraise and specious evaluation" that distracted them from producing truly meaningful work.[30]

Short-story writer, novelist, and physician Rudolph Fisher died of intestinal cancer within four days of Thurman, and the spirit of the movement dwindled even further. In "Uncle Tom's

Mansion," Van Vechten had described Fisher's story "The City of Refuge," which appeared in the *Atlantic Monthly* in February 1925, as "the finest short story yet written by a man of Negro blood, except Pushkin."[31] The two men had been constant companions in Harlem during its heyday.

In 1928, Fisher published a novel, *The Walls of Jericho*, with Knopf at Van Vechten's urging. Like *Infants of the Spring*, *The Walls of Jericho* is a satire, and its scenes of the fabulous days of Harlem are sneering denunciations of intraracial snobbery and white "do-gooders." An exception to the panoply of foolish white characters is one Conrad White, modeled on Carl Van Vechten, who is at home among black people and similarly weary of black conservatism and white earnestness. The relationship that he and his wife enjoy with black friends is simultaneously grounded in and transcends the boundaries of racial difference. In this book, and in every other black-authored Harlem Renaissance novel that includes a character inspired by Carl Van Vechten, most other characters, both black and white, fail to appreciate the authentic communion of Van Vechten and his black intimates—except those modeled on black artists of the Harlem Renaissance.

For black Harlem Renaissance writers who set out to remember the era in fiction, it seemed impossible to capture the New Negro movement without a depiction of the unique and complicated place Van Vechten held within it as an opportunist, an exception, a co-conspirator, and a friend.

"Occasionally, some one is heard to croak hoarsely that the Negro 'Renaissance' that was launched so bravely in 1926–1927 has not continued its voyage on the seas of art as triumphantly as might have been wished. Personally I feel no sympathy with these complaints, no disappointment in the results," Carl Van Vechen wrote in a commentary for *Challenge,* a literary journal founded by Dorothy West in 1934.[32] Langston Hughes disagreed. "I was there. I had a swell time while it lasted," he wrote in *The Big Sea.* But, he acknowledged, the Harlem Renaissance was ultimately only a fantasy of the black elite. "The ordinary Negroes hadn't heard of the Negro Renaissance. And if they had, it hadn't raised their wages any."[33]

Many black writers had turned their attention away from the debates of the period, like Hughes, but Van Vechten always refused to subscribe to this bleak vision of the Harlem Renaissance years. In fact, he believed that the Negro Renaissance had accomplished exactly the goals James Weldon Johnson had outlined in his 1922 introduction to *The Book of American Negro Poetry.* Then, at the dawn of the New Negro era, Johnson had explained that art was the most effective means for Negroes to demonstrate that they were worthy of recognition as artists and citizens. His book amounted to the first concerted attempt to achieve this ambition. Carl Van Vechten believed that Johnson himself embodied the dignity of the Negro Renaissance, and in his 1934 commentary for *Challenge,* he cited *Along This Way,* Johnson's autobiography, as an example of how far the Negro Renaissance had come.

Four years later, James Weldon Johnson died, too.

A NUDE BLACK BARD IN CENTRAL PARK

Johnson was on a drive near his summer home in Wiscasset, Maine, when a train struck his car on June 26, 1938. He was sixty-seven years old, nine years older than Van Vechten. The two men shared the same birthday, June 17, and celebrated together every year, along with Alfred A. Knopf Jr., known as Pat. More than two thousand people attended the funeral of the man Van Vechten called one of the greatest men he had ever known. Van Vechten was executor of Johnson's estate (Van Vechten had likewise named Johnson executor of his).

A week after Johnson's death, Van Vechten wrote a letter to his widow. "What can I write? You know how I feel." There was too much to say, and nothing at all, so he reflected on the church, the flowers, and the music, which were all beautiful and befitting. "With the pall bearers I sat between Arthur Spingarn & Rabbi Wise. Theodore Roosevelt & W. C. Handy were adjacent. Could any one else bring out such a strange combination of people in united love?"[34]

Van Vechten described how Johnson's death had affected him in a letter to the *New York Amsterdam News*. "I feel a selfish grief over the death of James Weldon Johnson, because one of my dearest friends has passed away, but more than that, it is easy to realize that the world has lost one of its great men. Putting aside his work as an artist, which is very important, I believe it can be said that no one ever has done more for inter-racial understanding (and when I say inter-racial, I am referring to ALL races) than James Weldon Johnson. He had a genius for tactful decisions and on many occasions his mere presence has been sufficient to make new friends for his race. He was widely known

Birthday celebration at the Knopf home in Purchase, New York, June 17, 1931: *standing from left to right:* Ettie Stettheimer, Carl Van Vechten, James Weldon Johnson with his arms around Fania Marinoff, Witter Bynner, Grace Nail Johnson; *crouching:* Blanche Knopf and Alfred A. Knopf Jr. (Photograph by Alfred A. Knopf. Courtesy of Alice L. Knopf. Yale Collection of American Literature, Beinecke Rare Book and Manuscript Library.)

from coast to coast in America and he will be missed and remembered as long as anyone in American history is missed and remembered."[35]

During a talk he gave in memoriam of Johnson at Fisk University in Nashville, where Johnson had served as the Spence Chair of Creative Literature since 1930, Van Vechten compared Johnson to his own father: "It has always been my belief that my father was a thoroughly good man: kind, gentle, helpful, generous, tolerant of unorthodox behavior in others, patriarchal in offering good advice, understanding in not expecting it to be followed, moderate in his way of living, and courageous in accepting the difficulties of life itself." In important ways, however, the two men were different. "Jim possessed at least two other desirable qualities which were lacking in my father: tact and discretion." Van Vechten meant to immortalize his great friend, he told the audience at Fisk: "It is because he was like that that Jim can never die."[36]

Within a year of Johnson's death, Van Vechten formed the James Weldon Johnson Memorial Committee to begin the project of establishing a proper memorial to Johnson's life. The committee consisted of Johnson's pallbearers as well as other prominent men and women in politics and the arts, including Marian Anderson, Eleanor Roosevelt, W. E. B. Du Bois, Duke Ellington, and Langston Hughes. Theodore Roosevelt was chairman; the Honorable Fiorello La Guardia, mayor of New York, was the honorary chairman; Walter White served as secretary. The committee debated various options, including the creation of an educational scholarship, until it was agreed that the memorial should benefit the larger New York community, not just a single person at a time.

Eventually, the committee decided to explore an idea proposed by sculptor Augusta Savage, who had suggested that a statue commemorating Johnson be erected at Seventh Avenue and 110th Street, just at the entrance to Central Park—the intersection of black and white New York. The location was exactly twenty-five blocks south of where Wallace Thurman had once predicted that a race uplift organization would someday erect a statue in honor of Carl Van Vechten as a modern-day abolitionist, once the furor over *Nigger Heaven* died down.

New York was the only place for such a monument, Van Vechten reasoned, because the city boasted the largest Negro community in the world, he declared, but it had no Negro memorial of any kind, unlike Boston, Philadelphia, and Washington, which had their own vibrant black communities. But the most important reason that New York must be the site of the memorial had to do with Johnson's own passion for the city, which he always claimed was his true home, though he was born in Jacksonville, Florida. He proclaimed his love for the unique sensory and material features of New York in a poem he sent to Van Vechten in the heyday of the Negro Renaissance entitled "My City," whose final stanza reads:

> But, ah! Manhattan's sights and sounds, her smells,
> Her crowds, her throbbing force, the thrill that comes
> From being of her a part, her subtle spells,
> Her shining towers, her avenues, her slums—
> O God! the stark, unutterable pity,
> To be dead, and never again behold my city![37]

Johnson's widow, Grace Nail Johnson, was enthusiastic about the idea of a monument and suggested "My City" for the inscription. But the committee was keen on another Johnson poem, "O Black and Unknown Bards," in which Johnson pays homage to his creative ancestors, those "black slave singers, gone, forgot, unfamed."[38] Ultimately, the committee prevailed.

The committee did honor another request made by Johnson's widow, which was to give the commission for the statue to Richmond Barthé instead of Savage, even though Savage had already completed a model. Mrs. Johnson's reasoning was sentimental, Van Vechten explained to readers of *Opportunity* magazine. The untimely death of her husband had prevented him from fulfilling a promise he had once made to sit for Barthé. Van Vechten supported her selection on pragmatic grounds. Barthé, who had studied at the Art Institute of Chicago and had shown his work all over the country, was "the best-known sculptor of his race," Van Vechten said, so the choice, like the choice of New York, was obvious.[39] It was also true that Van Vechten didn't like Savage personally, and he had no desire to host a competition for the sculpture. He didn't want to chance the possibility that the commission would go to "an obscure white girl in Oshkosh."[40] The choice of Barthé elicited jealousy among his contemporaries, who begrudged the young sculptor's apparently easy successes and grumbled about the bountiful support he received from white admirers.[41]

The proposed monument would be cast in bronze, and its marble base would bear an image of Johnson's head in bas-relief on one side, and on the other side a stanza from "O Black and Unknown Bards." The monument would be less a memorial to Johnson and more homage to the unknown bards, whom Johnson's poetry always remembered, with "their arms and faces uplifted to heaven, an inspiration to their race, a challenge to the defamers of that race."[42] Initially, the composition featured an upright soloist surrounded by several small figures. Barthé's final design featured a single male figure balanced on a rock. His ankles are shackled but the bard emanates triumph and purpose. His entire being is "stretched out upward, seeking the divine," just like the bards in Johnson's poem. His stance is sure and powerful; his body is muscular and defined—and naked.

As soon as Barthé finished a model of the statue in March 1941, Walter White, in his capacity as secretary of the James Weldon Johnson Memorial Committee, entreated committee members, as well as other prominent New Yorkers, to visit Barthé's Union Square studio and appraise the statue. But America was on the eve of war, and White found it difficult to convince the group to make the task a priority. One by one, however, the responses came in. Elmer Carter, who served on the Unemployment Insurance Appeal Board by appointment of the governor of New York, and who had succeeded Charles Johnson as the editor of *Opportunity* magazine, called it "magnificent." Then Barthé telephoned Walter White with even more exciting news: Theodore Roosevelt was delighted with the model; he declared it "the best thing Barthé had ever done," White reported to Van Vechten.[43]

The opinions of Gene Buck, the president of the American Society of Composers, Authors, and Publishers (ASCAP), and Mayor La Guardia were more difficult to pin down. La Guardia told White that he was busy and would defer to whatever decision was reached by the rest of the committee, but White insisted that La Guardia must view the statue for himself. Only La Guardia had the power to accelerate the process of gaining the approval

The Singing Slave (aka *The Birth of the Spirituals*) by Richmond Barthé, c. 1940 (Photograph © Morgan and Marvin Smith.)

of the City Art Commission, and only La Guardia had the authority to secure the location the committee had chosen, the strip of land bisecting Seventh Avenue and 110th street. "As soon as this is done we will proceed to raise the funds and proceed with the actual making of the statue," White explained in a letter to La Guardia on June 17, 1941, what would have been Johnson's seventieth birthday.[44]

All plans came to a halt when both White and La Guardia were waylaid by the furor surrounding President Roosevelt's Executive Order 8802, also known as the Fair Employment Act, which was designed to prohibit racial discrimination in the national defense industry. In a letter to Van Vechten, White described how he and La Guardia were working alongside A. Philip Randolph, civil rights activist and founder of the influential labor union Brotherhood of Sleeping Car Porters, to compel Roosevelt to stand behind the order in the face of fierce opposition from the U. S. Office of Personnel Management, the army, and the navy. Certain officials in Washington were trying to force the president to stack the Committee on Fair Employment Practices, which Roosevelt had designed to implement the executive order, with "non entities," White reported, in order to derail, or at least stall, the process. "La Guardia, A Philip Randolph and I have had to fight tooth and toe-nail, night and day, to block this."[45]

President Roosevelt signed the order only after White, Randolph, and other activists threatened to organize a protest march on Washington. Eleanor Roosevelt wrote a letter to Randolph asking him to reconsider his ultimatum. For his part, La Guardia, whom the president had appointed to direct the Office of

Civilian Defense, issued an ultimatum of his own: either the president sign the executive order, or he would have to find a new head of the Office of Civilian Defense. Roosevelt signed the order one week before the protest was scheduled to take place. In return, La Guardia did not resign his post and Randolph called off the demonstration, but he was inspired by the episode to form the March on Washington movement, which motivated Dr. Martin Luther King to stage his historic March on Washington in 1963.

In the meantime, the mayor promised to send a representative—another sculptor—to Barthé's studio to evaluate the statue. Everything hinged on La Guardia's decision, and Barthé postponed his plans to leave New York while he waited and worried. He couldn't afford to leave, anyway, having received no payment for his work. No efforts to raise funds could begin in earnest until La Guardia approved the statue. The sculptor chosen by La Guardia eventually approved the statue in August. It was finally time for White to fill out the appropriate forms from officials at the Art Commission. The forms would have to be signed by the commissioner of parks, the powerful and controlling Robert Moses, who would come to be known as the man who shaped New York.

In September White wrote a letter to Moses in which he explained why the commissioner should support the committee's plans for the memorial. First, the statue was unique. It would be the first statue of a Negro in New York City, although not in New York State (a statue of Frederick Douglass is located in Rochester). White was confident that Moses would see the value in the project. He predicted that the historic significance of the monument would appeal to Moses, a man known for his considerable ego. White's letter evidenced his characteristic talent for persuasion. He urged Moses to come to Barthé's studio to view the statue as soon as possible.[46]

Moses did not respond as White had hoped. "The approval of the Park Dept. is not perfunctory," he informed White. He resented the fact that the letter from White was the first he had heard of the plans for a James Weldon Johnson statue. He would not cut corners just to meet White's deadline, he said, and he did not like to be pressured.[47]

White kept Van Vechten apprised of his communications with Moses, sending Carl a copy of Moses's letter the next day. "Don't be too alarmed by the tempestuousness of Bob Moses' letter," he warned. He explained that Moses was "a very irascible person though otherwise able and fine."[48] White had already tried to placate the commissioner. His letter began with profuse apologies if he had sounded too demanding in his previous correspondence. His eagerness had nothing to do with his own convenience, he assured Moses. He was simply trying to accommodate Barthé, who had had to delay plans to leave New York for several months. There had been so many delays with the project, White said, that he was only trying to stay on top of the process so that it would advance in a timely manner.[49]

In letter after letter, White tried to convince Moses to support the plans for the statue as it was. Once he sent him the article Van Vechten had written about the memorial for *Opportunity*. White confided his frustration about Moses's resistance to Van

Vechten, and Carl offered tactical advice. Moses should be reminded that nudes were "noble, classical, and modern," he suggested to Walter, naming examples. Furthermore he said, if the bard were in pants, the statue would be "'picturesque darky folklore, unobjectionable and unnoticed."[50] He included examples of cities with public nude sculptures, including New York.

"Thank you for your excellent listing of the country's most sexy nudes," White responded. "Published as a pamphlet this ought to have an enormous sale as a guide book for old maids!"[51] Soon there were other objections to the statue, however, this time concerning the chains that shackled the feet of Barthé's bard.

The chains "might be offensive to Negroes as a reminder of the dark days of slavery," worried Edward Blum of the prominent department store Abraham and Straus. On the contrary, White replied. "Were the figure one of a Negro with head bowed in a spirit of defeat and despair I would most certainly object to the chains," he assured Blum. "But in the exultant, buoyant treatment by Mr. Barthé the figure rises *from* the chains as a demonstration of the Negro's rising above the manacles not only of physical slavery but of discrimination as well." But Blum shouldn't take only his word for it, he said, offering that Elmer Carter, another Negro on the committee who had "wide acquaintance with Negroes of all types throughout the country," agreed with him.[52]

Frank C. Crosswaith, chairman of the Negro Labor Committee, was comfortable with the chains but not the nudity. He spoke for the entire Negro Labor Committee in a letter to White: "In the matter of his sex organ: While we are most appreciative of the modernistic and realistic sides, I think it would not fit so well in a community like Harlem because the average person would not react to it as we would and too, in that neighborhood are a large number of children and it is likely to have a harmful social effect upon their thinking and acting."[53] If Johnson had been an athlete, he said, then he might have considered the nudity appropriate.

Hoping that Crosswaith would listen to Van Vechten, Walter entreated Carl to meet Crosswaith at Barthé's studio and explain the symbolism to him. But Van Vechten did not want to get involved. He told White that since he did not know Crosswaith personally, such an invitation might appear presumptuous. Carl had more advice for White, however. "You might also suggest to him that if white children are not corrupted by a sight of nude statues, colored children need not be. Incidentally the Vatican is full of them."[54]

Moses refused to approve the statue until White collected enough pledges from prominent Negroes attesting that the statue would not offend Negroes as a whole. White sent more letters to influential New Yorkers, but was surprised to discover more opposition than support. A. Philip Randolph, for instance, also objected strongly to the chains. "With the chains unbroken it might carry with it the idea that Negroes are content to sing even with their chains," he told White, "and this may give solace to some of our enemies in the country." He was concerned, too, about the psychological effect on young people. "It may also arouse a sort of bitter antagonism among some of our younger Negroes who constantly express themselves as being opposed to being reminded of slavery." Nonetheless, he judged the statue a "colossal" artistic accomplishment.[55]

Walter approached Carl again, asking him to intervene and reason with Randolph, but Van Vechten was content to stay behind the scenes. On the matter of the chains, Carl was adamant, however. "To me the statue loses all propaganda or controversial value with the chains broken and becomes merely a handsome piece of sculpture," he told White, "but anybody can be wrong and I seem to be in the minority opinion."[56] By now, it was January 1942.

Moses remained unmoved when black members of the James Weldon Johnson Memorial Committee came forward to endorse the chains. They were intellectuals, Moses responded dismissively, and therefore viewed the statue through a sophisticated lens. What about the man on the street, the everyday Negro? White sent him more letters, but Moses refused to budge in his opinion. He finally stonewalled White into surrender, and the latter sent out a statement to the members of the committee: "As a concession to Mr. Moses's point it was agreed that the chains should be broken, which would emphasize the symbolism that when the Negro slave sang his body moved upwards out of chains and into freedom."[57]

Ultimately, Moses simply did not want the statue to be located in Central Park under any circumstances, and he reverted to the issue of nudity once White and the committee had agreed to the unbroken chains. White sent a letter to Van Vechten: "I regret the necessity of sending you herewith a copy of a letter dated March 30 from Commissioner Robert Moses in which it appears that neither he nor the Art Commission will approve the Barthé memorial to James Weldon Johnson, apparently on the grounds that it is a nude."[58] But White still maintained hope, informing Van Vechten of his plans to convene the committee to meet with Moses in person. Would Van Vechten be willing to join them?

It wasn't a good idea, Carl replied. White summarized Van Vechten's perspective on the matter in a letter to Colonel Theodore Roosevelt. "Dear Ted," he began, and reported Van Vechten's opinion that before any meeting was held with the commissioner, the committee should meet and "decide on a thoroughly integrated point of view." Van Vechten suggested that Barthé address the committee members at this meeting and let them know whether he would be willing to sculpt another model. White implored Roosevelt to lend his political muscle to the cause.[59]

He asked the same of Elmer Carter who, although he had called Barthé's statue "magnificent," flatly refused. Carter had had enough of the entire ordeal. He wanted the committee to stand firm and concede nothing else. The sculpture was beautiful, he said, and entirely appropriate for the park and its patrons. "Surely they see enough of ugliness and if only a fleeting glance at a beautiful object is offered them, it appears to me that they should not be denied the chance," he wrote to White. Besides, he knew exactly what was behind the resistance on the part of Moses and the Art Commission: "an illy disguised resistance to the figure of a Negro at the entrance of the city's great park." He was finished with the issue, and with Moses, too. "And I am not going to write Mr. Moses any letters and I do not agree with him that this should not be a public fight, and so far as I am concerned

I want the battle pitched right out on Fifth Avenue and Forty-second Street. I am not going to attend any meetings designed to cook up some phony compromise." Barthé himself was willing to compromise, however, White reported to Van Vechten. He would consider putting a fig leaf on the statue, but he would not put pants on it or remove the chains entirely.[60]

White dug his heels in deeper, continuing to solicit letters from eminent New Yorkers, black and white, who praised the statue, and sending the letters on to Moses. In May, the James Weldon Johnson Memorial Committee, the Art Commission, and the Park Department finally met, and the committee received a final answer after a "heated" discussion: no. Robert Moses explained the decision in a letter to White: "Our position is this: We don't think that a statue of this kind in the place selected will commend itself to the majority of our citizens inside and outside of Harlem. We think that many of them will object to the symbolism. We believe that, even with slight modifications, it will be difficult to protect this particular kind of statue from vandalism. We further believe that you are making a mistake in confining the sculptor to what is nothing more than a narrow island separating traffic, and that another location with adequate space removed from traffic would give the sculptor an opportunity to do a much finer work. Few people, other than automobilists, will see the statue at the location you propose and no one will be able to read the inscription unless he risks being run over."[61]

Just as the First World War had effectively shut down *Three Plays for a Negro Theater,* the 1917 production by Ridgely Torrence, the Second World War terminated plans for the James

Weldon Johnson memorial. In the meantime, Van Vechten had become occupied with plans for another project to memorialize Johnson, something much grander and more far-reaching than a statue. He had decided to create an archive of Negro materials in Johnson's name. As the site for this venture, he chose the library at Yale University in New Haven, Connecticut.

ANYTHING NEGRO

Van Vechten returned to the pages of the *Crisis* to explain the genesis of this new venture: "For a very long time I pondered, in my own mind, the question of what would be my ultimate disposal of my collection of Negro books, manuscripts, letters, photographs, phonograph records, and music; not a large collection, perhaps, but an extremely interesting and valuable one, since it has been my privilege during the past two decades to know intimately many of the most prominent members of the race. In this quandary, and spurred on by the world conditions to arrive at my decision in some haste, I was invited by Bernhard Knollenberg, the head librarian of Yale University, to deposit this material in the Yale Library. Fortuitously, he employed precisely the right words to convince me that Yale was the place for it: 'We haven't any Negro books at all.' "[62]

New Haven was appropriate, he explained, because it was near New York and Boston and "in the heart of the thickest section of the collegiate world." [63] New Haven might even be a better location than New York because that city already had the Schomburg Collection at the New York Public Library, founded by Puerto Rican bibliophile Arthur Alphonso Schomburg in 1926, which included his collection of five thousand books, pamphlets, manuscripts, and prints written by or concerning blacks in the United States, Spain, and Latin America. A grant from the Carnegie Corporation made it possible for the New York Public Library to purchase the collection, which would grow to ten thousand materials by the late 1930s. Today the collection, a repository of 10 million items relating to blacks all over the world, is called the Arthur Schomburg Center for Research in Black Culture and is housed at the library's 135th Street branch.

Yale was the first white college to lobby for black materials, and housing Negro materials at a white institution seemed fitting to Van Vechten, who reminded readers of the *Crisis* that Johnson had devoted his life to, among other ideals, bridging the divide between black and white. What Van Vechten did not reveal to his readers was his desire to compete with the Schomburg and every other repository as the premier site in the country for housing black materials. He confided to Yale librarian Bernhard Knollenberg in a letter that he had "a very real anxiety to make the JWJ Collection the BEST, if not the largest, collection of Negro source material in the world."[64] The official title of the collection would be the James Weldon Johnson Collection of Negro Arts and Letters, founded by Carl Van Vechten. Years later, he explained that had named the collection after Johnson rather than himself because he wanted others to donate materials, "and I didn't want them to think I was hogging the collection."[65] But Van Vechten also suspected that his reputation had been so badly damaged by *Nigger Heaven* that some people would not be willing to donate materials if the collection bore his name.

In a letter to Knollenberg in late May 1941, Van Vechten wrote, "Some time ago we discussed briefly the possibility of my giving the Yale University Library my Negro books and papers. If you still want them I've decided to go ahead with this idea. It isn't a vast collection, like the Schomburg or the Spingarn, nor does it contain many old books (tho' I have the rarest of them all, Phillis Wheatley's Poems) but it makes up for that, perhaps, in personality and association items." His collection contained many artifacts, among them "a very valuable, important, and personal collection of letters from many of the more important Negroes of the day." He planned to begin sending material to the library within a few weeks, and saw no end to the process. "I think it is extremely likely that I shall be sending it to you until I die, for even after the present collection is all on its way to New Haven, further material will rapidly accumulate."[66]

He had a few conditions. Above all, the collection must be preserved as an entity. The material was not to be divided across the university under any circumstances. For instance, the music department "may think they have first claim to the music and phonographic records. I am convinced, however, that the collection will have a greater value if it is kept together as a group of books and papers gathered by the author of Nigger Heaven." In essence, Van Vechten said, Knollenberg must uphold the same conditions he would apply to any other rare material in the library.

A few days later, Carl presented Knollenberg with more conditions. First, all of the book jackets must be preserved. "They are an integral part of the collection and often impart important information." None of the records were to be played more than five times a year, "and then on a phonograph in first class condition with the best available needles, and under the supervision of a library attendant." No reproductions of photographs would be permitted without permission. And finally, some correspondence and other personal material (such as his pornographic scrapbooks) would be sealed until twenty-five years after his death.[67]

"I am happy to have your letter of May 29, 1941, concerning your collection of Negro books, papers, phonograph records, scrapbooks and photographs," wrote Knollenberg. "It goes without saying that we shall be delighted to have this collection at the Yale University Library." Knollenberg had long admired Van Vechten for the work he had undertaken on behalf of the Negro. He had complimented Van Vechten a few months before: "I am beginning to have a little hope that the colored man may be in for a better deal, and I have not any doubt that if he does get a better deal one of the persons most largely responsible will be you." Knollenberg invited Van Vechten to begin sending his body of Negro material.[68]

Van Vechten implored readers of the *Crisis* and *Opportunity* to donate money—even pennies, he said—as well as "any manuscripts or books written by anyone with Negro blood, and the best books about Negroes written by white men belong in this collection. Further, interesting photographs, rare first editions of music (I wish somebody would give us the St. Louis Blues in this form!) phonograph records, programs of plays or concerts, and especially letters, should find a fitting, permanent resting place here."[69] In a 1941 letter to Dorothy Peterson about his ambitions for the collection, he was more frank. "My dear," he wrote, "we want anything we can get that is Negro. . . . Music also is desirable, manuscripts, letters, ANYTHING Negro except stocking caps and reefers."[70] He enthused to Langston Hughes about his vision for the collection: "I have a DEFINITE FEELING that in LESS than five years Yale will have a chair of Negro life and culture and whoever sits in that chair will have the best source material in the country to guide him."[71] Carl's prediction was overly optimistic: Yale would not begin a program in Afro-American studies until 1968.

Van Vechten had dispensed with writing by the time he began to focus his energies on the James Weldon Johnson Collection. His seventh and final novel, *Parties* (1930), was considered a failure by most critics. Clinton Simpson of the *Saturday Review of Literature* called the book, a satirical take on the frivolity of the Jazz Age, "flippant" and "cheap," while others misread the book as a celebration of the debauchery that Van Vechten meant to condemn.[72] "The English notices of Parties are almost as violent as those directed against Jude the Obscure," Van Vechten wrote to Alfred A. Knopf in November 1930.[73] Nonetheless, Van Vechten believed *Parties* was his greatest literary achievement, though it was a commercial failure. But he had lost his taste for writing. "Writing became harder and harder," he remembered in later life. "I was very conscientious and tried for a perfection that I could not always realize."[74] His last book was *Sacred and Profane Memories*, which includes "Feathers," a portrait of one of his beloved cats; "Folksongs of Iowa," in which he considered the unique qualities of the state; and "The Tin Trunk," in which he lovingly described the ferrotypes of his mother and father that had so captivated him in his youth.[75]

The same year in which he published *Sacred and Profane Memories,* Van Vechten turned to photography. "It has always been my habit when I finish anything, to start something else," he said in 1960. Van Vechten's first amateur photograph was a portrait of his paternal grandmother, taken with a box camera in the 1890s. Not long afterward, he took a photograph of two young black girls sitting on the front steps of Harriet Beecher Stowe's house in Cincinnati, Ohio. From the box camera, he graduated to an early Kodak, then to a more sophisticated box camera. And when Mexican-born artist Miguel Covarrubias introduced him to the Leica in 1932, a new addiction was born. "Now Mr. Van Vechten has found something to thrill him anew," announced a reporter for the *New York Telegraph* in 1933. The reporter was fascinated by Carl's studio. "Out of nowhere came lights and tripods and the most amazing backgrounds," he gushed. "Each [photograph] is more breathtaking than the other, each with life and sparkle, vision and intelligence."[76]

In the first decade of his career as a photographer, Van Vechten experimented with chiaroscuro lighting, props, and dramatic poses for his subjects. By the 1940s, he called his photographs "purely documentary." But Van Vechten always saw the act of taking a photograph as entirely personal, and his prolific success was made possible by his vast collection of friends and acquaintances. "I knew so many people I had no difficulty getting subjects," he said in 1960.[77] Carl set up a studio in his apartment and subjects filed in: dancers, activists, singers, journalists, actors, artists, educators, and people whom he just found personally interesting. Van Vechten chose subjects only according to his tastes. He never exchanged photographs for pay, so he was not beholden to anyone. He saw the process through from beginning to end, and enjoyed the developing and printing most of all because it required absolute solitude. He printed up some of his photographs as postcards, which are included among his correspondence.

Every photograph bore his particular signature. "In taking photographs in black and white, I consider backgrounds very seriously."[78] He was fussy about composition, and used elaborate props—"robes, costumes, banshee hats, Easter eggs, masks, feathers, cats, marionettes," recalled Bruce Kellner. In *Carl Van Vechten and the Irreverent Decades* Kellner described his experience of being photographed by Van Vechten. It "was never the easiest thing to survive with savior-faire": "Carl always puttered a little; an assistant set up the lights. Carl adjusted his camera on a wooden easel; the assistant supplied stools, chairs—indeed, chaise longues or beds—against the draped or otherwise decorated fourth wall. Then the subject sat. The lights were excruciatingly hot, and the room was stuffy. Carl stood behind his camera, staring like a mad scientist in the movies, waiting for the 'exact moment,' in which he always believed. Then the shutter began to snap, sometimes quickly, sometimes with syncopated hesitations, always with Carl's embalmed stare above."[79] Van Vechten himself described being photographed as "an awful job." He understood his own idiosyncrasies: "I'm very particular, and I want certain backgrounds, I want all sorts of things." Van Vechten began using color film when it became available but he preferred black and white. "Color prints are no good," he said, "because they don't last."[80]

Bessie Smith survived a session with Van Vechten in 1936. He had admired Smith since he first heard her earliest records, which he "played and played in the early 'twenties and everybody who came to my apartment was invited to hear them."[81] Van Vechten doted on these records; he released them to the James Weldon Johnson Collection attended by strict instructions: patrons would be permitted to listen to them only once every two weeks and only under supervision.

Van Vechten had seen Smith perform at the Orpheum Theatre in Newark on Thanksgiving Day in 1925. Like the rest of her audience (a "blue-black crowd, notable for the absence of mulattoes"), he was captivated by her presence, her attire ("a crimson satin robe, sweeping up from her trim ankles, and embroidered in multicolored sequins in designs"), her face ("beautiful with the rich ripe beauty of southern darkness, a deep bronze-brown, matching the bronze of her bare arms"), and her voice ("full of shouting and moaning and praying and suffering, a wild, rough, Ethiopian voice, brash and volcanic, but seductive and sensuous too, released between rouged lips and the whitest of teeth").[82]

A few years later, Smith gave another extraordinary performance at Van Vechten's West 55th Street apartment. Like her performance at the Orpheum, it was "the real thing: a woman cutting her heart open with a knife until it was exposed for us all to see, so that we suffered as she suffered, exposed with a rhythmic ferocity, indeed, which could hardly be borne." Fania

Marinoff was greatly moved by Smith's style, voice, and presence, and she started to kiss Smith in gratitude at the end of the evening. Marinoff's dramatic personal style alarmed and bewildered Smith, who pushed Van Vechten's wife to the floor. Van Vechten never described this incident in any of his writing about Smith, of course, to avoid embarrassing his wife. But Smith's behavior did not change his or his wife's high opinion of her as a performer, and it did not prevent Van Vechten from pronouncing the entire evening a success. "In my own experience, this was Bessie Smith's greatest performance," he wrote in a 1947 article, "Memories of Bessie Smith."[83]

In 1936, Smith came to be photographed in Van Vechten's home studio. Between shows, she revealed a different side of herself than the one she displayed onstage. She was "cold sober and in a quiet reflective mood," Van Vechten recalled. "She could scarcely have been more amiable or cooperative," even changing costumes at Van Vechten's behest. In each of the photographs, she wears an elaborate dress. In some, her eyes are cast downward, her expression pained. In others, she is serene, looking off to the side, holding a bouquet of feathers. Van Vechten felt he knew Bessie Smith, and he always considered his photographs "the only adequate record of her true appearance and manner that exist."[84] Bessie Smith died the following year as a result of two successive car accidents, both of which took place in a single night.

The magic of Van Vechten's portraits of Bessie Smith begot the magic that shines through in his photographs of Billie Holiday. Holiday was "here all night," Van Vechten remembered, "and she was very difficult to break down. I didn't know her, and she was

Bessie Smith, February 3, 1936 (Yale Collection of American Literature, Beinecke Rare Book and Manuscript Library. Courtesy of the Carl Van Vechten Trust.)

Bessie Smith, February 3, 1936 (Yale Collection of American Literature, Beinecke Rare Book and Manuscript Library. Courtesy of the Carl Van Vechten Trust.)

very difficult, and it took me at least two hours to break her down, and then she became so friendly she didn't want to go at all." He finally "broke her down" by showing her the pictures he'd taken of Bessie Smith, whom she held in great esteem. "The first way she broke down, she began to cry, and I took photographs of her crying, which nobody else had done. But more than that, later I took photographs of her laughing, which nobody else had done either." In one photograph, Holiday is shrouded in a regal-looking drape, one shoulder exposed, with the light behind her. Four years before he died, after nearly thirty years and thousands of photographs, Van Vechten called his photographs of Billie Holiday not only some of his best, but the best ones of Holiday ever taken.[85]

Two years before he photographed Bessie Smith, Van Vechten photographed the equally inimitable Nora Holt, with her prominent freckles and carefully shaped brow. The same year Nella Larsen, dressed in a lively polka-dotted blouse, sits in front of an almost psychedelic backdrop and looks up at something beyond the frame, her face markedly tired. The photograph was taken three years before she disappeared from Van Vechten's life. For Langston Hughes, he created a background made of a pastiche of clippings from newspapers all over the country, perhaps a comment on Hughes's demanding travel schedule. In 1941, he captured Countee Cullen standing in front of a tree in Central Park, looking round and middle-aged in a three-piece suit. A few weeks later, he used a plain background to frame a defiant-looking George Schuyler, decked out in a white suit, his arms folded. James Weldon Johnson managed to create a towering presence, even

Billie Holiday, March 23, 1949 (Yale Collection of American Literature, Beinecke Rare Book and Manuscript Library. Courtesy of the Carl Van Vechten Trust.)

while sitting. He emanates vitality in a photograph taken by Van Vechten in 1932, six years before he died. That same year, he took the first of many photographs of Dorothy Peterson. She looks young and mysterious at thirty-five, her head turned romantically to the side, and her eyes cast upward. She appears considerably older in a color photo taken eight years later in front of the Savoy Ballroom, next to a poster announcing a performance by Ella Fitzgerald. Van Vechten used a soft lens to capture his dear friend in 1949. In this photo, she gazes out of an apartment window, her face enhanced by a brilliant light shimmering within its frame.

Van Vechten captured a kinetic Walter White at thirty-nine. He peers good-naturedly at the camera from the lower right-hand corner of the frame. Two years later, in 1934, Carl photographed an aristocratic Claude McKay with his legs crossed and his knees positioned by interlaced fingers. McKay faces the camera with raised eyebrows, as if Van Vechten had stolen his attention from something more important. Zora Neale Hurston was particularly pleased with a pair of photographs Van Vechten took of her the same year. "I love myself when I am laughing," she told him. "And then again when I am looking mean and impressive."[86] A winsome Harold Jackman laughs in a 1932 photo, which appears nearly animated by his elegance and charisma.

"I've photographed everybody, from Matisse to Isamu Noguchi," Van Vechten bragged to a *New Yorker* reporter in 1963. "My first subject was Anna May Wong, and my second was Eugene O'Neill."[87] The subjects of his first studio portraits were his wife and Wong, the first Chinese American movie star, but earlier

Nella Larsen, November 23, 1934 (Yale Collection of American Literature, Beinecke Rare Book and Manuscript Library. Courtesy of the Carl Van Vechten Trust.)

Langston Hughes, February 24, 1936 (Yale Collection of American Literature, Beinecke Rare Book and Manuscript Library. Courtesy of the Carl Van Vechten Trust.)

Countee Cullen, June 20, 1941 (Yale Collection of American Literature, Beinecke Rare Book and Manuscript Library. Courtesy of the Carl Van Vechten Trust.)

George Schuyler, July 2, 1941 (Yale Collection of American Literature, Beinecke Rare Book and Manuscript Library. Courtesy of the Carl Van Vechten Trust.)

James Weldon Johnson, December 1932 (Yale Collection of American Literature, Beinecke Rare Book and Manuscript Library. Courtesy of the Carl Van Vechten Trust.)

Dorothy Peterson, March 26, 1932 (Yale Collection of American Literature, Beinecke Rare Book and Manuscript Library. Courtesy of the Carl Van Vechten Trust.)

Dorothy Peterson, c. 1940 (Yale Collection of American Literature, Beinecke
Rare Book and Manuscript Library. Courtesy of the Carl Van Vechten Trust.)

Dorothy Peterson, September 3, 1949 (Yale Collection of American Literature, Beinecke Rare Book and Manuscript Library. Courtesy of the Carl Van Vechten Trust.)

Walter White, August 17, 1932 (Yale Collection of American Literature, Beinecke Rare Book and Manuscript Library. Courtesy of the Carl Van Vechten Trust.)

Claude McKay, April 13, 1934 (Yale Collection of American Literature, Beinecke Rare Book and Manuscript Library. Courtesy of the Carl Van Vechten Trust.)

Zora Neale Hurston, November 9, 1934 (Yale Collection of American Literature, Beinecke Rare Book and Manuscript Library. Courtesy of the Carl Van Vechten Trust.)

Zora Neale Hurston, November 9, 1934 (Yale Collection of American Literature, Beinecke Rare Book and Manuscript Library. Courtesy of the Carl Van Vechten Trust.)

Harold Jackman, September 11, 1932 (Yale Collection of American Literature, Beinecke Rare Book and Manuscript Library. Courtesy of the Carl Van Vechten Trust.)

photographs featured Nora Holt, Gladys Bentley, a peerlessly daring entertainer who sang and played piano in bow ties and dress tails in Harlem nightclubs, and Prentiss Taylor, a white artist who designed Van Vechten's bookplate and the dust jacket for *Sacred and Profane Memories*. He assisted Van Vechten with the lighting in his early photographs. By the end of his life, Van Vechten had taken fifteen thousand photographs, over nine thousand of which are housed at the Beinecke Rare Book and Manuscript Library at Yale University, which also contains the negatives for the remaining six thousand along with all of his contact prints.

Van Vechten was particularly proud of the range of his photographs of blacks. "One of the unique features of the collection is a set of photographs of Negroes (already there are eleven boxes with an average of forty photographs in a box) which I have made myself during the past ten years," Van Vechten told readers of the *Crisis* in 1942, "perhaps the largest group of photographs of notable Negro personalities ever made by one man."[88] Bernhard Knollenberg did not need to be convinced that the photographs would constitute a vital part of the collection he and Van Vechten were building. But while Knollenberg had not hesitated to accept Van Vechten's black materials on behalf of Yale, when it came to adding a living, breathing Negro to the library staff—well, that became a different matter altogether.

RACE FEELING

In March 1941, Bernhard Knollenberg sent Carl Van Vechten a copy of a letter he had written to a "young colored woman" by the name of Lillian G. Lewis, a student at Hampton University, in response to her inquiry about joining the staff of the Yale University library. If hired, she would be the first black person to work in such a capacity. In his correspondence with Van Vechten, Knollenberg seemed excited by the inquiry, but his letters to Lewis were colored by caution and doubt. He warned her that it wouldn't be easy and that he expected substantial resistance, but he would do what he could.

Knollenberg sent Lewis's letter to Van Vechten, but only as a point of interest. He bristled when Van Vechten asked permission to share the letter with the famously tireless Walter White, who was then serving as the secretary of the NAACP. Knollenberg agreed, but he was emphatic that he didn't want the issue of Lewis's employment to become a public matter. He would canvass his colleagues, Knollenberg said, but he would do it *his* way. "I think that those of us who have no race feeling to overcome (my parents had colored friends in the house from the time I was a baby and hence I never had the slightest anti-race feeling to overcome) should realize that others react different from ourselves, and try to get over our point of view by tact, not by pressure."[89]

Lewis did not get the job. It had nothing to do with race, Knollenberg assured her; the decision was based on her lack of library training. She wrote back to ask if Knollenberg would consider her for a job involving menial duties, as she would do anything to be close to the collections. He was touched by the offer, but he did not want to hire another black person in a menial labor job. "What I hope for," he told Lewis, "is to find colored men or women who have the capacity and training to take and hold non-menial positions."[90] Van Vechten then suggested Harold Jackman.

Van Vechten was keen on Jackman, insisting to Knollenberg that Jackman was the perfect candidate for a curatorial position at Yale, specifically to assist in the organization of the collection. Van Vechten took it upon himself to secure the position for Jackman, embracing his familiar role of go-between as ardently as if it were his own civil rights campaign. He sweetened the pot for Knollenberg. Jackman wouldn't have to quit his job as a high school teacher to take the position in the library at Yale, he told Knollenberg. Instead he could take a sabbatical. That way, Knollenberg wouldn't feel pressured to keep Jackman on if the arrangement did not work out to his satisfaction and Jackman's.[91] A few days later, Jackman wrote Knollenberg a letter officially announcing his interest in working at Yale.

Racial discrimination was wrong, began Knollenberg in his reply to Jackman. He was repulsed by the irony that Americans were currently fighting a war for democracy while rank prejudice against Negroes was still legal. "I am determined to do all I can at Yale to bring our practice into conformity with our preaching," he promised. However, although he had been searching for a trained Negro librarian for some time, he had found none who could "measure up to our standard of ability, professional training, and personality." He agreed with Van Vechten that Jackman was the right person "from the standpoint of ability and personality," but Jackman, like Lewis, simply lacked the appropriate training. Knollenberg admitted that he himself had no library training, but he had trained staff at his disposal; Jackman would have no such supports. He suggested that Jackman take a sabbatical year from teaching in order to obtain the necessary training for the position.[92]

But even when he completed his training, Knollenberg warned Jackman, there would be race feeling to consider. Knollenberg predicted that his own staff would fall in behind him, but the university administration might not be as supportive. The war might provide enough distraction for the appointment to be made, but "the real test will come with the ebb tide after the war." If Jackman performed his duties satisfactorily, however, then he could count on a united front of Yale library staff to take up his cause.[93]

Perhaps because Knollenberg's view was discouraging, perhaps because of the practical realities, Jackman quickly reconsidered. Upon further consideration, he informed Knollenberg a week later, he had decided that pursuing a position at Yale would not be wise. After all, why would he abandon his position as a teacher in the New York public school system, which came with good retirement benefits, and which he had held for seventeen years, for a job at a lower salary, no benefits, and no promise of permanence, to boot?[94]

But Jackman encouraged Knollenberg to continue his efforts to bring the library into line with his liberal convictions. "I very definitely feel that this Collection can be made an opening wedge for a capable Negro at Yale, and I earnestly hope some Negro will profit by it," he wrote. "The fact that you have been willing to consider me makes me hopeful that you will still continue your search for a Negro to take charge of the Collection."[95]

Knollenberg did not have to search very far, as it turned out. Dorothy Peterson was interested.

Peterson and Van Vechten had been close friends since they met in 1925 on the same historic night that Carl also met Harold Jackman and Nella Larsen. Dorothy, Nella, and Carl quickly co-alesced into a trio of kindred spirits, spending a great deal of time together at parties and each other's homes. Dorothy ac-companied Nella to Carl's home the night she dropped off *Quick-sand.* When Nella disappeared, Carl and Dorothy chased down clues about her whereabouts, although Peterson, unlike Van Vechten, eventually grew tired of Larsen's strange behavior and lost interest in finding her. The bond between Peterson and Van Vechten was strong, and she kept him abreast of the important events in her life. "I have a grand Arabian boyfriend acquired on our recent trip to Tetuán," she wrote Carl while on a vacation in Spain with Nella.[96] (Dorothy returned to Spain in the 1950s, seeking relief from the crippling arthritis with which she had suffered for years.)

Dorothy entrusted Carl with her bad news, too, such as her struggles with depression, which sometimes kept her from at-tending parties at his home. They shared inside jokes about race. Carl sent her a copy of "A Prediction," a caricature the artist Miguel Covarrubias had made of him in 1928. Dorothy re-sponded with an ad for hair pomade. "In case this prediction should come true," she teased, "I am providing you with a rem-edy (see inside page) for all these ills."[97] She wrote him frankly about her personal worries, entrusting him with her distress

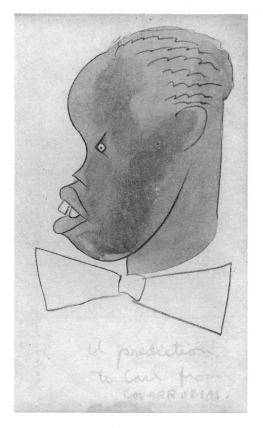

"A Prediction," 1926, by Miguel Covarrubias (Courtesy of the National Portrait Gallery, Smithsonian Institution.)

upon discovering that her beloved married brother Sidney was involved in relationship with a white woman. After Dorothy came to Carl's house to discuss the matter, he summarized their conversation in his daybook: "Sidney, she tells me, is mixed up with a white girl."[98]

Carl gave Dorothy advice. She should stop worrying about Sidney's marriage. If Sidney didn't love his wife, then he shouldn't live with her, but infidelity was "one of the silliest reasons" to

Letter from Dorothy Peterson to Carl Van Vechten, May 24, 1928 (Yale Collection of American Literature, Beinecke Rare Book and Manuscript Library. Courtesy of Carla L. Peterson.)

separate.[99] He kept her secrets close. "Eventually I'm giving YOUR letters to Yale. I haven't been over them yet, so I don't know, but I dare say they will have to be sealed till after your death." He teased her when he read through love letters between her and Jean Toomer, author of the 1923 collection *Cane,* a montage of prose and poetry that is generally considered to be the first important work of the Harlem Renaissance. By the time Dorothy and Carl began going back over their letters, Toomer had long since abandoned his affiliation with the Negro race, identifying only as an American. "I think Jean Toomer's letters are also of the highest interest as a document," Carl wrote Dorothy. "His love-making I find rather algebraic. Was he more HUMAN in the flesh?"[100] Dorothy knew Carl's secrets, too. "If you have any of mine saved," he asked, "I wish you'd give these too (after yours go in) and probably these will have to be sealed too!"[101]

Van Vechten became close to Peterson's family, also. Sidney, a physician, spent drunken nights at his house. He came to Van Vechten himself to solicit advice about his interracial romance. "Sidney Peterson comes in to see me & asks what I think about miscegenation. It seems he is in love with a white girl," he recorded in his daybook.[102] When Dorothy's father died in 1943,

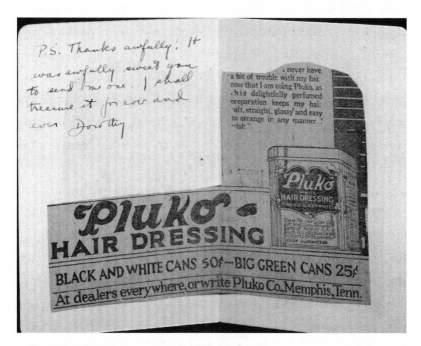

Ad for "Pluko hair dressing" (Yale Collection of American Literature, Beinecke Rare Book and Manuscript Library. Courtesy of the Carl Van Vechten Trust.)

Carl was devastated. "Dorothy Darling," he wrote. "Just this minute I hear of your father's death and I am hurt and shocked and lonely. . . . It never occurred to me he wouldn't be here always: he was so YOUNG."[103] Carl was a great admirer of Jerome Bowers Peterson, who had served as U.S. consul to Venezuela for two years, and then as the deputy collector of the Internal Revenue Service in San Juan, Puerto Rico, where Dorothy had grown up and attended college. Jerome Peterson had also been one of the founders of the influential black newspaper the *New York Age.*

In 1944, Van Vechten established the Jerome Bowers Peterson Memorial Collection of Celebrated Negroes at Wadleigh High School in Harlem, where Dorothy was then working as a Spanish teacher. The photographs in the collection belonged to Dorothy; since Van Vechten had begun his career as a photographer, she had been collecting his photographs of "prominent Negroes," as he told the Wadleigh audience at the dedication ceremony.[104] The Jerome Bowers Peterson Collection is now housed at the University of New Mexico.

Van Vechten was one of the elder Peterson's pallbearers, but even on that day of grief his mind was on the James Weldon Johnson Collection. "I sat at the funeral next to Walter White," he wrote to Knollenberg, "who told me that he believed that Arthur Spingarn was no longer sure he wanted to leave his fabulous Negro library to Howard and thought he could easily be persuaded to turn it in to the James Weldon Johnson Collection."[105] He suggested that Knollenberg write Spingarn directly. Ultimately, Spingarn divided his papers between the Moorland-

Spingarn Research Center at Howard University and the Library of Congress.

"It has never occurred to me to ask Dorothy Peterson if she would like to go into the Yale Library because she has a job at least three times as good as Harold Jackman's," Carl wrote to Knollenberg in August 1942.[106] Even more than Harold, Carl continued, Dorothy was suited to the work necessary to build the James Weldon Johnson Collection. At the time, Peterson was employed full-time as a teacher but, like Van Vechten, she treated her work on the collection like a second career, even donating money for the endowment while she was in the middle of financial woes. "Don't forget that I am spending *all my time* working for the RACE: Night and Day," Van Vechten reminded Peterson in October 1942.[107] So was Dorothy. They were kindred spirits when it came to almost everything, including the art of collecting. Once he sent her a piece from the *New York World-Telegram:* "Negro Swimmer Tows Raft Full of Wounded Soldiers to Safety." In the accompanying letter he wrote: See if you can get the name of the Powerful Negro Swimmer for Posterity!" Peterson was delighted by his challenges and inspired by his glee. As he told her in a 1941 letter, "I am up to my ears in Negro doings!"[108]

Peterson and Knollenberg had already met. A year before she set her sights on the job at Yale, they were introduced at a party at Van Vechten's home. On behalf of his wife and himself, Knollenberg thanked Van Vechten for the evening in a letter he sent the following day. "We had a delightful time last evening

Carl Van Vechten (Photograph by Saul Mauriber), June 23, 1958, postcard to Dorothy Peterson (Yale Collection of American Literature, Beinecke Rare Book and Manuscript Library. Courtesy of the Carl Van Vechten Trust.)

at your house. Once or twice when I have been in company with Negroes there has been an air of constraint. Last night I felt as much at home as I have ever felt in a party composed largely of people I was meeting for the first time, and I thought everyone else 'felt as free and easy' as I did." He was particularly taken with Gladys White, Walter's wife, and Dorothy.[109]

Van Vechten replied to Knollenberg immediately. "Thanks a lot for your letter and we are happy you and Mrs. Knollenberg had a good time, but those were not Negroes, they were old and valued friends of ours whom we have known intimately, and see frequently, for twenty years!" he explained.[110] It was not the first time he would provide Knollenberg with a little race education (a few weeks before, he had instructed Knollenberg to spell "Negro" with a capital N).[111] Dorothy Peterson enjoyed the party, too, and also sent a thank-you note to Van Vechten. In his reply, Carl confided only that Knollenberg had called Dorothy "one of his favorites!!"[112]

Carl had not anticipated Dorothy's interest in the job at Yale, but once she expressed it, he made it his mission to secure the position for her, and Knollenberg was pleased to include him in his discussions with Dorothy. Carl mailed her a copy of the letter he had written Knollenberg describing his surprise in Dorothy's interest in the job, and assured Knollenberg that he had tried to dissuade her but had resigned himself to the fact that Knollenberg's encouragement had clearly won out. Since Dorothy and Knollenberg were both determined to proceed, he said, he itemized Dorothy's singular qualifications. "She knows, or knew before they died, most of the writers intimately. Her background couldn't be better. Her knowledge of languages would be of immense assistance," Van Vechten wrote. "If she does go into this, it will be seriously, and with her face towards the future and what that may bring her and the Collection. Let me know what you decide."[113]

He was more cautious in his communication with Dorothy. "I am glad in my heart that you have the nerve to live on a biscuit, but don't ever say I MADE you do this," he warned.[114] But he was excited about the prospect of Dorothy working at Yale every day, knee deep as he was in Negro doings. She would adore the library itself, he told her. At the time, the James Weldon Johnson Collection was housed at Sterling Memorial Library, which was relatively new, having been built in 1930. In 2003, seventy years after she joined the library staff, Marjorie Wynne described her first impression of Sterling. "Everything was new and wonderful: the towering nave swept boldly forward (unhindered by a central staircase), and every surface—glass, iron, stone, and wood—was alive with scenes and inscriptions from books and manuscripts."[115] It was magnificent, Carl reported to Dorothy. Her brother Sidney would be impressed, too. "He'll think you are going to be Pope or something!"[116]

Behind the scenes, Van Vechten was managing a problem—Bernhard Knollenberg, who, Van Vechten believed, was dragging his feet on the issue of Dorothy's hire. He pestered him in a letter dated August 20. Dorothy was excited, he said, and "INSISTS that this is what her whole life has been leading up to and seems to be very serious about going ahead. I think it would be unfair to let her do this if you were opposed to her acceptance as a possible librarian."[117] She was eager for resolution—and so was he. Why wouldn't Knollenberg give them an answer? Carl implored Knollenberg to be frank with him, at least, and promised to keep his confidence, but he was primarily looking out for Dorothy, who was bothered by Knollenberg's silence, which bothered Carl in turn.

Knollenberg's initial enthusiasm had waned, as it turned out, and he was now disinclined to offer Peterson the job. First, there was the matter of her professional training. Like Lewis and Jackman, Peterson was not a trained librarian, Knollenberg said, and he didn't have the time or the resources to train her himself. Second, there was the matter of the salary; Knollenberg had decided that it wasn't high enough for her. "By its very nature, a curatorship has to be primarily a work of love," he informed Van Vechten, who had predicted this reaction from Knollenberg; he had coached Peterson two weeks earlier: "When you write Mr. K, Id write something short and simple like this: 'In spite of everything, I think Id like to try it. When may I come to talk to you about it?'"[118]

Finally, Knollenberg got to the point: race feeling. "With a few exceptions, the Caucasians in New Haven with whom Miss Peterson will come into contact, are less liberal in their attitude toward Negroes than the New York Caucasians with whom Miss Peterson has associated." Perhaps a southerner, used to staying in his place, would fare better? From the perspective of the South, New Haven would seem more tolerant than it actually was. As for Dorothy Peterson, "living as she has in New York she has come into association with an exceptionally liberal minded group of Caucasians, and any change will be a change for the worse in that particular." He didn't believe Peterson had fully considered this aspect of the job.[119]

Uncharacteristically, Van Vechten took a few days before responding to Knollenberg. "I think the engagement as Curator of the Collection of a Southerner who would be willing to remain in ANY WAY socially subservient, would completely defeat the purpose of the Collection," he said. "To my mind, the more sophisticated the person engaged, the better, and I think one of the essentials should be a wide acquaintance, white and black, with individuals who are interested in movements and problems of the RACE." With regards to Dorothy: "I do not anticipate any troubles along the lines you speak. In the first place, even if everybody in New Haven snubbed Miss Peterson, an eventuality I am not expecting, she knows plenty of people, East, West, North, and South, who would drop by to see her." And it wasn't true that Negroes found New Haven inhospitable, he contended. The writer Owen Dodson, for instance, was much admired by his peers at the Yale School of Drama. And what about Paul Robeson? He and his family were the only black residents in the very small town of Enfield, Connecticut. They were valued members of their community, and their son was one of the most popular and successful boys in school. "If you reply that these are special cases," Van Vechten cautioned, "I would say that is exactly what I mean: Anybody who would KNOW the authors and contents of the books in the James Weldon Johnson Memorial Collection and know how to enlarge the Collection and encourage endowments would have to be a very special case indeed!"[120]

Knollenberg felt misunderstood and offended. "Dear Mr. Van Vechten, You have inadvertently done me an injustice," he claimed. "No one could be more opposed to having a Negro who is of the subservient ('Uncle Tom' as Richard Wright calls it) type, but I know some southern Negroes who are decidedly not subservient."[121] Knollenberg took his lesson from *Uncle Tom's Children*, a 1938 collection of short stories by Richard Wright, a book that Carl also admired. He had written excitedly to Dorothy Peterson when the collection was published: "Have you read Uncle Tom's Children by Richard Wright? It is very horrible and very marvelous and I guess the race has found another great writer. Do you know him? He lives in Harlem and ought to be photographed by the Maestro."[122] Van Vechten eventually photographed Wright and his wife, Ellen Poplar, in 1945.

Van Vechten attempted to soothe Knollenberg's feelings in his reply. "I never questioned YOUR attitude in the matter of Negroes. I have great faith in that. What I did gather from your letter was that a Negro who was accustomed to concede the erratic behavior of Southern whites might find it easier going in your library. This may be a correct assumption. My own experience with Southern intellectual Negroes who pretend on the surface to accept conditions is that underneath they are generally bitter and neurotic and are likely to be good haters."[123] He asked permission from Knollenberg to be frank on all matters pertaining to the collection, requesting that Knollenberg receive his opinions in the spirit of honesty and respect. He deferred to Knollenberg's greater understanding of the library, and in response, Knollenberg conceded that Van Vechten might indeed have a point. Knollenberg's proposal continued to rankle Van Vechten, however, and although he encouraged Dorothy to make her own decision about whether to pursue the position at the library (which she did not receive), he pleaded with her: "ONLY DON'T MAKE ME HAVE TO PUT UP WITH A DARKY FROM ALABAMA."[124]

NEGRO DOINGS

The task of gathering materials for the James Weldon Johnson Collection called upon all of Van Vechten's diplomatic resources as he and Knollenberg worked in tandem to build the monument to Johnson's memory. It wasn't easy; other dramas unfolded.

Relations between Carl and Claude McKay had improved considerably since Van Vechten showed up drunk to meet him at the Café de la Paix in the summer of 1929, and then ran off in pursuit of a truck full of carrots. "I want to congratulate you again for the idea of a JWJ Collection," Claude wrote to Carl in 1941. "It seems precisely appropriate to me for I often think of his life as a series of rare items." Along with his letter, McKay included a "small trifle for the JWJ Collection—the rarest of my few literary items," the salesman's dummy for *Home to Harlem*. Alfonse Schomburg wanted them, he said, but he felt a special affinity for the collection that Van Vechten was building at Yale.[125]

McKay had come to respect Van Vechten a great deal, and regularly suggested black artists and writers for him to photograph, such as the painter Jacob Lawrence. "He has done the most marvelous paintings of Harlem types and scenes," McKay wrote. "And so I thought I would let you know about him as he seems to me an excellent subject for you."[126] Van Vechten contacted Lawrence immediately. In his letter of thanks to McKay for the dummy, he wrote, "I liked Jacob Lawrence and found him very handsome to look at, with very beautiful brown skin. Thanks for him too."[127] Van Vechten assumed that McKay would eventually choose Yale as the repository for all of his materials.[128]

Van Vechten's assumption upset McKay, and he accused Van Vechten of having misrepresented his intentions. Van Vechten had only asked him for "a manuscript," he said—not all of his manuscripts, and he had taken Van Vechten at his word. Besides, he said, the fact was that he had had similar requests for his work not only from the archivists at the Schomburg Library but also from other "black" institutions. "You know the Negro intelligentsia, perhaps more than myself," he wrote, "and what they may think, if I gave two or three manuscripts to a white person and none to colored collectors, who asked first!" But he admitted that his real reasons for complying with Van Vechten's wishes originally had nothing to do with race. "The fact is," he confessed, "that I had been lazy about getting back the manuscripts and I thought I would use you to get them for me, keep the one you preferred and let me have the others."[129] Van Vechten had already heard from others that McKay, who was having financial troubles, was hoping to make a profit from his manuscripts.

Van Vechten, who had been somewhat prepared for McKay's reversal, responded with a mea culpa. He was sorry if he had misunderstood, he told McKay, and would gladly return any material that McKay would rather keep for himself. He reminded Knollenberg a few days before receiving McKay's letter: "When I wrote you that Claude McKay had offered us his manuscripts, I warned you there might be a catch in it, as *strictly* between us, Claude is known to be difficult."[130] Ultimately, McKay wasn't able to sell his material and agreed to let Yale house it. Today, the majority of McKay's papers are in the James Weldon Johnson Collection—including, of course, the record of his ambivalence over where the material should be housed. When

Claude McKay died in 1948, Van Vechten served as one of his pallbearers.

Van Vechten had not been surprised by McKay's behavior, but he was alarmed when he encountered resistance from the most unlikely of sources: Grace Nail Johnson.

Mrs. Johnson had been driving the car the night her husband was killed. She was seriously injured and emotionally devastated by the accident. "It would be a mercy if Grace would die but I guess she won't," Van Vechten confided to his wife days after the accident, shortly after visiting Grace.[131] Her breasts and legs had been crushed, he told Marinoff, and her face was badly damaged. There was a great possibility that she would lose an eye. But soon Mrs. Johnson began to recover more quickly than anyone expected. Ultimately, she did not lose her eye, or even need plastic surgery. But the emotional damage would linger for the rest of her life, and it certainly affected her behavior with regards to the James Weldon Johnson Collection.

Initially Grace was as enthusiastic about the James Weldon Johnson Collection as she had been about the memorial. "Proudly shall I write Mr. Knollenberg, and with greater pride say, Thank you!!" she wrote.[132] Van Vechten suggested that she wait a while to write Knollenberg—a year to be exact—until the collection was firmly in place.

By the following year her feelings had changed, it seemed. "Dear Grace," Van Vechten wrote, "Whenever the subject of the James Weldon Johnson Collection at Yale comes up, as it does several times a day, somebody is sure to inquire, 'What has Grace given you?' and I have been obliged (and somewhat ashamed) to reply, 'Nothing.'" Her letters indicated a willingness to participate, but she had yet to donate anything to the collection. On the other hand, Johnson's friends had been delivering material in a steady stream. He asked her to be frank. Was she going to give anything or not? He resorted to threats: "I believe, however, if you keep such things in the cabin or your house in Great Barrington and either burns down or is invaded by flood, posterity," he warned, "let alone your contemporaries, will judge you harshly."[133] (Grace had informed Carl when, three years earlier, a hurricane had destroyed a substantial number of books stored in the Johnsons' house.)

Van Vechten alerted Knollenberg to the problem he was having with Grace Nail Johnson. "I think I had better take up another unpleasant matter with you," he began an August 1942 letter. "Matters have reached such a pass with Grace Johnson that I set a few spies to work and discover that she has several fancied and even manufactured grievances against me. As my relations with Jim were intimate and my relations with her almost on the same plane (if you ever go through the letters of the two I shall presently send you you will discover that in almost every one they are thanking me for something or other), but her conduct since the founding of the Collection at Yale has been most strange." Van Vechten became particularly angry when he learned that Grace had given her late husband's materials to the Library of Congress, but then quickly taken them back. "Outwardly, she has been amiable but she has never offered to give us anything or to help with the collection in any way," Van

Vechten continued. "Now, I learn of these grievances, based probably on some deeper rankling which she may not even understand herself. In any case, I can apparently at the moment get no further with her. I should hate to think the Collection would lose in any way through this and I suggest this solution, if it isn't too much trouble for you. Write her a warm letter and invite her to lunch with you and to inspect the Collection (this MAY be what she wanted all the time)."[134]

Knollenberg was baffled. "I had lunch with JWJ and her at Troutbeck not long before Mr. Johnson's death and recall that she is charming." But maybe she had been a little "phony," now that he thought about it. "The impression was, of course, very superficial," he allowed, "and I shall probably find, on further acquaintance, that I was mistaken." He took Van Vechten's advice and wrote a letter to Mrs. Johnson in which he invited her to come to Yale and have lunch with him and then spend an hour or two with the collection. In the interest of posterity, Van Vechten wrote a note at the bottom of Knollenberg's letter: "Mrs. Johnson did not reply to this letter & did not come to lunch."[135]

Van Vechten's unnamed spies had composed an unflattering portrait of Mrs. Johnson that Van Vechten conveyed to Knollenberg. The same Grace Nail Johnson who had participated eagerly in the project of the Johnson Memorial had devolved, Carl reported, into a petty, self-centered woman. She was "annoyed and hurt because more attention has not been paid to HER," Van Vechten reported to Knollenberg, "overlooking the fact that the Collection is a tribute to the race in general and her husband in particular. This motive, of course, is silly and even ignoble, but it is not too difficult to deal with if you come to it freshly. If, however, you find it undignified to deal with it at all I can sympathize with your attitude. As a matter of fact we might get better results by leaving her entirely alone. You can make up your mind about this." Van Vechten began to wonder if it was possible that Mrs. Johnson was hiding the fact that there were actually no James Weldon Johnson manuscripts at all. When Mrs. Johnson did not respond positively to Knollenberg's entreaties, Van Vechten advised him to join him in offering her "the benefit of a vast, deep, extremely cold silence."[136]

Several years later, Mrs. Johnson had returned to her old self and regained her original excitement about the collection. By that time, Bernhard Knollenberg had moved on, replaced by Donald Gallup, who reported to Van Vechten in 1947 that Grace had spent the evening with him and his wife and talked enthusiastically about the Yale collection.[137] Perhaps it had simply taken those five years for Johnson's widow to overcome her grief and sense of loss at the idea of giving away her husband's memorabilia.

Van Vechten predicted that working with Du Bois would present even greater difficulties. "I must warn you that he can be very rude, but I think you can take it!" Van Vechten told Knollenberg in August, at around the same time as the men began to strategize about how best to handle Grace. Du Bois was "one of the towering Negro figures of the epoch," Van Vechten acknowledged to Knollenberg, but he was convinced that Du Bois's personality had been a creative and professional handicap during the era of the Negro Renaissance.[138] Van Vechten counseled Dorothy Peterson to focus her archival energies on collecting back issues of *Opportunity* as opposed to the *Crisis*, which had been edited by Du Bois during the pivotal years of the Harlem Renaissance. Because of Du Bois's stubborn shortsightedness, he told Peterson, "the Crisis just passed this movement up," although the *Crisis* had sponsored numerous literary contests for emerging Harlem Renaissance writers and published the writing of several major figures of the movement, like Langston Hughes and Countee Cullen.[139]

Twenty-five years earlier, Van Vechten and Du Bois had experienced the same revelation. Both men had proclaimed Ridgely Torrence's 1917 tour de force *Granny Maumee* as the signal of the beginning of a new era in the life of the American Negro, but that had been the last time the two men had agreed on anything. Still, Van Vechten recognized that the James Weldon Johnson Collection would not be complete without some portion of Du Bois's letters, manuscripts, and personal papers, so Knollenberg would have to brave Du Bois's rudeness. Van Vechten cautioned him not to take it personally. "W. E. B. Du Bois is seldom very friendly with white people and has always been particularly unfriendly to me for reasons which I need not go into." Even so, Van Vechten was concerned about Du Bois's feelings, and warned Knollenberg that Du Bois might be "hurt" if he weren't invited to contribute his material to the collection, even if he were not interested in making a contribution. He advised Knollenberg to draft an introductory letter to Du Bois, but not to send it without his approval.[140]

Du Bois was seventy-four when Van Vechten sent Knollenberg to court him, and he had not slowed down in any way over the seventeen years since he and Van Vechten had first met. If anything, Du Bois's career had only taken on more speed as he had moved away from the official NAACP platform of integration toward a reconsideration of segregation, justifying his shift in a series of articles he published in the *Crisis* in 1934. He picked a fight with Walter White in the pages of the *Crisis* when Walter disagreed with him. Du Bois eventually (and not uncharacteristically) turned nasty, accusing White of being white. "He has more white friends than colored. He goes where he will in New York City and naturally meets no Color Line, for the simple and sufficient reason that he isn't 'colored.'"[141] Readers of the *Crisis* and members of the NAACP editorial board had had enough of Du Bois by this point. He was censured by the NAACP and effectively forced to resign from the organization as well as from his position as editor of the *Crisis* in July. He shifted his podium from the *Crisis* to the *Amsterdam News,* where in a column called "As the Crow Flies," he continued to lecture his readers on the state of American politics.

Knollenberg was as perplexed by Van Vechten's perspective on Du Bois as he had been by Van Vechten's descriptions of Grace Nail Johnson. On the occasions of their meetings, Knollenberg said, Du Bois had always been friendly. He knew nothing about the root of the discord between Du Bois and Van Vechten, or anything at all about the controversy that had attended the publication of *Nigger Heaven*. "Some day soon I hope to find out what has come between you and see if I cannot be a peacemaker," he offered.[142] He promised to keep Van Vechten's name out of his correspondence with Du Bois.

Knollenberg admired Du Bois for the same reason he admired Van Vechten. In his mind, both men were equally passionate and outspoken on issues of racial equality. In the same letter in which he offered his diplomatic services, Knollenberg described in affectionate detail a visit Du Bois had made to Yale a few months before, when he had been invited to address the student body; his topic was "The Future of Europe in Africa."

> We have a Sociology Club here, the head of which is a graduate student whom I have seen a little of. He called me a few days before Dr. Du Bois' visit to ask if we would be willing to have a literary exhibition of Dr. Du Bois' works as a friendly gesture in connection with his visit. I was, of course, delighted to accede to this request. He further said that they were having difficulty in finding a place to have dinner in honor of Dr. D. B. at which Negroes as well as Whites could be present. I was able to help arrange that. Finally, he asked if my wife would be willing to sit next to Dr. Du Bois at dinner (He had heard she was a southerner) and I told him that she was as utterly devoid of race prejudice as I am. I imagine that he passed some of this information on to Dr. Du Bois, because he was extremely cordial to both my wife and me. We accompanied him to his talk in the lounge at the Graduate School, and there I was repaid many times for the little

trouble I had gone to in connection with his visit by hearing him excoriate the Whites who were whooping it up for a war for democracy while stirring up latent anti-Semitism and doing nothing to curb manifestations of anti-Negroism. I had been at dinner only a few nights before with some distinguished Poles who had let loose some of the most virulent anti-Semitic talk that I had heard for some time. Because of a professional interest in Dr. Du Bois, these ladies and gentlemen were in the audience only a few yards away from Dr. Du Bois, and in a position where I could watch their faces. His thrusts really went home, and I have rarely seen such an uncomfortable group. I had wanted to say exactly what he said, but was bound by the rules of social civility not to do so at a dinner party. It was wonderful to have Dr. Du Bois do it for me.[143]

Van Vechten congratulated Knollenberg on the draft of the letter he planned to send to Du Bois. Knollenberg's story softened him, and he hurried to qualify his earlier judgment of Du Bois. "Perhaps I exaggerated when I wrote that he was 'particularly unfriendly to me,'" he wrote. "There is nothing that you can 'fix up' because we have never been friendly and have never quarreled. Nothing whatever has happened. I have known Dr. Du Bois for nearly twenty years and never advanced a step with him. I can attribute this in part to my great friendship with James Weldon as these two, while outwardly friendly, never really were so." He attributed the distance between them to Du Bois's coldness. "Dr. Du Bois has many admirers but few friends and that is what I mean when I say I exaggerated by 'particularly.'" Du Bois had dined at his house, but they had never developed a friendship, he explained. Then he got to the point. "He was the only Negro intellectual to give Nigger Heaven a bad review and it was a scorcher." It wasn't true that Du Bois had written the only negative review, but none rankled Van Vechten more than Du Bois's "hot crack," as Charles Chesnutt had referred to Du Bois's 1926 review. Van Vechten directed Knollenberg to his own cache of papers about Nigger Heaven if he wanted to learn more. Of course, it wasn't Du Bois's attitude toward whites that bothered Van Vechten; it was Du Bois's attitude toward him. "Recently, in referring enthusiastically to the JWJ Collection at Yale, he has pointedly omitted all reference to me."[144] Van Vechten did not believe this was a simple oversight.

By the time he died at the age of ninety-five in 1963, W. E. B. Du Bois had outlived Reconstruction, Jim Crow, and the Third Reich, and he witnessed the beginnings of the civil rights movement. He and Van Vechten may not have liked each other very much, but they both embodied controversial positions on black-white relations in their era. The disparities in their cultural and aesthetic beliefs were extreme, and they didn't care much for each other's fiction. (Carl considered Dark Princess, a 1928 novel by Du Bois, "asinine.")[145] Still, Du Bois took the time to sit before Van Vechten's camera in 1946, when he was seventy-eight. Van Vechten positioned his subject in front of a fanciful background of swirls, like pinwheels or lollipops. In the photograph, Du Bois's normally grave countenance looks amused.

W. E. B. Du Bois, 1946 (Yale Collection of American Literature, Beinecke Rare Book and Manuscript Library. Courtesy of the Carl Van Vechten Trust.)

Ultimately, Du Bois did donate some of his papers to Yale, but the majority of his material is at the W. E. B. Du Bois Library at the University of Massachusetts, Amherst.

Walter White wanted to assemble his papers for Yale, but he was busy. As secretary of the NAACP, White spent much of his time writing letters asking for donations and other kinds of support, just as he had done in his capacity as secretary of the James Weldon Johnson Memorial Committee. In 1942, Van Vechten received several letters from White on NAACP letterhead that detailed recent advances made by the organization. For instance, the NAACP had been involved in several court victories regarding institutional salary differentials based on color, and White was especially proud of the pledges he had secured from Hollywood motion picture producers to "present the Negro hereafter as a normal human being instead of always as a clown or comedian."[146]

But there was much more work to be done. Many war industries still refused to employ Negroes, despite the president's executive order banning such discrimination. A host of racist demagogues—Senators John Rankin and Theodore Bilbo of Mississippi, Governia Eugene Talmadge of Georgia, and Klan leader Horace Wilkinson of Alabama, among them—were "stirring up anti-Negro hatred throughout the South," White informed Van Vechten in a form letter sent to all NAACP supporters.[147] The Ku Klux Klan and similar hate groups were quickly replenishing their numbers. And lynchings had become more frequent— and more sadistic. In the same form letter, White reported that in October 1941, white men had used pliers to tear pieces of flesh from two fourteen-year-old black boys in Shubuta, Mississippi, in an attempt to force them to confess to a crime they had not committed.

Van Vechten was sympathetic to the aims of the NAACP, and he renewed his contributions to the organization every time he received a reminder, but he was single-minded when it came to his James Weldon Johnson Collection mission. "Dear Walter," he implored after receiving White's letter about the Shubuta lynching, "Is there ANYTHING I can do to get some action out of you in my direction? I have spent DAYS in preparing your material and have had some beautiful boxes made to contain it. Here they lie, waiting for your signature before they go to Yale. It would only take ten minutes, and besides we hanker for a sight of you. PLEASE." At the end of the letter he wrote, "Do I have to get lynched to get your attention?"[148]

Van Vechten begged White for his manuscripts and letters, and for him to come and sign his own books for the James Weldon Johnson Collection, well into the 1940s. White pleased him when he sent a manuscript of "The Creation," a classic sermon by James Weldon Johnson. Van Vechten thanked him, calling the manuscript one of the "gems of the Collection." But mostly he berated Walter for everything he hadn't done for the collection, once sending him a detailed list of all that he had neglected. "You see I am like an elephant and never never forget."[149] White would never get around to assembling his papers, but Van Vechten did receive them after White's death in 1955. They were sent by White's second wife, South African–born food writer

Poppy Cannon White. When Walter and Poppy married in 1949, many black people were outraged by the mixed marriage; some claimed, to White's horror, that his marriage had stripped him of his authority to act as a spokesman for his race.

Van Vechten had battled with ambivalent feelings about White over the entire course of their thirty-year friendship. Walter had both delighted and annoyed Carl, who considered him forward, but had also benefited from that forwardness, which gained him access to the inner circles of black New York. In some ways, White had played the same role in Van Vechten's life as White had played in the lives of black artists whose careers he had helped to build. Without White, there might have been no *Nigger Heaven*, just as there may have been no *Quicksand* or *The Weary Blues* without Van Vechten. (White had been a central force behind Larsen's career, too.) White certainly felt that the bond between them was deep; he had initially named his second son Carl Darrow White, after Van Vechten and a black surgeon friend who lived in Chicago. Dorothy, Nella, and Carl snickered together when White, ever concerned with his image, succumbed to pressure to change his son's name when he was criticized for naming him after a white man. For his part, Van Vechten was sufficiently fond of White to commemorate the day of their meeting every year.

"You really should not tell me you are going to give all my letters to Yale," Langston Hughes teased Van Vechten in 1941, "because now I will become self-conscious and no doubt verge toward the grandiloquent. Besides I was just about to tell you about a wonderful fight that took place in Togo's Pool Room in Monterey the other day in which various were cut from here to yonder and the lady who used to be the second wife of Noel's valet who came to New York with him that time succeeded in slicing several herself—but you know the Race would come out here and cut *me* if they knew I was relaying such news to posterity via the Yale library. So now how can I tell you?"[150]

Carl was delighted with Hughes's coy report. "Langston has sent me another manuscript and says he has ALL my letters safe for Yale," Carl wrote to Dorothy. "He says getting into Yale via his correspondence will make him self-conscious and then proceeds to write me the most exciting letter I've had from him in years."[151]

Two years later, Van Vechten was still waiting for Hughes's materials. "What letters *you* write!" began an August 1943 letter. "Maybe I do too. Sometimes I wonder if OUR letters wont be the pride of the Collection."[152] And then he waited for several more years. A lot had changed since 1925, when Carl could expect a letter from Langston nearly every day, and count on his young friend's prompt attention to all of his requests.

A NEW SONG

Van Vechten had been careful to keep money out of his relationship with Hughes, who was usually in a financial pinch, both because he was determined to live on his writing alone and he was a poor money manager. Early in their relationship, Hughes worked as a busboy at the Wardman Park Hotel in Washington, but his meager salary would not cover his tuition at Lincoln

University in Pennsylvania. "I'm trying to persuade somebody to lend me three hundred a year for the next three years, said amount to be returned to the lender within the same length of time after my graduation. That would put me through Lincoln, which is where I want to go," he angled. After the prejudice he had experienced during his first college stint at Columbia, Hughes had his sights set on Lincoln in large part because it was a black college. "Do you happen to know some philanthropic soul who might like to take a sporting chance on the development of genius and advance me said loan?"[153] Van Vechten wrote back immediately. "Unfortunately I don't know anybody at present I could ask for what you desire . . . but don't worry about it—if you really want to go to Lincoln, a way will provide itself: somehow they always do, when the desire is behind them." He urged Hughes to focus on his writing. "There may be money in *that* for you," he advised.[154] Ultimately, a philanthropic soul in the person of Amy Spingarn came to Hughes's rescue and lent him the three hundred dollars he needed to enroll in Lincoln in the spring. Carl did lend Langston money when Charlotte Mason dumped him—"His patron failed him & he borrows some money"—he recorded in his daybook[155]—but their relationship never developed a financial aspect. Problems arose between them, anyway—over the same issue that split Hughes and Mason, which was the change in Hughes's literary voice.

Van Vechten didn't like "Advertisement for the Waldorf-Astoria," a poetic rebuke of the imminent opening of the lush twenty-eight-million-dollar hotel in Manhattan, which did not admit black patrons. Hughes composed the poem in 1931, which he modeled on a multi-page advertisement for the hotel in *Vanity Fair*. In the poem, he encouraged the jobless to: "Dine with some of the men and women who got rich off of your labor, who clip coupons with clean white fingers because your hands dug coal, drilled stone, sewed garments, poured steel to let other people draw dividends and live easy." Hughes's strident anti-capitalist tone annoyed Van Vechten, who described it to Blanche Knopf as a "cheap way of thinking."[156] He didn't like the entire mood of the manuscript in which the poem was included, which Hughes was then calling *Good Morning Revolution*. Langston had already submitted the manuscript to Blanche Knopf, but Knopf never made decisions about the work of her black authors before checking with Van Vechten.

"The revolutionary poems seem very weak to me: I mean very weak on the lyric side," went Van Vechten's evaluation of Hughes's 1933 manuscript. "I think in ten years, whatever the social outcome, you will be ashamed of these. Why attack the Waldorf? This hotel employs more people than it serves and is at present one of the cheapest places any one can go to who wants to go to a hotel. It even seems a little ironic to me to ask a capitalist publisher to publish a book which is so very revolutionary and so little poetic in tone."[157]

Hughes took six weeks to respond. "Swell of you to write me so frankly about my poems," he began. "I agree with you, of course, that many of the poems are not as lyrical as they might be—but even at that I like some of them as well as anything I ever did—which is merely my taste against yours, and means nothing, as everyone has a right to his own likings, I guess. . . . About the Waldorf, I don't agree with you. At the time that I wrote the poem it was one of the best American symbols of too much against too little. I believe that you yourself told me that the dining room was so crowded that first week that folks wouldn't get in to eat $10.00 dinners. And not many blocks away the bread lines I saw were so long that other folks couldn't reach the soup kitchens for a plate of free and watery soup. . . . Blanche bases her note to me on your reactions."[158]

Hughes tried again the following year. "Re-submitted (revised and renamed) my book of proletarian poems to Blanche," he wrote to Van Vechten. He called the new version of the book *A New Song.* "I know you don't like them, but I do like them, and have been reading them with loud acclaim, even before the conservative Y. M. & Y. W. C. A. groups out here."[159]

Van Vechten still didn't like them. "In looking over your volume of poems again I find I like them even less than I did last year. In fact, I find them lacking in any of the elementary requisites of a work of art." A handwritten annotation placed in the margins of the letter reads: "This is a little too sweeping. I am speaking 'generally.' There are certain poems in the book that are very good indeed. Only less good than your best work in this form." He allowed that his assessment was subjective. "Doubtless I am wrong. At least you can rely on my being frank with you."[160]

When Blanche Knopf received the manuscript, she sent it directly to Carl, who wrote back the same day: "I think the revolutionary poems are pretty bad, more revolutionary than poetic; all this has been done a million times better." He gave her detailed advice on how to handle Hughes: "Of course, there can be no talk of his going elsewhere with the book. He should be written that of course you will print it if he insists upon it. I think stress should be laid on the fact that he has another book coming out and that it is impossible for a publisher to do justice to two books at once," Van Vechten instructed. "However, at all times, it should be stressed that you will print the book of course, if he wants it done. Langston is never unreasonable and I don't think he will be in this case. However, as you are going away, you'd better talk the situation over pretty thoroughly with Alfred, as many letters and telegrams may go through about this."[161] Blanche Knopf paraphrased whole sections of Van Vechten's letter in her response to Hughes.

The collection may not have been strong, certainly not nearly as strong as *The Weary Blues* or *Fine Clothes*, but Langston himself was as proud of the poems as he was of any of his work. He replied to Blanche the following day. "Dear Mrs. Knopf," he began, whereas he had previously addressed her as Blanche. He did not mean for the Knopf house to publish the book just to appease him, he said. Rather, he believed the collection represented an important response to the sociopolitical conditions of the moment. Would she please release the book so that he might turn it over to a publishing house that would produce it in an affordable format for a working-class audience? He had resigned himself to his predicament and reassured Blanche, "I have written Carl Van Vechten of this plan, and he thinks it is a good one."[162] In April 1938, the International Workers Order sponsored a printing of fifteen thousand copies at fifteen cents a copy.

In 1925, Alain Locke had described Van Vechten's championship of Hughes as the greatest contribution Van Vechten had made to the Negro Renaissance. Carl himself was proud of their relationship and was not shy about taking a substantial amount of credit for how far Hughes had come. But now the charming young poet had grown into a middle-aged man who sometimes disappointed him. "Am beginning to believe Langston must dislike me very much," Carl wrote to Dorothy Peterson in 1950. "Not a word about me in his library poem altho he mentions Sinclair Lewis and Bucklin Moon! Not a word about me at the opening of the Gershwin Collection at Fisk. Naturally he has written me more about Yale because HE is in it, but only at the threat of a whip, after long months, as you know."[163] But four days later, when Hughes read "Prelude to Our Age: A Negro History Poem" at the ceremony for the opening of the Schomburg Collection, Van Vechten's name did appear among a litany of whites friends of the Negro ("whose fingers intertwine / With mine tell our story, too").[164]

Langston had not forgotten his old friend, and he tried to demonstrate his enduring affection in 1957 when Knopf was preparing to publish his *Selected Poems*. Langston asked Carl to write the preface, "since you did it of my first, and this—so we would have come full circle together, poetically speaking!"[165] But Van Vechten's name no longer carried the literary weight that it once had, and editor Herbert Weinstock turned down Hughes's request to associate Van Vechten with his book.[166] Hughes shielded his friend from Weinstock's negative response in February. "My SELECTED POEMS is so big that Herbert Weinstock does not think it needs an introduction, so he recently informed me, so I reckon you can cross that off your writing schedule. But I would have liked it."[167]

Van Vechten began to tally up the number of letters and phone calls he received from Langston; he also began to scrutinize the quality of Hughes's letters. He may not have admitted it to Hughes, but he was still bothered by the mundane language Langston used in his salutations, as he informed Dorothy in a 1957 letter addressed to "Miss Dorothy Peterson, Dame of the American Commonwealth": "In a letter this AM from Mr. Hughes, he subscribes himself as 'affectionately,' I fainted."[168]

The previous year, Carl *did* faint, or keel over, as he described the episode in a letter to Dorothy. It was "a miscarriage, or a sunburst, or a bad housemaid's knee [bursitis], or something." Despite health concerns, he remained annoyed by what he perceived as neglect on Hughes's part. At the bottom of his letter to Dorothy, he noted that he had had no word from Langston.[169]

But Van Vechten was proud of the correspondence that *had* passed between them over the years. "Dear Langston," he wrote, "At last I have read all your back letters and arranged them chronologically, a terrific job, but one well worth the doing: they will go to Yale presently. They are among the most valuable lots in the Collection: warm (showing how colored and white get along on occasion), intimate, full of references to every living thing, and a mine of information about Negro habits and doings, full of enclosures, rich in folklore, and fabulous in friendship."[170]

The correspondence between Langston and Carl is gathered, like all of the correspondence between Van Vechten and his black friends, under a legend of his own creation: "Letters from Blacks."

A SENSITIVE AND SKILLFUL INTERPRETER

Van Vechten described his philosophy of friendship to an interviewer in 1960. He borrowed the sentiment of the English writer Nancy Mitford, who once called friendship "a work of art," something that must be cultivated in order to thrive. Van Vechten said, "There are some people who have no sense of values who are careless about friendship, and when they're careless with me, it's just the end."[171]

On his eighty-fourth birthday, four months before he died, Van Vechten received a card from Grace Nail Johnson that included an excerpt from "The Art of Friendship," a poem by Wilferd Peterson. "The first step in the art of friendship is to be a friend," the excerpt begins. Carl Van Vechten certainly excelled in the arena of friendship, and inspired fierce attachment in those who loved him.

Upon receiving her usual birthday greetings from Carl in 1953, Nora Holt waxed sentimental about their relationship. "Of all my friends you are the arch offender, envoyer of sweet dreams and never to be forgotten experiences, that give life and illumination to waning years." She missed the parties Van Vechten had hosted at his West 55th Street apartment in the heyday of Harlem, and reminisced about the "enchanting friends, now gone, who gave zest and charm to nights of revelry and mornings of spent emotions."[172]

Through careful tending on the part of both Nora and Carl, the friendship between them thrived for forty years, since the first time he saw her dancing nude at a party at the studio of German-born artist Winold Reiss in 1925. "I was out last night with the Sheka of Harlem," Van Vechten wrote to H. L. Mencken after one of the first of many thrilling evenings he would spend with Holt. He compared her to another opera singer, a white Scottish soprano. "She looks like Mary Garden & and her trail is strewn with bones, many of them no longer hard."[173] Thirty years later, still as grand as ever, she was on Van Vechten's arm in New Haven where Donald Gallup, then curator of the Yale University Library, had arranged an exhibition of items from the collections Van Vechten had established at Yale.

It was ultimately the particular artistry of his style of friendship that made the James Weldon Johnson Collection at Yale possible. He knew the materials as intimately as he had known many of those who had produced them. The main catalogue to the collection, which is six hundred fifty-eight pages long, is annotated with Carl's personal commentary. It is more than simply a practical guide to the materials: it is a record of his passion for the people who had enraptured him since his college days in Chicago forty years earlier. His guide leads the researcher into the heart of what the people and the work of the Harlem Renaissance meant to him. He introduced researchers to the correspondence of James Weldon Johnson with his own nostalgia: "During his lifetime, I always had the feeling that James Weldon Johnson was a great man, perhaps the greatest it has ever been my good fortune to know personally."[174]

In his notes on the phonograph records, Van Vechten instructed the uninitiated: "The Blues are the Negro's prayers to a cruel Cupid. They are songs of disappointed love."[175] He noted that certain letters might be of "high interest," such as those

Nora Holt, 1930 (Photograph by James Marqis Connely. Yale Collection of American Literature, Beinecke Rare Book and Manuscript Library. Courtesy of the Carl Van Vechten Trust.)

Nora Holt and Carl Van Vechten at Yale, June 22, 1955 (Photograph by Saul Mauriber. Yale Collection of American Literature, Beinecke Rare Book and Manuscript Library. Courtesy of the Carl Van Vechten Trust.)

in the collections of Nora Holt and Paul Robeson's wife, Essie. He lauded the talents of Ethel Waters: "Her performances are notable for their deep expressiveness, correct intonation, clear enunciation, and marvelous rhythm," and then detailed which of her records are "obscene." He provided a context for researchers to understand the language she used in her letters to him. "Such addresses as "My Nordic Lover" in the second letter and subscriptions like "your native mama" in the first are Ethel's idea of good clean fun."[176] Just as he did in his daybooks upon first making the acquaintance of a person, he made a note about each contributor's race: (N) for Negro, (W) for white. Carl insisted on the racial classification when a curator challenged its significance. "I would like to point out here that one of the first questions asked about a new author of a new story of Negro life is whether it was written by a Negro or a white man and that any curator of this material or librarian will have to answer similar questions 20 times a day," wrote Van Vechten to Yale curator James Babb.[177]

In his catalogue for the James Weldon Johnson Collection, Van Vechten was critical of the current generation of black writers, particularly those who would come to define the post–Negro Renaissance period. "James Baldwin (N): Go Tell It On The Mountain. First edition in dust jacket. An authentic book, extremely well written, intelligent and felt, but curiously not very interesting."[178] Van Vechten called Baldwin one of his "favorite writers" in a 1956 letter to Dorothy Peterson.[179] He was more impressed with Baldwin's nonfiction writing than his stories, and annotated his catalogue entry for *Notes of a Native*

Son, Baldwin's 1955 collection of essays thus: "This is practically the first important appearance of the Negro as essayist. Mr. Baldwin makes a magnificent start in the right direction. He is, however, somewhat iconoclastic in his ideas."[180]

Van Vechten had strong opinions about Baldwin's contemporaries as well. On Richard Wright's *The Outsiders:* "The novel has vitality, tells a story vividly, and the author's narrative sense is extremely good, but the characters do not awaken compassion or any other emotion. One follows the crimes breathlessly, but the criminals do not awaken interest. Probably Wright is trying to eschew propaganda, to deal with pure narration. He is on his way, but certainly has not reached his goal." But he was thrilled about Ralph Ellison's tour de force, *Invisible Man.* "This sensational novel by a new Negro author will be published on April 14. The Communist chapters are terrific."[181] Ellison was not, however, enthralled with Van Vechten. "I despised his photography," he told biographer Arnold Rampersad. "In fact, I didn't care for the whole Van Vechten influence. It introduced a note of decadence into Afro-American literary matters which was not needed."[182] Ellison was also a photographer but he, like the actor Sidney Poitier, refused to sit before Van Vechten's camera.

The James Weldon Johnson Collection of American Negro Arts and Letters opened on January 7, 1950. Charles S. Johnson, who was then president of Fisk University, was asked to give a formal address to mark the occasion. "Of all the magnificent writings of Carl Van Vechten, and his contributions, as sensitive and skillful an interpreter of a period and class of American life," he told his audience, "one of the most important of his services

Cover of 1951 edition of *Nigger Heaven* (Avon Books. Yale Collection of American Literature, Beinecke Rare Book and Manuscript Library.)

has been that of the introduction to American literature of the Negro as a person rather than a type, thus breaking the dismally persistent stereotype that has obscured and distorted virtually every external view of this race in America."[183]

Van Vechten believed he had even more to celebrate when, a year later, Avon publishers reissued *Nigger Heaven* in a twenty-five-cent paperback edition, but the resurrection of the 1926 novel did not last long. As Van Vechten wrote to Donald Gallup in November 1951, "Some Negro has objected to Nigger Heaven again and the cheap edition has been withdrawn by the publisher."[184] Avon editor in chief Charles R. Byrne had tried to convince Van Vechten to change the title, but he was adamant: "THE TITLE CANNOT BE CHANGED" was his response to Byrne's request.[185] Byrne issued a formal statement to announce the withdrawal of *Nigger Heaven:* "Since it is our practice not to give offense to any racial or religious minority, we decided that the proper thing to do would be to withdraw this book from newsstand sale."[186]

In 1955, Van Vechten received an honorary doctorate of letters from Fisk, "a university he has befriended more than once," a reporter for the *Nashville Tennessean* explained.[187] Van Vechten called receiving the honor "the biggest event of the Fifties." Carl appreciated the singularity of the honor. "Fisk University in its eighty years has given very few people honorary degrees—I think eight, maybe ten—and they're all people like Ralphe Bunche, very very important people, so that's quite an honor." He was as proud of his honorary doctorate as he was of the party that followed. "The Negroes gave me a very big party, very successful.

The party was at Jimmy Daniels' nightclub in the Village, on 8th Street, called Bon Soir."[188] The guest list was limited to twenty of the friends he had had for twenty years and more. George Schuyler was on hand to praise him: "We, in our poor way, pay tribute tonight to our good friend who put the hex on jim crow, who has been tireless in his persistence, who has opened countless minds and hearts in circles where it has done incalculable good for all concerned."[189]

Van Vechten received the honorary degree from Fisk in part because he had established the George Gershwin Memorial Collection of Music and Musical Literature at the university. A reporter for *Time* magazine (in whose pages Van Vechten had been ridiculed in 1925 for spending his time with Negroes) applauded the racial angle of Van Vechten's archival projects in 1944: "One way to get Negroes to visit white schools and vice versa is to tempt them. Novelist Carl Van Vechten has done just that with a scheme involving Yale and Fisk Universities."[190] The George Gershwin Memorial Collection, officially opened in 1947, includes letters, musical scores, first editions, recordings, and scrapbooks of American musical history.

Two years later, Van Vechten persuaded Georgia O'Keeffe to donate a collection of paintings to Fisk, which was christened the Alfred Stieglitz Collection after her late husband, and which included the work of Marsden Hartley, Henry Demuth, Arthur Dove, and Van Vechten's dear friend Florine Stettheimer. The collection is housed in the Carl Van Vechten Gallery at Fisk University. He also chose Fisk as the site for the Florine Stettheimer Memorial Collection of Books about the Fine Arts.

Van Vechten created other collections. He had been collecting material for the Anna Marble Pollock Memorial Library of Books about Cats since he wrote *Tiger in the House* in 1920. He donated the entire library, named for his first friend in New York, the wife of playwright Channing Pollock, to Yale in 1948. He donated a selection of his photographs to his hometown high school. He created the Rose McClendon Memorial Collection of Celebrated Negroes at Howard University.

And the New York Public Library received several collections of his books, photographs, and correspondence. The Carl Van Vechten Collection of the New York Public Library contains all materials relating to his books as well as artifacts of his personal life, including family photographs, correspondence, college themes, and his daybooks. The New York Public Library exhibited a collection of his material for public view on his birthday in 1955. It was the first time the library had so honored a living author. Five years later, he would be absorbed into the library's bones. "The New York Public Library is carving my name in stone on one of the columns of the library," Van Vechten announced to interviewer William Ingersoll in 1960. "There are very few authors, if any, on the list," he said. He would be in the company of "Rockefeller and Astor and Ford and Tilden and all those people. I feel like a millionaire up with all those millionaires, and I'm sure it will enhance my credit."[191]

In 1963 Van Vechten would attend the dedication ceremony of the Beinecke Rare Book and Manuscript Library, which is now the repository of the James Weldon Johnson Collection. The modernist personality of the Beinecke building is a stunning contrast to the gothic style of Sterling Library, where the collection was originally held. Built under the leadership of curator James Babb, the Beinecke is a structure of "Platonic purity: exactly twice as deep as high, and three times as long." Its opaque walls serve as a "marble and granite mirror, gathering and giving out natural light in ways that intensify experience and sometimes even produce beauty."[192] Visible from the reading room is a sculpture court designed by Isamu Noguchi, whom Van Vechten photographed in 1935. Grace Nail Johnson went to visit the Beinecke Library for the first time in 1964, seven months before Van Vechten died. It was beautiful, she told him.[193]

BACK BEFORE MY TIME

In 1960, Van Vechten described the experience of rereading his old letters. "A great deal of it was pleasant, some was nostalgic, some downright interesting," he said. "You never know what letters are going to interest the future generations." The 1960 interview served as a good time to reflect upon a life eighty years in the making. He explained himself, then reversed himself. His social life in Cedar Rapids was not nearly as dismal as he had characterized it at an earlier point in the interview, he confessed, especially his complaint about having few people to talk to. "I don't remember what I had to talk about that was so damn interesting." He described some of the cultural changes he had witnessed. When he was a child in Cedar Rapids, there were no phones, so people communicated across backyard fences.[194]

In another interview he talked about falling in love with New York when he first arrived in 1906. "The streets were rather magnificent then, with horse-drawn carriages on them. Lord, I go back *before* my time!"[195] But although he could no longer walk long distances easily, and his hearing had deteriorated, significant features of his life had not changed at all, he told Ingersoll. "Some people think in old age you feel differently from what you were when you were young. That's not true at all. I feel exactly the same way I felt when I was eighteen years old."[196] Except he had more sense, he told black writer Chester Himes.[197]

Van Vechten's commitment to nurturing the talents of black writers never waned, not even in old age when, in his oral history interview, he publicized the talents of black writer Chester Himes, whose 1947 novel *Lonely Crusade* he called "the best novel ever written yet by a Negro." Van Vechten was also drawn to Himes because of his dramatic past (as a young man, he had spent eight years in prison for armed robbery) and uncompromising personality. "Chester is very intransigent and I'm about the only person, black or white, that he's ever got along with more or less permanently."[198] He was protective of the notoriously tough Himes, and tender with him, too. "If my letters touch you, it is nothing to what your letters do to me," he wrote to Himes in 1961. Just as he had done over the years with many friends who brought him their troubles, including Eric Walrond, Essie Robeson, Nella Larsen, and Dorothy Peterson, Van Vechten gave Himes counsel. "You are at last, I believe, growing up and beginning to understand what any one has to face sooner or later, the mysteries, and agonies, and wonders of life," wrote Van Vechten, who was almost thirty years Himes's senior. "There is seemingly no solution for any of this. We actually have to learn to grin and bear it." He encouraged Himes to channel his rage and sadness into his writing. "I have always wanted you to write a book to top Lonely Crusade and I think you can," he assured Himes. "You can write about Negroes or white people, but no race problems this time, please."[199]

Van Vechten had predicted to H. L. Mencken in 1925 that he would eventually grow out of his interest in the Negro, but he never did. As he wrote to Langston Hughes in 1964: "You and I have been through so many new negroes that we are a little tired of it all. BUT I was really excited about the group you have brought together. Le Roi Jones who appears to be somebody. . . . I wonder when he & Baldwin will have a fight! It will be a big one."[200]

Van Vechten died seven months later, on December 21, 1964.

"Carl Van Vechten Is Dead," announced the *Amsterdam News*, the paper in which journalist Hubert Harrison had years before seared him and his novel *Nigger Heaven*. The reporter remembered Van Vechten fondly, particularly his passion for photography, as did the author of Carl's *New York Times* obituary. Both papers noted that he had gone to bed unusually early on the night of his death, and then died overnight.[201] Van Vechten was eighty-four years old.

Langston Hughes delivered a tribute to Van Vechten a few months later at the American Academy of Arts and Letters, then known as the National Institute of Arts and Letters. (Van Vechten himself had been inducted a few years earlier. He informed Chester Himes in a 1961 letter: "At this advanced age I have been voted into the Institute of Arts and Letters. I was too daring for the sober set that governed the Institute when I was writing books, but now that Henry Miller is a member there is little reason to keep me out").[202] Hughes remembered Carl's life in the world of letters and friendship as "a long and happy sojourn." He told his listeners that while Van Vechten had aged he had not grown old, because the surest "sign of old age is when a man begins to disapprove of the young."[203] In his own eulogy, George Schuyler remembered Van Vechten as "the indomitable Dutchman" through whom "the best of Harlem and the stream of Caucasian culture came to a meeting of the ways. Americanism took on new dimensions which all now see and know and share."[204]

Nora Holt sent a telegram to Fania Marinoff immediately upon hearing of Carl's death. In a subsequent letter to Van Vechten's widow, she wrote: "I think of you everyday and wonder how you are. Days are very sad for me as I miss the cards and letters from darling Carlo. I am desolate when I contemplate the years to come and he is not here. Then I can only look back on the years that were. Lovely, gentle years!"[205]

The remaining years of Fania Marinoff's life were not gentle. She had never wanted to live without Carl, and never fully recovered from the loss. In the end, she gradually lost all her senses except touch. Seven years after her husband died, Fania Marinoff, Van Vechten's "maid of many moods," as he had once described her, was gone, too.

"When someone vanishes, he disappears into two kinds of history, private and public," wrote Lincoln Kirstein in a 1965 tribute to Carl Van Vechten.[206] To a large degree, Van Vechten has disappeared into the public history occasioned by the commotion over his 1926 novel *Nigger Heaven*. But the questions at the heart of the book—the relationship between race and art as well as the power of language—are much bigger than the novel itself. Similarly, the Harlem Renaissance, the first moment in African American history during which African Americans were able to wrestle with these questions collectively, is much larger than Van Vechten's role within it. But grander than either Van Vechten's novel or the Harlem Renaissance is the archive of the James Weldon Johnson Collection. It is the epic theater of blackness that Du Bois, Johnson, and Van Vechten believed they were witnessing as they sat in the audience of Ridgley Torrence's play *Granny Maumee;* it is a catalogue of the excitement of that moment as well as the disappointments, frustrations, and triumphs—large and small—that African American artists experienced in subsequent years. As much as it is a repository of manuscripts, records, and photographs, the collection is a storehouse of conversations, ideas, passions, and grudges; and of political and personal ambitions to uplift the status of blacks in this country. The collection, made possible by the intersecting lives of Carl Van Vechen and the Harlem Renaissance, is not only Van Vechten's greatest bequest, it is the greatest bequest of the era. It is itself a living history of the life of Carl Van Vechten and of the black artists and writers who shared his passion for blackness. Like *Granny Maumee*, the collection is a tour de force: a New Negro dream come true.

AUTHOR'S NOTE

Nigger Heaven was my beginning. The title jumped out from a list of essay topics in a junior seminar on African American literature. I was shocked, unsettled, and intrigued. When I learned that a white man had written the novel, my trinity of emotions deepened.

I have followed these emotions for the last twenty years, trying to get to the root of them, to settle on a feeling. I wavered once in college after I decided to concentrate my senior thesis on white patronage during the Harlem Renaissance. The topic was a ruse: I was really interested only in Carl Van Vechten. But my courage faltered when a friend and fellow student pointed out, "Of all the people to write about who lived during the Harlem Renaissance, you choose to write about a white man." His face was full of disappointment. I had let him down; I had let the race down. It was too late to change topics, so I proceeded, shamefacedly. It would be years before I learned to love the seeming paradox: a black woman inspired by the black addiction of a white man.

But I understood what my friend meant. He felt about Van Vechten the way many black people who lived, read, and wrote in the 1920s felt about him: that he was an intruder into the world of blackness. And many people, of all races, find the very idea that a white man would use the word *nigger* in the title of a book—would use the world *nigger* at all—unsavory, to say the least. Carl Van Vechten's intentions were and continue to be questionable. But I could not resist my own passion, which is much like the passion—perhaps questionable but certainly binding—that ineluctably interlaces the story of Carl Van Vechten and the story of the Harlem Renaissance.

Another friend once said to me that we are always writing our own biographies, no matter the subject. This book certainly has been occasioned by my personal history. Appropriately—and to me, prophetically—I was a student at Yale University when I began to read and write about Carl Van Vechten. The James Weldon Johnson Collection was, literally, steps away from my dorm when I was an undergraduate. In those early years, when my own addiction begin to take hold, I felt about Van Vechten the way he himself felt about his relationship to black people and culture—as if something like fate was at work.

My interest in the Harlem Renaissance in general began in adolescence. I grew up in the shadow of Fisk University. My mother often told me stories about being a student there, particularly about the gentility of Arna Bontemps, Langston Hughes's best friend, who took an appointment as librarian at Fisk in the early 1940s. My mother told stories, too, of the poet Robert Hayden, who taught a seminar with Hughes and Bontemps in the late 1940s. Hayden was only thirteen during the heyday of the Harlem Renaissance but, like other poets and fiction writers of his generation, he was an inheritor of the tradition. Hayden's legendary poor sight, my mother said, was only slightly enhanced by his Coke-bottle glasses. He would often not recognize my mother, herself a poet whom Hayden mentored, until he came to the point of nearly passing her by on campus walkways. He was a very gracious man, she said.

My mother also told me a story about Langston Hughes. Hayden had arranged for her to meet Hughes when he and Bontemps invited the poet to Fisk to lecture and visit their classes. My mother, who was always prone to respiratory illness, contracted the whooping cough on the day of the meeting. She told me this story without regret, but my twelve-year-old heart stung for her, and for what might have been.

After my mother died, the nature of my research trips to New Haven seemed to take on a new character, and once when I crossed the threshold of the Rare Book and Manuscript room at the Beinecke, it occurred to me that the reasons why I kept coming back were, in essence, to remember the dead and, hopefully, to contribute something to the future. "We all yearn for transcendence, for immortal life, to be part of the future," wrote the late Yale historian of African art, Professor Sylvia Ardyn Boone.[1] Perhaps those people who spend their lives in libraries yearn also to be of service to the past and the future. Carl Van Vechten entrusted some of his dearest stories to the Beinecke library, and several other libraries, and it has been my pleasure to bear witness to and wrestle with the rich and dense legacy he left behind.

When he was eighty years old, Carl Van Vechten discussed the experience of aging with William Ingersoll. "A great many people who are dead are more alive than a great many people who are alive," Van Vechten said.[2] And so he has been for me.

My life with Carl Van Vechten has been a long and happy sojourn, and I feel some sadness as I reach its end. But as I write these final lines, I am soothed by the words of blues musician Willie Dixon, "I can't quit you baby, / but I got to put you down a little while."

NOTES

All material located in the James Weldon Johnson Memorial Collection is in the Yale Collection of American Literature, Beinecke Rare Book and Manuscript Library, Yale University, New Haven, Connecticut, is cited as James Weldon Johnson Collection. All material located in the Carl Van Vechten Papers in the New York Public Library is cited as Carl Van Vechten Papers.

INTRODUCTION

1. Carl Van Vechten, "The Reminiscences of Carl Van Vechten," 193, interview with William Ingersoll, Oral History Research Office, Columbia University, New York, March 3, 1960.
2. Countee Cullen to Carl Van Vechten, June 29, 1925, James Weldon Johnson Collection.
3. Eric Walrond to Carl Van Vechten, March 20, 1925, James Weldon Johnson Collection.
4. Rudolph Fisher's inscription to Van Vechten, May 16, 1926, James Weldon Johnson Collection.
5. Fannie Hurst, "Zora Neale Hurston: A Personality Sketch," *Yale University Library Gazette,* July 1960, 18.
6. Nora Holt to Carl Van Vechten, June 27, 1954, James Weldon Johnson Collection.
7. Harold Cruse, *The Crisis of the Negro Intellectual: A Historical Analysis of the Failure of Black Leadership* (New York: Morrow, 1967), 37, 85.

1 A NICHE SOMEWHERE

1. Carl Van Vechten, *Sacred and Profane Memories* (New York: Knopf, 1932), 27.
2. Van Vechten, "Reminiscences," 5.
3. Ibid., 16.
4. Van Vechten, *Sacred and Profane Memories,* 12.
5. Ibid., 191.
6. Ibid., 2, 12.
7. Ibid., vii, 2.
8. Ibid., 10.
9. Ibid., 6–7, 3–4.
10. Bruce Kellner, *Carl Van Vechten and the Irreverent Decades* (Norman: University of Oklahoma Press, 1968), 16–17.
11. Ibid., 46.
12. Bruce Kellner, "Carlo's Wife," in *Kiss Me, Again: An Invitation to a Group of Noble Dames* (New York: Turtle Point, 2002), 186.
13. Van Vechten, "Reminiscences," 150.
14. *New York World-Telegram,* March 20, 1932, Carl Van Vechten, scrapbooks, Carl Van Vechten Papers.
15. Carl Van Vechten, *The Tattooed Countess* (New York: Knopf, 1924), 267–68.
16. Van Vechten, *Sacred and Profane Memories,* 30.
17. Ibid., 225, 230.
18. Ibid., 215; Kellner, *Carl Van Vechten and the Irreverent Decades,* 33.
19. Quoted in ibid., 80–81.
20. Carl Van Vechten, *In the Garrett* (New York: Knopf, 1920), 312.
21. Carl Van Vechten, "Biondina," 1, 3, Miscellaneous College Themes, Carl Van Vechten Papers.
22. Carl Van Vechten, "The Inky Ones,"1, Miscellaneous College Themes, Carl Van Vechten Papers.
23. Van Vechten, *Sacred and Profane Memories,* 225.
24. Van Vechten, "Reminiscences," 15.
25. Carl Van Vechten, *Letters of Carl Van Vechten,* ed. Bruce Kellner (New Haven: Yale University Press, 1987), 78.

26. Wallace Thurman, "Harlem Facets," *World Tomorrow,* November 1927, reprinted in *The Collected Writings of Wallace Thurman,* ed. Amritjit Singh and Daniel M. Scott III (New Brunswick: Rutgers University Press, 2003), 35.
27. Alain Locke, ed., *The New Negro* (New York: Albert & Charles Boni, 1925), 6.
28. *New York Herald Tribune Books,* December 20, 1925, 5.
29. A. Philip Randolph, "A New Crowd—A New Negro," in *Voices from the Harlem Renaissance,* ed. Nathan Irvin Huggins (New York: Oxford University Press, 1976), 18–20.
30. Locke, *The New Negro,* 3.
31. Langston Hughes, "My Early Days in Harlem," *Freedomways* 3 (Summer 1963), reprinted in *The Collected Works of Langston Hughes,* vol. 9, *Essays on Art, Race, Politics, and World Affairs,* ed. Christopher C. De Santis (Columbia: University of Missouri Press, 2002), 395–96.
32. Langston Hughes, *The Big Sea* (New York: Hill & Wang, 1940), 81, 85.
33. Ibid., 224, 223.
34. James Weldon Johnson, *Black Manhattan* (New York: Da Capo, 1930), 186.
35. Carl Van Vechten, "Prescription for the Negro Theatre," *Vanity Fair,* October 1925, 46.
36. Thurman, "Harlem Facets," 33, 35.
37. James Weldon Johnson, *Along This Way* (New York: Viking Penguin, 1933), 380.
38. Hughes, *The Big Sea,* 273–78.
39. Claude McKay, *A Long Way from Home* (New York: Harcourt Brace Jovanovich, 1970), 133.
40. Hughes, *The Big Sea,* 225.
41. Thurman, "Harlem Facets," 37.
42. Rudolph Fisher, "The Caucasian Storms Harlem," in *The Portable Harlem Renaissance Reader,* ed. David Levering Lewis (New York: Viking Penguin, 1995), 115.
43. Hughes, *The Big Sea,* 224–25.

44. Langston Hughes, "Who's Passing for Who?" in *Langston Hughes: Short Stories,* ed. Akiba Sullivan Harper (New York: Hill & Wang, 1996), 170, 173–74.

45. Van Vechten, "Reminiscences," 207.

46. McKay, *A Long Way from Home,* 132–33.

47. Johnson, *Black Manhattan,* 175.

48. Quoted in Susan Curtis, *The First Black Actors on the Great White Way* (Columbia: University of Missouri Press, 1998), 8.

49. Quoted in ibid., 3.

50. Ibid., 5, 8, 20.

51. Ridgely Torrence, *Granny Maumee, The Rider of Dreams, Simon the Cyrenian* (New York: Macmillan, 1917), 3.

52. Ibid., 23.

53. Ibid., 30.

54. Carl Van Vechten, "The Negro Theatre," in *In the Garret,* 318.

55. Ibid., 319.

56. See Eric Lott, *Love and Theft: Blackface Minstrelsy and the American Working Class* (New York: Oxford University Press, 1995), for its singular discussion of blackface minstrelsy as a tradition that represents white ambivalence toward black people, born of both admiration and ridicule.

57. Carl Van Vechten, "A Note on American Letters," in *"Keep A-Inchin' Along": Selected Writings of Carl Van Vechten on Black Art and Letters,* ed. Bruce Kellner (Westport, Conn.: Greenwood, 1979), 28.

58. Van Vechten, "The Negro Theatre," 312–16.

59. Ibid., 312.

60. James Weldon Johnson to Carl Van Vechten, February 28, 1925, James Weldon Johnson Collection.

61. Charles S. Johnson, "The Negro Renaissance and Its Significance," in *The Harlem Renaissance,* ed. Harold Bloom (Broomall, Pa.: Chelsea House, 2004), 174.

62. McKay, *A Long Way from Home,* 112.

63. Quoted in Johnson, "The Negro Renaissance and Its Significance," 177.

64. Ibid., 174.

65. Carl Van Vechten, *The Splendid Drunken Twenties: Selections from the Daybooks, 1922–1930,* ed. Bruce Kellner (Urbana: University of Illinois Press, 2003), 99.

66. Quoted in Jervis Anderson, *This Was Harlem* (New York: Farrar, Straus & Giroux, 1981), 201.

67. Quoted in Arna Bontemps, "The Awakening: A Memoir," in *The Harlem Renaissance Remembered,* ed. Arna Bontemps (New York: Dodd, Mead, 1972), 13.

68. McKay, *A Long Way from Home,* 102.

69. Quoted in Bontemps, "The Awakening," 13–14.

70. Hughes, *The Big Sea,* 218.

71. A critical review that Cullen wrote of *The Weary Blues,* Hughes's first book, prompted his closest friend Harold Jackman, a high school teacher in Harlem, to warn him that it might create speculation that he was jealous of Hughes, a suspicion that Cullen dismissed as "pure rubbish." Countee Cullen to Harold Jackman, January 6, 1926, James Weldon Johnson Collection. Langston Hughes, "The Weary Blues," in *The Collected Poems of Langston Hughes,* ed. Arnold Rampersad and David Roessel (New York: Knopf, 1998), 50.

72. Van Vechten, "Reminiscences," 20.

73. Carl Van Vechten, daybooks, November 10, 1924, Carl Van Vechten Papers. Florence Mills was a much-beloved dancer and singer, a star in the world of black theater. Rosamond Johnson was a composer and musician. He collaborated with his brother, James Weldon Johnson, on what is still known as the Negro National Anthem, "Lift Ev'ry Voice and Sing." Bill "Bojangles" Robinson was a song and dance man, a success in vaudeville and later on Broadway.

74. Carl Van Vechten to Edna Kenton, c. August 1924, in *Letters of Carl Van Vechten,* 69.

75. Van Vechten, "Reminiscences," 20.

76. Martin Duberman, *Paul Robeson* (New York: New Press, 1989), 80.

77. Carl Van Vechten to Fania Marinoff, August 4, 1929, James Weldon Johnson Collection.

78. Duberman, *Paul Robeson,* 229.

79. Ethel Waters, *His Eye Is on the Sparrow* (New York: Doubleday, 1951), 194.

80. Ibid.

81. Ibid., 195, 196.

82. Carl Van Vechten, "Negro 'Blues' Singers," *Vanity Fair,* March 1926, 106.

83. Waters, *His Eye Is on the Sparrow,* 194–96.

84. Zora Neale Hurston, *Dust Tracks on a Road* (Urbana: University of Illinois Press, 1942), 243, 245.

85. Ibid., 309–10.

86. Hurst, "Zora Neale Hurston," 19.

87. Carl Van Vechten, "Some 'Literary Ladies' I Have Known," *Yale University Gazette,* January 1952, 113.

88. Zora Neale Hurston, *Zora Neale Hurston: A Life in Letters,* ed. Carla Kaplan (New York: Doubleday, 2002), 290.

89. Thomas H. Wirth, ed., *Gay Rebel of the Harlem Renaissance: Selections from the Work of Richard Bruce Nugent* (Durham: Duke University Press, 2002), 226.

90. Van Vechten, "Reminiscences," 198.

91. Kellner, *Carl Van Vechen and the Irreverent Decades,* 162.

92. Van Vechten, daybooks, April 4, 1925.

93. Hughes, *The Big Sea,* 254.

94. Nora Holt to Fania Marinoff, August 13, 1925, James Weldon Johnson Collection.

95. Emily Bernard, ed., *Remember Me to Harlem* (New York: Knopf, 2001), 32.

96. Hughes, *The Big Sea,* 253–54.

97. Carl Van Vechten to Langston Hughes, November 12, 1939, James Weldon Johnson Collection.

98. Van Vechten, "Reminiscences," 355.

99. Carl Van Vechten, "Fragments from an Unwritten Autobiography," 7, Yale University Library, New Haven, 1955.

100. Van Vechten, daybooks, May 19, 1927.

101. "A 'Stewed' Author," *New York Age,* November 27, 1926, Carl Van Vechten Papers.

102. Van Vechten, daybooks, September 14, 1926.

103. Ibid., June 25, 1926.
104. Van Vechten, scrapbooks, vols. 24, 25, Carl Van Vechten Papers.
105. Ibid., vols. 27, 28.
106. "Reunion," *New Yorker,* March 26, 1927, Van Vechten, scrapbooks, vol. 21, Carl Van Vechten Papers.
107. Waters, *His Eye Is on the Sparrow,* 195.
108. Van Vechten, "Reminiscences," 336.
109. Kevin J. Mumford, *Interzones: Black/White Sex Districts in Chicago and New York in the Early Twentieth Century* (New York: Columbia University Press, 1997), 30.
110. Ibid., 178.
111. Ibid., 32.
112. Mezz Mezzrow and Bernard Wolfe, *Really the Blues* (New York: Random House, 1946).
113. Marianna Torgovnick, *Gone Primitive: Savage Intellects, Modern Lives* (Chicago: University of Chicago Press, 1990).
114. Sigmund Freud, *Civilization and Its Discontents,* ed. James Strachey (New York: Norton, 1961), 39.
115. Quoted in Colin Rhodes, *Primitivism and Modern Art* (London: Thames & Hudson, 1994), 69.
116. Van Vechten, "Reminiscences," 206.
117. Carl Van Vechten, *Nigger Heaven* (New York: Knopf, 1926), 89.
118. Mabel Dodge Luhan, *Movers and Shakers* (New York: Harcourt, Brace, 1936), 80.
119. Van Vechten, "Fragments," 37–38.
120. Luhan, *Movers and Shakers,* 15, 45.
121. Ibid., 80.
122. Ibid.
123. Van Vechten, "The Negro Theatre," 316.
124. Langston Hughes, "The Negro Artist and the Racial Mountain," in Henry Louis Gates Jr. and Nellie Y. McKay, eds., *The Norton Anthology of African American Literature* (New York: Norton, 2004), 1311–12.
125. Hughes, *The Big Sea,* 10, 106, 11.
126. Hughes, "The Negro Artist and the Racial Mountain," 1314.

127. Robert B. Stepto, *From behind the Veil: A Study of Afro-American Narrative* (Urbana: University of Illinois Press, 1991), xiv.

128. Langston Hughes to Carl Van Vechten, October 30, 1941, James Weldon Johnson Collection.

129. Carl Van Vechten to Langston Hughes, after October 29, 1925, December 31, 1932, January 22, 1946, April 6, 1954, James Weldon Johnson Collection.

130. Carl Van Vechten to Langston Hughes, November 19, 1957, James Weldon Johnson Collection.

131. Langston Hughes to Carl Van Vechten, November 30, 1957, James Weldon Johnson Collection.

132. Carl Van Vechten to Langston Hughes, October 30, 1958, James Weldon Johnson Collection.

133. George Chauncey, *Gay New York: Gender, Urban Culture, and the Making of the Gay Male World, 1890–1940* (New York: Basic Books, 1994), 304.

134. Ibid., 328.

135. Hughes, *The Big Sea*, 273–74.

136. Mumford, *Interzones*, 84.

137. See Eric Garber, "A Spectacle in Color: The Lesbian and Gay Subculture of Jazz Age Harlem," in *Hidden from History: Reclaiming the Gay and Lesbian Past*, ed. Martin Duberman, Martha Vicinus, and George Chauncey (New York: New American Library, 1989), 318–33.

138. Mumford, *Interzones*, 84.

139. Jonathan Weinberg, " 'Boy Crazy': Carl Van Vechten's Queer Collection," *Yale Journal of Criticism* 7 (Fall 1994): 28.

140. Carl Van Vechten, scrapbooks, vol. 3, James Weldon Johnson Collection.

141. Weinberg, " 'Boy Crazy,' " 31.

142. Van Vechten, scrapbooks, vol. 9, James Weldon Johnson Collection.

143. Ibid., vol. 8.

144. Ibid., vol. 3.

145. Elizabeth Alexander, *The Black Interior* (Minneapolis: Graywolf, 2004) 21.

146. Hughes, "The Negro Artist and the Racial Mountain," 1312.

147. Carl Van Vechten to Langston Hughes, November 4, 1941, James Weldon Johnson Collection.

148. Arnold Rampersad, *The Life of Langston Hughes* (New York: Oxford University Press, 1988), 1:81.

149. Ibid., 1:66–71.

150. Langston Hughes, *I Wonder as I Wander: An Autobiographical Journey* (New York: Hill & Wang, 1993), 256; Rampersad, *The Life of Langston Hughes*, 1:288.

151. "Clippings about Hughes," James Weldon Johnson Collection.

152. Van Vechten, scrapbooks, vol. 8, James Weldon Johnson Collection.

153. Douglas Sadownick, "Protest from Poet's Estate Keeps Film out of Gay Festival, *Los Angeles Times*, July 12, 1989, part 6, p. 2.

154. Duberman, Vicinus, and Chauncey, *Hidden from History*, 3.

155. Quoted in Countee Cullen, *My Soul's High Song: The Collected Writings of Countee Cullen, Voice of the Harlem Renaissance*, ed. Gerald Early (New York: Doubleday, 1991), 23.

156. W. E. B. Du Bois, "The Negro in Art: How Shall He Be Portrayed?" in *The New Negro: Readings, Representation, and African American Culture, 1892–1938*, ed. Henry Louis Gates Jr. and Gene Andrew Jarrett (Princeton: Oxford University Press, 2007), 190.

157. Ibid.

158. Carl Van Vechten, response to *Crisis* symposium "The Negro in Art: How Shall He Be Portrayed?" in Gates and Jarrett, *The New Negro*, 191.

159. Carl Van Vechten, "Folksongs of the American Negro," *Vanity Fair*, July 1925, 52.

160. Carl Van Vechten, "The Black Blues," *Vanity Fair*, August 1925, 57–58.

161. Van Vechten, "Prescription for the Negro Theatre," 46, 92, 98.

162. W. E. B. Du Bois, "Criteria of Negro Art," in *W. E. B. Du Bois: Writings*, ed. Nathan Huggins (New York: Viking, 1986), 1002.

163. Van Vechten, "The Negro Theatre," 322.

164. Du Bois, "Criteria of Negro Art," 1002.

165. Ibid., 1001.

166. James Weldon Johnson, *The Book of American Negro Poetry* (New York: Harcourt Brace, 1922), 9.

167. James Weldon Johnson, "The Dilemma of the Negro Author," *American Mercury,* November 1928, 481.

168. James Weldon Johnson, "Race Prejudice and the Negro Artist," in *The Politics and Aesthetics of "New Negro" Literature,* ed. Cary Wintz (New York: Garland, 1996), 290.

169. Johnson, "Dilemma," 481.

170. Ibid., 480.

171. Hughes, "The Negro Artist and the Racial Mountain," 1314.

172. Countee Cullen to Harold Jackman, January 6, 1926, James Weldon Johnson Collection.

173. Countee Cullen, "Review of *The Weary Blues* by Langston Hughes." *Opportunity,* February 1926, 73.

174. Countee Cullen to Carl Van Vechten, December 25, James Weldon Johnson Collection.

175. Johnson, "Dilemma," 481.

176. Ibid., 477.

177. Ibid., 481.

178. See Jeffrey B. Ferguson, *The Sage of Sugar Hill: George S. Schuyler and the Harlem Renaissance* (New Haven: Yale University Press, 2005), 183–211.

179. George Schuyler, "Negro-Art Hokum," in Huggins, *Voices from the Harlem Renaissance,* 310.

180. Ibid., 312.

181. Van Vechten, "Reminiscences," 199–200.

182. Carl Van Vechten, "Moanin' wid a Sword in Mah Han'," *Vanity Fair,* February 1926, 100; Van Vechten, response to *Crisis* symposium "The Negro in Art: How Shall He Be Portrayed?" 191.

183. Van Vechten, "'Moanin'," 102.

184. Ibid., 100.

185. Van Vechten, response to symposium "The Negro in Art: How Shall He Be Portrayed?" 191.

2 *NIGGER HEAVEN*

1. Carl Van Vechten, *Firecrackers: A Realistic Novel* (New York: Knopf, 1925), 168.

2. Carl Van Vechten to Langston Hughes, June 4, 1925, James Weldon Johnson Collection.

3. Van Vechten, daybooks, August 16, 1925.

4. Carl Van Vechten to Langston Hughes, September 5, 1925, James Weldon Johnson Collection.

5. Van Vechten, *Letters of Carl Van Vechten*, 84.

6. Carl Van Vechten to Langston Hughes, after December 8, 1925, James Weldon Johnson Collection.

7. Carl Van Vechten to Gertrude Stein, June 30, 1925, in *The Letters of Gertrude Stein and Carl Van Vechten, 1913–1946*, ed. Edward Burns (New York: Columbia University Press, 1986), 1:116.

8. Ibid.

9. Van Vechten, scrapbooks, vol. 24, Carl Van Vechten Papers.

10. *Chicago Whip*, December 18, 1926, Van Vechten, scrapbooks, Carl Van Vechten Papers.

11. Van Vechten, daybooks, December 10, 1926.

12. Van Vechten, *Nigger Heaven*, 80. Subsequent page references to this work will be given parenthetically in the text.

13. Nora Holt to Carl Van Vechten, August 17, 1926, Carl Van Vechten Papers.

14. "Nora Ray-Patterson Scandal," *Inter-state Tattler*, January 22, 1926, 2, Carl Van Vechten Papers.

15. Carl Van Vechten to Gertrude Stein, July 24, 1926, in *The Letters of Gertrude Stein and Carl Van Vechten*, 1:130–31.

16. Nora Holt to Carl Van Vechten, October 18, 1926, James Weldon Johnson Collection.

17. Gertrude Stein to Carl Van Vechten, December 26, 1926, in *The Letters of Gertrude Stein and Carl Van Vechten*, 1:139.

18. Countee Cullen to Harold Jackman, August 15, 1926, James Weldon Johnson Collection.

19. Harold Jackman to Carl Van Vechten, February 14, 1925, Carl Van Vechten Papers.

20. *Variety*, May 19, 1926, Carl Van Vechten Papers.

21. Quoted in Kellner, *Carl Van Vechten and the Irreverent Decades*, 211.

22. *Publishers Weekly,* June 26, 1926; *New Yorker,* August 28, 1926; *Messenger,* September 1926, all in Van Vechten, scrapbooks, vol. 18, Carl Van Vechten Papers.

23. Carl Van Vechten to Alfred A. Knopf, December 20, 1925, in *The Letters of Carl Van Vechten,* 85–86.

24. Van Vechten, daybooks, November 25, 1925.

25. Carl Van Vechten, "Notes and Suggestions concerning Carl Van Vechten's Nigger Heaven," James Weldon Johnson Collection.

26. Van Vechten, daybooks, November 27, 1925.

27. Countee Cullen to Harold Jackman, July 1, 1923, James Weldon Johnson Collection.

28. Van Vechten, daybooks, November 28, 1925.

29. Countee Cullen, *Heritage,* in Gates and McKay, *The Norton Anthology of African American Literature,* 1311–14.

30. Countee Cullen to Alain Locke, May 1925, James Weldon Johnson Collection.

31. Countee Cullen to Harold Jackman, October 7, 1925, James Weldon Johnson Collection.

32. Countee Cullen, *One Way to Heaven* (New York: Harper & Brothers), 417.

33. Countee Cullen to Carl Van Vechten, June 25, 1926, James Weldon Johnson Collection; Countee Cullen to Carl Van Vechten, July 1, 1926, James Weldon Johnson Collection; Countee Cullen to Carl Van Vechten, July 24, 1926, Carl Van Vechten Papers.

34. Carl Van Vechten, catalogue, 224, James Weldon Johnson Collection.

35. Charles Duane Van Vechten to Carl Van Vechten, August 10, 1923; Charles Duane Van Vechten to Carl Van Vechten, April 15, 1922; Charles Duane Van Vechten to Carl Van Vechten, November 28, 1925, all in Carl Van Vechten Papers.

36. Charles Duane Van Vechten to Carl Van Vechten, December 7, 1925, Carl Van Vechten Papers.

37. Van Vechten, "Reminiscences," 281.

38. Charles Johnson to Carl Van Vechten, August 10, 1926, Carl Van Vechten Papers.

39. Edward Lueders, *Carl Van Vechten* (New York: Twayne, 1965), 102.

40. Van Vechten, *The Tattooed Countess*, 132.

41. Van Vechten, daybooks, July 28, 1926.

42. Ronald Firbank, *Prancing Nigger* (New York: Brentano's, 1924), 8.

43. Carl Van Vechten, introduction to Firbank, *Prancing Nigger*, vi.

44. Neither was Van Vechten the first white writer to capitalize on black themes, nor the only white writer to do so during the Harlem Renaissance years. Some well-known examples include Waldo Frank, whose 1920 novel *Holiday* drew upon Frank's travels in the rural South. Julia Peterkin won the Pulitzer Prize for her 1928 folk comedy, *Scarlet Sister Mary*. DuBose Heyward's 1925 novel *Porgy* was eventually transformed into Gershwin's famous opera *Porgy and Bess*. In 1929 Heyward wrote another novel, *Mamba's Daughters*, upon which he and his wife, Dorothy Heyward, based a play of the same name in 1939, which starred Ethel Waters. There were many triumphs on the stage, including Paul Green's Pulitzer Prize–winning 1926 play *In Abraham's Bosom*. Eugene O'Neill had enormous success with *The Emperor Jones* in 1922 and *All God's Chillun Got Wings* in 1924. Marc Connelly received a Pulitzer for his 1930 musical *The Green Pastures*, which James Weldon Johnson deemed "something very little short of a miracle" (*Black Manhattan*, 219).

45. W. E. B. Du Bois, "An Array of Books," *Crisis*, September 1924, 219.

46. W. E. B. Du Bois, "Books," in *The Critics and the Harlem Renaissance*, ed. Cary D. Wintz (New York: Garland, 1996), 173.

47. Editorial, *Chicago Whip*, December 18, 1926.

48. Charles S. Johnson to Carl Van Vechten, August 10, 1926, Carl Van Vechten Papers.

49. Carl Van Vechten, *Peter Whiffle* (New York: Knopf, 1922). Subsequent page references to this work will be given parenthetically in the text.

50. Carl Van Vechten, eulogy for A'Lelia Walker, 2, James Weldon Johnson Collection.

51. A. C. Sterling, "Those Were the Fabulous Days!" *Pittsburgh Courier*, October 11, 1952.

52. Hughes, *The Big Sea*, 252.

53. Ibid., 227.

54. Van Vechten, "Reminiscences," 208.

55. *Time*, August 23, 1926, 32.

56. Carl Van Vechten to James Weldon Johnson, June 21, 1930, James Weldon Johnson Collection.

57. Carl Van Vechten to James Weldon Johnson, September 7, 1926, James Weldon Johnson Collection.

58. Countee Cullen to Harold Jackman, May 6, 1926, James Weldon Johnson Collection.

59. Van Vechten, daybooks, September 22, 1926, September 4, 1926, September 8, 1926.

60. Lewis Baer to Carl Van Vechten, September 28, 1926, Carl Van Vechten Papers.

61. Van Vechten, daybooks, September 29, 1926.

62. Ibid., October 26, 1926.

63. Ibid., November 3, 1926.

64. Hughes, *The Big Sea*, 270.

65. *New York Times*, December 20, 1926, Carl Van Vechten Papers.

66. Aubrey Bowser to Carl Van Doren, September 4, 1926, Carl Van Vechten Papers.

67. *Pittsburgh Courier*, November 6, 1926, 8.

68. Ernestine Rose to Carl Van Vechten, October 20, 1926, Carl Van Vechten Papers.

69. *Pittsburgh Courier*, November 6, 1926, 8, November 26, 1926.

70. George S. Schuyler, "Views and Reviews," *Pittsburgh Courier*, October 1, 1955, 6.

71. Alice Dunbar-Nelson, "Une Femme Dit," *Pittsburgh Courier*, September 18, 1926.

72. Claude McKay, *Home to Harlem* (New York: Harper & Brothers, 1928), 113.

73. Henry Miller, *Plexus* (New York: Grove, 1963), 562.

74. Hubert Harrison, "'No Negro Literary Renaissance,' Says Well Known Writer," *Pittsburgh Courier*, March 12, 1927, Van Vechten, scrapbooks, vol. 19, Carl Van Vechten Papers.

75. Hubert Harrison, *A Hubert Harrison Reader*, ed. Jeffrey B. Perry (Middletown: Wesleyan University Press, 2001), 342.

76. Hubert Harrison, "Homo Africanus Harlemi," *Amsterdam News,* September 1, 1926, reprinted in *A Hubert Harrison Reader,* 344. Editor Perry explains the title: "The phrase 'Homo Africanus' had been used by L. M. Hussey in a 1925 *American Mercury* piece which discussed how African Americans had learned to survive by wearing the mask and playing roles that made whites feel comfortable" (341).

77. Ibid., 341.

78. Ibid.

79. Harrison, " 'No Negro Literary Renaissance.' "

80. Nora Holt to Carl Van Vechten, Carl Van Vechten Papers.

81. Eric Walrond to Carl Van Vechten, c. August 1926; Paul Robeson to Carl Van Vechten, August 12, 1926; Walter White to Carl Van Vechten, August 19, 1926; Alain Locke to Carl Van Vechten, July 27, 1926; Gertrude Stein to Carl Van Vechten, c. September 1926, all in Carl Van Vechten Papers.

82. Anita Loos to Carl Van Vechten, September 25, 1926; Harold Jackman to Carl Van Vechten, August 19, 1926; Ellen Glasgow to Carl Van Vechten, July 28, 1926, all in Carl Van Vechten Papers.

83. Charles S. Johnson to Carl Van Vechten, August 10, 1926; Charles S. Johnson to Carl Van Vechten, August 17, 1926, both in Carl Van Vechten Papers.

84. Quoted in Leon Coleman, *Carl Van Vechten and the Harlem Renaissance: A Critical Assessment* (New York: Garland, 1998), 129.

85. James Weldon Johnson, "Romance and Tragedy in Harlem—A Review," *Opportunity,* October 1926, 316, 330.

86. Dunbar-Nelson, "Une Femme Dit."

87. Nella Larsen to Carl Van Vechten, "Wednesday, eleventh," Carl Van Vechten Papers.

88. W. E. B. Du Bois, "Books," *Crisis,* December 1926, 81.

89. Ibid.

90. Ibid., 82.

91. Charles Chesnutt to Carl Van Vechten, September 7, 1926, Carl Van Vechten Papers.

92. Carl Van Vechten, "Uncle Tom's Mansion," *New York Herald Tribune,* December 20, 1925, 6.

93. Walter White to W. E. B. Du Bois, November 26, 1926, Carl Van Vechten Papers.

94. Van Vechten, daybooks, November 30, 1926.

95. Hughes, *The Big Sea*, 140, 263–64.

96. Rampersad, *The Life of Langston Hughes*, 1:141.

97. Hughes, *The Big Sea*, 266.

98. Floyd Calvin, "Calvin's Weekly Diary of the New York Show World," *Pittsburgh Courier*, February 5, 1927.

99. Langston Hughes, "Those Bad New Negroes: A Critique on Critics," *Pittsburgh Courier*, April 9, 1927.

100. Ibid., April 16, 1927.

101. Allison Davis, "Our Negro 'Intellectuals,'" *Crisis*, August 1928, 268–69.

102. Ibid.

103. Langston Hughes, "To the Editor of *The Crisis*," July 28, 1928, James Weldon Johnson Collection.

104. Carl Van Vechten to Langston Hughes, August 2, 1928, James Weldon Johnson Collection.

105. Benjamin Brawley, "The Negro Literary Renaissance," *Southern Workman*, April 1927, 177, 178, 182–83.

106. Quoted in Carl Van Vechten to Langston Hughes, April 1927, James Weldon Johnson Collection.

107. Ibid.

108. Gates and Jarrett, *The New Negro*, 237.

109. McKay, *A Long Way from Home*, 282–83.

110. McKay, *Home to Harlem*, 8, 298, 93.

111. Ibid., 274.

112. W. E. B. Du Bois, "The Browsing Reader," *Crisis*, June 1928, 202.

113. McKay, *Home to Harlem*, 57.

114. Du Bois, "The Browsing Reader," 202.

115. McKay, *Home to Harlem*, 315.

116. Claude McKay to W. E. B. Du Bois, June 18, 1928, quoted in *The Passion of Claude McKay*, ed. Wayne Cooper (New York: Schocken Books, 1973), 149–50.

117. Quoted in Wayne F. Cooper, *Claude McKay: Rebel Sojourner in the Harlem Renaissance* (Baton Rouge: Louisiana State University Press, 1987), 289.

118. Claude McKay to James Weldon Johnson, May 9, 1928, James Weldon Johnson Collection the Courtesy of the Literary Representative for works of Claude McKay, Schomburg Center for Research in Black Culture, The New York Public Library, Astor, Lenox and Tilden Foundations; second letter quoted in Cooper, *Claude McKay*, 289.

119. McKay, *A Long Way from Home*, 319. Van Vechten day books, August 9, 1929.

120. Ibid., 313.

121. Alain Locke, "Spiritual Truant," *New Challenge*, Fall 1937, 81–84.

122. McKay, *A Long Way from Home*, 320.

123. Ibid.

124. Ibid., 319.

125. Ibid., 314.

126. Herschel Brickell, review of *Home to Harlem*, in Wintz, *The Critics and the Harlem Renaissance*, 189.

127. Dewey Jones, "More 'Nigger Heaven,'" *Chicago Defender*, March 17, 1928.

128. Johnson, *Along This Way*, 381.

129. Langston Hughes to Wallace Thurman, n.d., James Weldon Johnson Collection.

130. Foreword to *Fire!! A Quarterly Devoted to the Younger Negro Artists*, November 1926, 1.

131. Wallace Thurman, "Cordelia the Crude," *Fire!! A Quarterly Devoted to the Younger Negro Artists*, November 1926, 5.

132. Bruce Nugent, "Smoke, Lillies and Jade," *Fire!! A Quarterly Devoted to the Younger Negro Artists*, November 1926, 38.

133. Langston Hughes to Wallace Thurman, n.d., James Weldon Johnson Collection.

134. Arthur Huff Fauset, "Intelligentsia," *Fire!! A Quarterly Devoted to the Younger Negro Artists*, November 1926, 46.

135. Arthur Huff Fauset, "Homage to Sterling Brown," in *Sterling A. Brown: A UMUM Tribute*, ed. Black History Museum Committee (Philadelphia: Black History Museum UMUM Publishers, 1982), 2.

136. Fauset, "Intelligentsia," 45.

137. Langston Hughes to Wallace Thurman, n.d., James Weldon Johnson Collection.

138. Wallace Thurman, "Fire Burns," *Fire!! A Quarterly Devoted to the Younger Negro Artists,* November 1926, 47.

139. Ibid.

140. Ibid.

141. Ibid.

142. Ibid., 48.

143. Eleanor Van Notten, *Wallace Thurman's Harlem Renaissance* (Amsterdam: Rodopi, 1994), 135.

144. Hughes, *The Big Sea,* 237.

145. *Crisis,* January 1927, 158.

146. Carl Van Vechten, scrapbooks, vol. 19, Carl Van Vechten Papers.

147. Du Bois, "Criteria of Negro Art," 1001.

148. Hughes, *The Big Sea,* 270.

149. Van Vechten, "Reminiscences," 207.

150. Randall Kennedy, *Nigger: The Strange Career of a Troublesome Word* (New York: Pantheon, 2002), 45.

151. Quoted in ibid., 28.

152. Ibid.

153. Kennedy, *Nigger,* 4; Jabari Asim, *The N Word: Who Can Say It, Who Shouldn't, and Why* (Boston: Houghton Mifflin, 2007).

154. Hughes, *The Big Sea,* 269.

155. Johnson, "Romance and Tragedy in Harlem," 116.

156. Van Vechten, scrapbooks, vol. 131, Carl Van Vechten Papers.

157. Judith Butler, *Excitable Speech: A Politics of the Performative* (New York: Routledge, 1997), 100.

158. Quoted in Asim, *The N Word,* 224.

159. Ann duCille, *Skin Trade* (Cambridge, Mass.: Harvard University Press, 1996), 6.

160. Kennedy, *Nigger,* 109.

161. John Gennari, unpublished essay, forthcoming in *Passing for Italian.*

162. Ibid.

163. Carl Van Vechten to Langston Hughes, March 25, 1927, James Weldon Johnson Collection.

164. Quoted in Robert Worth, "*Nigger Heaven* and the Harlem Renaissance," *African American Review* 29, no. 3 (1995): 472.

3 LETTERS FROM BLACKS

1. Nella Larsen to Carl Van Vechten, c. March 1927, James Weldon Johnson Collection.

2. *Letters of Gertrude Stein and Carl Van Vechten,* 1:146–47, 234–35.

3. Nella Larsen to Carl Van Vechten, June 30, 1926, James Weldon Johnson Collection.

4. Kellner, *Carl Van Vechten and the Irreverent Decades,* 133.

5. Ethel Waters to Carl Van Vechten, October 9, 1929, January 11, 1930, James Weldon Johnson Collection.

6. George Hutchinson, *In Search of Nella Larsen: A Biography of the Color Line* (Cambridge, Mass.: Harvard University Press, 2006), 222. My appreciation of the relationship between Van Vechten and Larsen has been greatly enhanced by this wonderful biography.

7. Terrence E. Williams, "Writer Scores Best Girls Who Entertain 'Nordics,'" *Pittsburgh Courier,* October 1, 1927, Van Vechten, scrapbooks, vol. 19, Carl Van Vechten Papers.

8. W. E. B. Du Bois, "Two Novels," *Crisis,* June 1928, 202.

9. *Crisis,* April 1930, 1929.

10. Nella Larsen to Carl Van Vechten, "Sunday," c. July 28, 1929, James Weldon Johnson Collection.

11. Nella Larsen to Carl Van Vechten, August 1928, James Weldon Johnson Collection.

12. Hutchinson, *In Search of Nella Larsen,* 303; Kathleen Pfeiffer, *Race Passing and American Individualism* (Amherst: University of Massachusetts Press, 2002), 135.

13. Nella Larsen, *Quicksand and Passing* (New Brunswick: Rutgers University Press, 1987), 200. Subsequent page references to this work will be given parenthetically in the text.

14. Van Vechten, daybooks, April 4, 1929.

15. Ibid., April 10, 1929.

16. Wallace Thurman to Langston Hughes, n.d., James Weldon Johnson Collection.

17. Ibid.

18. Ibid.

19. Hughes, *The Big Sea*, 238, 235.

20. Dorothy West, "The Elephant's Dance," in *The Richer, The Poorer: Stories, Sketches, and Reminiscences* (New York: Anchor, 1996) 215.

21. Rampersad, *The Life of Langston Hughes*, 1:172.

22. Wallace Thurman, *The Blacker the Berry* (New York: Simon & Schuster, 1996), 21. Subsequent page references to this work will be given parenthetically in the text.

23. Bruce Nugent, "Gentleman Jigger," in Wirth, *Gay Rebel of the Harlem Renaissance*, 169–70.

24. Van Vechten, daybooks, February 4, 1929.

25. Wallace Thurman, *Infants of the Spring* (New York: Macaulay, 1932), 187, 283.

26. Langston Hughes, "Harlem Literati in the Twenties," *Saturday Review of Literature*, June 22, 1940, 13.

27. West, "The Elephant's Dance," 226.

28. Ibid., 225.

29. Eleonore van Notten, *Wallace Thurman's Harlem Renaissance* (Amsterdam: Editions Rodopi B. V., 1994), 300.

30. West, "The Elephant's Dance," 225.

31. Van Vechten, "Uncle Tom's Mansion," *New York Herald Tribune Books*, December 20, 1925, 6.

32. Carl Van Vechten, "Carl Van Vechten Comments," *Challenge: A Literary Quarterly* 1 (Fall 1934): 28.

33. Hughes, *The Big Sea*, 228.

34. Carl Van Vechten to Grace Nail Johnson, July 2, 1938, James Weldon Johnson Collection.

35. Carl Van Vechten, letter to the *Amsterdam News*, 1938, in *"Keep A-Inchin' Along,"* 113.

36. Carl Van Vechten, "James Weldon Johnson: The Man," n.d., typescript original, 1, 4, James Weldon Johnson Collection; presented at Fisk University as "My Friend: James Weldon Johnson."

37. James Weldon Johnson, "My City," in *St. Peter Relates an Incident* (New York: Viking, 1935), 37.

38. James Weldon Johnson, "O Black and Unknown Bards," in Johnson, *The Book of American Negro Poetry*, 123–24.

39. Carl Van Vechten, "The Proposed James Weldon Johnson Memorial," *Opportunity*, February 1940.

40. Carl Van Vechten to Grace Nail Johnson, December 29, 1938, James Weldon Johnson Collection.

41. See Margaret Rose Vendryes, *Barthé: A Life in Sculpture* (Jackson: University of Mississippi Press, 2008), 103.

42. Carl Van Vechten, "The James Weldon Johnson Memorial Project," *Crisis*, February 1940, 41, 40.

43. Elmer Carter to Walter White, March 1941; Walter White to Carl Van Vechten, April 14, 1941, both in James Weldon Johnson Collection.

44. Walter White to the Hon. Fiorello La Guardia, June 17, 1941, James Weldon Johnson Collection.

45. Walter White to Carl Van Vechten, July 16, 1941, James Weldon Johnson Collection.

46. Walter White to Robert Moses, September 9, 1941, James Weldon Johnson Collection.

47. Robert Moses to Walter White, September 11, 1941, James Weldon Johnson Collection.

48. Walter White to Carl Van Vechten, September 12, 1941, James Weldon Johnson Collection.

49. Walter White to Robert Moses, September 12, 1941, James Weldon Johnson Collection.

50. Carl Van Vechten to Walter White, September 24, 1941, James Weldon Johnson Collection.

51. Walter White to Carl Van Vechten, September 24, 1941, James Weldon Johnson Collection.

52. Edward Blum to Walter White, September 24, 1941; Walter White to Edward Blum, September 24, 1941, both in James Weldon Johnson Collection.

53. Frank Crosswaith to Walter White, October 24, 1941, James Weldon Johnson Collection.

54. Carl Van Vechten to Walter White, October 29, 1941, James Weldon Johnson Collection.
55. A. Philip Randolph to Walter White, January 1942, James Weldon Johnson Collection.
56. Carl Van Vechten to Walter White, January 12, 1942, James Weldon Johnson Collection.
57. Walter White to members of the James Weldon Johnson Committee, March 24, 1942, James Weldon Johnson Collection.
58. Walter White to Carl Van Vechten, April 2, 1942, James Weldon Johnson Collection.
59. Walter White to Col. Theodore Roosevelt, April 6, 1942, James Weldon Johnson Collection.
60. Elmer Carter to Walter White, April 1942, James Weldon Johnson Collection.
61. Robert Moses to Walter White, May 4, 1942, James Weldon Johnson Collection.
62. Carl Van Vechten, "The James Weldon Johnson Memorial Collection," in *"Keep A-Inchin' Along,"* 124.
63. Ibid.
64. Carl Van Vechten to Bernhard Knollenberg, October 22, 1941, Carl Van Vechten Papers.
65. Bernhard Knollenberg to Carl Van Vechten, March 15, 1941, Carl Van Vechten Papers.
66. Carl Van Vechten to Bernhard Knollenberg, May 29, 1941, Carl Van Vechten Papers. Arthur B. Spingarn, who had provided pro bono legal counsel for the NAACP and served as both vice president and president of the organization, was, like Van Vechten, an accomplished collector of books by and about blacks. The Arthur B. Spingarn Collection of Negro Authors was established in 1946 at the Moorland-Spingarn Research Center at Howard University in Washington, D.C.
67. Carl Van Vechten to Bernhard Knollenberg, June 5, 1941, Carl Van Vechten Papers.
68. Bernhard Knollenberg to Carl Van Vechten, June 2, 1941, Carl Van Vechten Papers.

69. Carl Van Vechten, "The J. W. Johnson Collection at Yale," *Crisis,* March 1942, 222.

70. Carl Van Vechten to Dorothy Peterson, August 18, 1941, James Weldon Johnson Collection.

71. Carl Van Vechten to Langston Hughes, August 16, 1943, James Weldon Johnson Collection.

72. Clinton Simpson, "So This Is New York," *Saturday Review of Literature,* September 6, 1930, 101.

73. Carl Van Vechten to Alfred A. Knopf, November 18, 1930, in *Letters of Carl Van Vechten,* 117.

74. Van Vechten, "Reminiscences," 218, 229.

75. Carl Van Vechten, foreword to *Sacred and Profane Memories,* vii.

76. Van Vechten, scrapbooks, vol. 25.

77. Van Vechten, "Reminiscences," 252, 232.

78. Ibid., 316.

79. Kellner, *Carl Van Vechten and the Irreverent Decades,* 271–72.

80. Van Vechten, "Reminiscences," 305, 316.

81. Carl Van Vechten, "Memories of Bessie Smith," *Jazz Record,* September 1947, 6.

82. Ibid.

83. Ibid., 7.

84. Ibid., 7, 29.

85. Van Vechten, "Reminiscences," 305.

86. Zora Neale Hurston to Carl Van Vechten, December 10, 1934, James Weldon Johnson Collection.

87. "Talk of the Town," *New Yorker,* January 12, 1963.

88. Van Vechten, "The J. W. Johnson Collection at Yale," 223.

89. Bernhard Knollenberg to Carl Van Vechten, March 18, 1941, Carl Van Vechten Papers.

90. Bernhard Knollenberg to Carl Van Vechten, March 26, 1941, Carl Van Vechten Papers.

91. Carl Van Vechten to Bernhard Knollenberg, March 31, 1941, Carl Van Vechten Papers.

92. Bernhard Knollenberg to Harold Jackman, April 11, 1941, Carl Van Vechten Papers.

93. Ibid.

94. Harold Jackman to Bernhard Knollenberg, April 18, 1941, Carl Van Vechten Papers.

95. Ibid.

96. Dorothy Peterson to Carl Van Vechten, December 16, 1930, James Weldon Johnson Collection.

97. Dorothy Peterson to Carl Van Vechten, May 24, 1928, James Weldon Johnson Collection.

98. Van Vechten, daybooks, January 5, 1929.

99. Carl Van Vechten to Dorothy Peterson, 1940, James Weldon Johnson Collection.

100. Carl Van Vechten to Dorothy Peterson, August 3, 1942, James Weldon Johnson Collection. Jean Toomer became a devotee of the philosophy of Greek-Armenian mystic Georges Gurdjieff, whose teachings on spiritual development appealed to Peterson, too, never more so than during her romance with Toomer in the mid-1920s. Hutchinson, *In Search of Nella Larsen*, 253.

101. Carl Van Vechten to Dorothy Peterson, September 5, 1941, James Weldon Johnson Collection.

102. Van Vechten, daybooks, February 18, 1929.

103. Carl Van Vechten to Dorothy Peterson, February 19, 1941, James Weldon Johnson Collection.

104. Van Vechten, address given at the opening exhibition of the Jerome Bowers Peterson Memorial Collection of Celebrated Negroes, Wadleigh High School, Harlem, April 26, 1944, James Weldon Johnson Collection.

105. Carl Van Vechten to Bernhard Knollenberg, February 27, 1943, Carl Van Vechten Papers.

106. Carl Van Vechten to Bernhard Knollenberg, August 3, 1942, Carl Van Vechten Papers.

107. Carl Van Vechten to Dorothy Peterson, c. October 26, 1942, James Weldon Johnson Collection.

108. Carl Van Vechten to Dorothy Peterson, September 5, 1941, James Weldon Johnson Collection.

109. Bernhard Knollenberg to Carl Van Vechten, October 15, 1941, Carl Van Vechten Papers.

110. Carl Van Vechten to Bernhard Knollenberg, October 16, 1941, Carl Van Vechten Papers.

111. Carl Van Vechten to Bernhard Knolleberg, September 8, 1941, Carl Van Vechten Papers.

112. Carl Van Vechten to Dorothy Peterson, October 26, 1941, James Weldon Johnson Collection.

113. Carl Van Vechten to Bernhard Knollenberg, August 3, 1942, Carl Van Vechten Papers.

114. Carl Van Vechten to Dorothy Peterson, August 5, 1942, James Weldon Johnson Collection.

115. Marjorie G. Wynne, "Crossing Wall," in *The Beinecke Library of Yale University,* ed. Stephen Parks (New Haven: Beinecke Rare Book and Manuscript Library, 2003), 61.

116. Carl Van Vechten to Dorothy Peterson, August 5, 1942, James Weldon Johnson Collection.

117. Carl Van Vechten to Bernhard Knollenberg, August 20, 1942, Carl Van Vechten Papers.

118. Bernhard Knollenberg to Carl Van Vechten, August 21, 1942, Carl Van Vechten Papers; Carl Van Vechten to Dorothy Peterson, August 5, 1942, James Weldon Johnson Collection.

119. Bernhard Knollenberg to Carl Van Vechten, August 21, 1942, Carl Van Vechten Papers.

120. Carl Van Vechten to Bernhard Knollenberg, August 24, 1942, Carl Van Vechten Papers.

121. Bernhard Knollenberg to Carl Van Vechten, August 26, 1942, Carl Van Vechten Papers.

122. Carl Van Vechten to Dorothy Peterson, April 2, 1938, James Weldon Johnson Collection.

123. Carl Van Vechten to Bernhard Knollenberg, August 26, 1942, Carl Van Vechten Papers.

124. Carl Van Vechten to Dorothy Peterson, September 1, 1942, Carl Van Vechten Papers.

125. Claude McKay to Carl Van Vechten, July 31, 1941, Carl Van Vechten Papers.

126. Claude McKay to Carl Van Vechten, July 27, 1941, Carl Van Vechten Papers.

127. Carl Van Vechten to Claude McKay, July 31, 1941, Claude McKay Letters and Manuscripts, Archives and Rare Books Division, Schomburg Center for Research in Black Culture, The New York Public Library.

128. Carl Van Vechten to Bernhard Knollenberg, October 22, 1941, Carl Van Vechten Papers.

129. Claude McKay to Carl Van Vechten, October 26, 1941, Carl Van Vechten Papers.

130. Carl Van Vechten to Bernhard Knollenberg, October 22, 1941, Carl Van Vechten Papers.

131. Carl Van Vechten to Fania Marinoff, between June 29 and July 2, 1938, in *Letters of Carl Van Vechten*, 159–60.

132. Grace Nail Johnson to Carl Van Vechten, June 4, 1941, Carl Van Vechten Papers.

133. Carl Van Vechten to Grace Nail Johnson, August 5, 1942, Carl Van Vechten Papers.

134. Carl Van Vechten to Bernhard Knollenberg, August 31, 1942, Carl Van Vechten Papers.

135. Bernhard Knollenberg to Carl Van Vechten, September 2, 1942, Carl Van Vechten Papers.

136. Carl Van Vechten to Bernhard Knollenberg, September 20, 1942, Carl Van Vechten Papers.

137. Donald Gallup to Carl Van Vechten, November 7, 1947, Carl Van Vechten Papers.

138. Carl Van Vechten to Bernhard Knollenberg, August 29, 1942, Carl Van Vechten Papers.

139. Carl Van Vechten to Dorothy Peterson, December 2, 1941, James Weldon Johnson Collection.

140. Carl Van Vechten to Bernhard Knollenberg, August 29, 1942, Carl Van Vechten Papers.

141. W. E. B. Du Bois, "Segregation in the North," *Crisis*, March 1934, reprinted in *Writings in Periodicals Edited by W. E. B. Du Bois: Selections*

from The Crisis, vol. 2, *1926–1934*, ed. Herbert Aptheker (Millwood, N.Y.: Kraus-Thompson, 1983), 745–50.

142. Bernhard Knollenberg to Carl Van Vechten, August 31, 1942, Carl Van Vechten Papers.

143. Ibid.

144. Carl Van Vechten to Bernhard Knollenberg, August 26, 1942, Carl Van Vechten Papers.

145. Van Vechten, daybooks, June 6, 1928.

146. Walter White to Carl Van Vechten, December 9, 1942, James Weldon Johnson Collection.

147. Walter White to Carl Van Vechten, December 19, 1942, James Weldon Johnson Collection.

148. Carl Van Vechten to Walter White, October 23, 1942, James Weldon Johnson Collection.

149. Carl Van Vechten to Walter White, May 12, 1946, James Weldon Johnson Collection.

150. Langston Hughes to Carl Van Vechten, October 30, 1941, James Weldon Johnson Collection.

151. Carl Van Vechten to Dorothy Peterson, November 3, 1941, James Weldon Johnson Collection.

152. Carl Van Vechten to Langston Hughes, August 16, 1943, James Weldon Johnson Collection.

153. Langston Hughes to Carl Van Vechten, October 29, 1925, James Weldon Johnson Collection.

154. Carl Van Vechten to Langston Hughes, after October 29, 1925, James Weldon Johnson Collection.

155. Van Vechten, daybooks, May 26, 1930.

156. Bernard, *Remember Me to Harlem*, 106. Langston Hughes, "Advertisement for the Waldorf-Astoria," in *The Collected Poems of Langston Hughes*, 143.

157. Carl Van Vechten to Langston Hughes, April 3, 1933, James Weldon Johnson Collection.

158. Langston Hughes to Carl Van Vechten, May 23, 1933, James Weldon Johnson Collection.

159. Langston Hughes to Carl Van Vechten, March 5, 1934, James Weldon Johnson Collection.

160. Carl Van Vechten to Langston Hughes, March 20, 1934, James Weldon Johnson Collection.

161. Carl Van Vechten to Blanche Knopf, c. March 1934, Carl Van Vechten Papers.

162. Langston Hughes to Blanche Knopf, May 15, 1934, Harry Ransom Center, University of Texas, Austin, reprinted in Randolph Lewis, "Langston Hughes and Alfred Knopf, Inc., 1925–1935," *The Library Chronicle of the University of Texas at Austin,* Vol. 22, No. 4, 59.

163. Carl Van Vechten to Dorothy Peterson, October 11, 1950, James Weldon Johnson Collection.

164. Langston Hughes, "Prelude to Our Age," in *The Collected Poems of Langston Hughes,* 383.

165. Langston Hughes to Carl Van Vechten, December 3, 1957, James Weldon Johnson Collection.

166. Rampersad, *The Life of Langston Hughes,* 2:277.

167. Langston Hughes to Carl Van Vechten, February 18, 1958, James Weldon Johnson Collection.

168. Carl Van Vechten to Dorothy Peterson, August 26, 1957, James Weldon Johnson Collection.

169. Carl Van Vechten to Dorothy Peterson, June 27, 1956, James Weldon Johnson Collection.

170. Carl Van Vechten to Langston Hughes, September 4, 1952, James Weldon Johnson Collection.

171. Van Vechten, "Reminiscences," 354.

172. Nora Holt to Carl Van Vechten, November 8, 1953, James Weldon Johnson Collection.

173. Carl Van Vechten to H. L. Mencken, c. 1925, in *The Letters of Carl Van Vechten,* 87.

174. Van Vechten, catalogue, 384.

175. Ibid., 43.

176. Ibid., 324.

177. Carl Van Vechten to James Babb, March 11, 1946, Carl Van Vechten Papers.

178. Van Vechten, catalogue, 568.

179. Carl Van Vechten to Dorothy Peterson, January 24, 1956, James Weldon Johnson Collection.

180. Van Vechten, catalogue, 598.

181. Ibid., 566, 533.

182. Quoted in Rampersad, *The Life of Langston Hughes,* 2:277.

183. Charles Spurgeon Johnson, "Literature and the Practice of Living," James Weldon Johnson Collection.

184. Carl Van Vechten to Donald Gallup, November 7, 1951, James Weldon Johnson Collection.

185. Carl Van Vechten to Charles R. Byrne, c. June 1950, in *The Letters of Carl Van Vechten,* 240–41.

186. *Jet,* December 13, 1951, 65.

187. Amon Evans, "For a Collector, a New Degree," *Nashville Tennessean,* May 31, 1955, 13.

188. Van Vechten, "Reminiscences," 329, 327.

189. George Schuyler, "Remarks of George Schuyler at Carl Van Vechten's 75th Birthday Party at Bon Soir," 3–4, Carl Van Vechten Papers.

190. *Time,* March 6, 1944.

191. Van Vechten, "Reminiscences," 329.

192. Patrick L. Pinnell, "The Building," in Parks, *The Beinecke Library of Yale University,* 26.

193. Grace Nail Johnson to Carl Van Vechten, May 25, 1964, James Weldon Johnson Collection.

194. Van Vechten, "Reminiscences," 53, 351, 352.

195. "The Talk of the Town," *New Yorker,* January 12, 1963, 21.

196. Van Vechten, "Reminiscences," 299, 53.

197. Carl Van Vechten to Chester Himes, June 24, 1961, James Weldon Johnson Collection.

198. Van Vechten, "Reminiscences," 268.

199. Carl Van Vechten to Chester Himes, August 8, 1961, James Weldon Johnson Collection.

200. Carl Van Vechten to Langston Hughes, June 2, 1964, James Weldon Johnson Collection.

201. "Carl Van Vechten Is Dead," *New York Amsterdam News,* December 26, 1964, 39; "Carl Van Vechten Is Dead at 84: Author, Critic and Photographer," *New York Times,* December 22, 1964, 29.

202. Carl Van Vechten to Chester Himes, June 24, 1961, James Weldon Johnson Collection.

203. Langston Hughes, address to the National Institute of Arts and Letters, New York, January 8, 1965, James Weldon Johnson Collection.

204. George S. Schuyler, "A Fond Farewell to Carlo," December 23, 1964, James Weldon Johnson Collection.

205. Nora Holt to Fania Marinoff, March 14, 1965, James Weldon Johnson Collection.

206. Lincoln Kirstein, "Carl Van Vechten (1880-1964)," *Yale University Library Gazette,* April 1965, 157.

AUTHOR'S NOTE

1. Sylvia Ardyn Boone, *West African Travels: A Guide to People and Places* (New York: Random House, 1974), 3.

2. Van Vechten, "Reminiscences," 354.

INDEX

Covarrubias, Miguel, 69, 198–99, 232, 258–60

Crisis, 7, 30–31, 44, 91–93, 95, 107, 124, 133, 140, 149–54, 159–60, 165, 173, 178, 197–98, 227–28, 230, 254, 276–77

Crosswaith, Frank C., 222–23

Cullen, Countee, 5, 45, 47–48, 50, 89, 91, 99–102, 107, 112–13, 116–21, 131, 133, 135–36, 152, 159, 178, 238, 243, 276; works: *Heritage,* 118; *One Way to Heaven,* 119–20

Cullen, Ida, 121

"Cy est Pourtraicte, Madame Ste Ursule, et les Unze Mille Vierge" (Stevens), 129

d'Alvarez, Marguerite, 65

Dalí, Salvador, 61

Dark Princess (Du Bois), 280

Darktown Follies, The (see *My Friend from Kentucky*)

Davis, Allison, 158–61

Day, Carita, 23

DeMille, Cecil B., 195

Demuth, Henry, 300

Dewey, John, 46

"Dilemma of the Negro Author, The" (Johnson), 97–101

Dinesen, Isak, 103

Dixon, Willie, 312

Dodson, Owen, 268

Doro, Marie, 64

Douglas, Aaron, 6, 47, 51, 117, 172–73, 178

Douglass, Frederick, 88, 220

Dove, Arthur, 300

Draper, Muriel, 198

Du Bois, W. E. B., 27, 35, 37, 39, 41, 44–47, 52, 88, 91–93, 95–97, 100–103, 107, 149, 159–60, 165–66, 173–74, 178–79, 188, 196–98, 214; relationship to CVV, 7–8, 30, 50, 95–97, 109, 124–26, 149–51, 154, 165, 275–82; as spokesperson for NAACP, 30, 277; works: "Criteria of Negro Art," 95–96, 173, 178; *Dark Princess,* 280; "The Negro in Art: How Shall He Be Portrayed," 91–93

Dunbar-Nelson, Alice, 142, 145, 148

Duncan, Isadora, 24

Duse, Eleanora, 42

Dust Tracks on a Road (Hurston), 58

Eastman, Max, 34, 52, 167 (see also *Liberator* and *New Masses*)

Ellington, Duke, 32, 71, 214

Ellison, Ralph, 297

Excitable Speech: A Politics of the Performative (Butler), 183

exoticism, 70

Fair Employment Act, Executive Order 8802, 219, 289

Faulkner, William, 34

170–71, 173, 175–77, 179, 189, 191, 193, 204, 206–10, 223, 226, 262, 269–70, 292, 305; homosexual culture, 2, 32, 79–80, 82–83; nightlife, 2, 7, 18, 31–35, 49, 61, 65–66, 70–71, 107, 116, 129–30, 150, 164, 167, 171, 175–76, 208, 254

Harlem, 203

Harlem Renaissance, *also* Negro Renaissance and New Negro Renaissance, 1–2, 4, 7–9, 18, 24, 31–33, 35, 37, 48, 52–53, 60, 69, 88, 90, 116, 124, 133, 140, 142–43, 145, 149, 155–56, 159, 161, 166, 169, 184, 190, 198, 202–3, 205–6, 208–11, 215, 260, 276, 289, 293, 296, 306–7, 309–10; history of, 25–28, 44, 47–48; race and art, 8, 41, 43, 61, 74–75, 91–93, 97, 103, 107–8, 156; scholarship, 5–6, 9, 184–85

Harmonium (Stevens), 129

Harper's, 98

Harris, Jim, 137

Harrison, Hubert, 136, 142–45, 179, 304; works: " 'Nigger Heaven'—A Review of the Reviews," 144; "No Negro Literary Renaissance," 145

Hartley, Marsden, 300

Harvard University, 158

Hayden, Robert, 310–11

Hayes, Roland, 152

Heritage (Cullen), 118

Heyward, DuBose, 92

Hicks, Granville, 177–78

Himes, Chester, 302–3, 305

His Eye Is on the Sparrow (Waters), 55–56

Hogan, Ernest, 23

Holiday, Billie, 235, 238–39

Holstein, Casper, 49

Holt, Nora, 7, 64, 108, 111–13, 145, 195, 238, 254, 292–95, 305

Home to Harlem (McKay), 163–68, 197, 270

Howard University, 262–63, 301

Hughes, Langston, 7–8, 28–30, 32–33, 47–53, 59, 77–78, 87–91, 99, 107, 131, 152, 159, 169, 171–79, 203–4, 208, 211, 214, 276, 310–11; on race and art, 8, 32–33, 45, 51–52, 71, 74–75, 77–78, 88, 94, 98, 100–103, 156–58, 178; relationship with CVV, 7, 30, 45, 49–50, 53, 64–65, 67, 78–79, 88, 91, 108–9, 131, 133, 137–38, 154–63, 176, 181, 187–88, 192, 231, 238, 242, 284–91, 303–5; sexuality of, 79, 87–91; works: *The Big Sea*, 28–29, 32, 64–65, 75–76, 79, 88, 133, 155–56, 178–79, 204, 211; *Fine Clothes to the Jew*, 155–63, 187, 191, 198;

Van Vechten (cont.)

Fania); foundation of Alfred Stieglitz Collection, 300; foundation of Anna Marble Pollock Memorial Library of Books about Cats, 300–301; foundation of Florine Stettheimer Memorial Collection of Books about the Fine Arts, 300; foundation of George Gershwin Memorial Collection of Music and Musical Literature, 290, 300; foundation of James Weldon Johnson Memorial Collection, 9, 214, 227–31, 254–58, 262–79, 282–85, 291, 293, 296–97, 301–2, 306, 310; journalist,11, 20, 151; for *Chicago American*, 20; for *New York Times*, 21; for *Vanity Fair*, 23, 30, 56, 93–94, 104, 119, 162, 193; for *New York Herald Tribune*, 26; for *New York Press*, 39, 41; literary works, *Peter Whiffle* (1922), 24, 50, 73, 121, 128, 144, 146, 155–66; *The Blind Bow-Boy* (1923), 107, 121, 144; *The Tattooed Countess* (1924), 24, 50, 73, 121, 128, 144; *Fire-crackers* (1925), 107; *Nigger Heaven* (1926) (see *Nigger Heaven*); *Sacred and Profane Memories* (1932), 14, 231–32, 254; "Feathers," 231; "Folk-songs of Iowa," 231–32; "The Tin Trunk" (1932), 14, 232; *Parties* (1930), 110, 231; *The Tiger in the House* (1920) 200, 301; "Fragments from an Unwritten Autobiography" (1955), 72–73; letters of, 4–7, 9, 14, 18, 50, 54, 65, 77–79, 94, 108, 110, 112–13, 120–22, 136–37, 146–47, 150–52, 162, 191–208; literary reputation of, 1, 7, 8–10, 24, 30, 47–48, 50, 55, 60, 109, 111, 116, 120, 125–27, 133, 135–50, 158–60, 175–76, 198, 290, 297; parties of, 55, 58–59, 61–69, 73, 195; patron of *Fire!!*, 173; as photographer, 11, 15, 232–54, 262, 269, 280–81, 297; race and art, 1–3, 5, 8, 10, 39–43, 46–47, 93–95, 97, 100, 103–5, 141, 156–57, 177, 211; relationship with Langston Hughes, 7, 30, 45, 49–50, 53, 64–65, 67, 78–79, 88, 91, 108–9, 131, 133, 137–38, 154–63, 176, 181, 187–89, 192, 231, 238, 242, 284–91, 303–305; relationship with James Weldon Johnson, 7, 9, 43, 61, 114, 116, 136, 147, 179, 181–83, 212–19, 221–28, 238,